Curiosities Series

New York
CURIOSITIES

Quirky characters,
roadside oddities &
other offbeat stuff

Withdrawn

Cindy Perman

gpp

Guilford, Connecticut

Interior photos by the author unless otherwise specified
Text design by Bret Kerr
Layout by Mary Ballachino
Maps by Daniel Lloyd © Morris Book Publishing, LLC

Library of Congress Cataloging-in-Publication Data
Perman, Cindy.
  New York curiosities : quirky characters, roadside oddities & other
offbeat stuff / Cindy Perman.
     p. cm. — (Curiosities series)
  Includes index.
  ISBN-13: 978-0-7627-4339-1
  1. New York (State)—Miscellanea. 2. New York (State)—
History—Anecdotes. 3. Curiosities and wonders—New York
(State) 4. New York (State)—Description and travel. I. Title.
  F119.P47 2008
  917.4704'44—dc22

                                    2008020228

Printed in the United States of America
10 9 8 7 6 5 4 3 2 1

For my mom, who's always up for a good adventure and ready to strike a pose when we get there

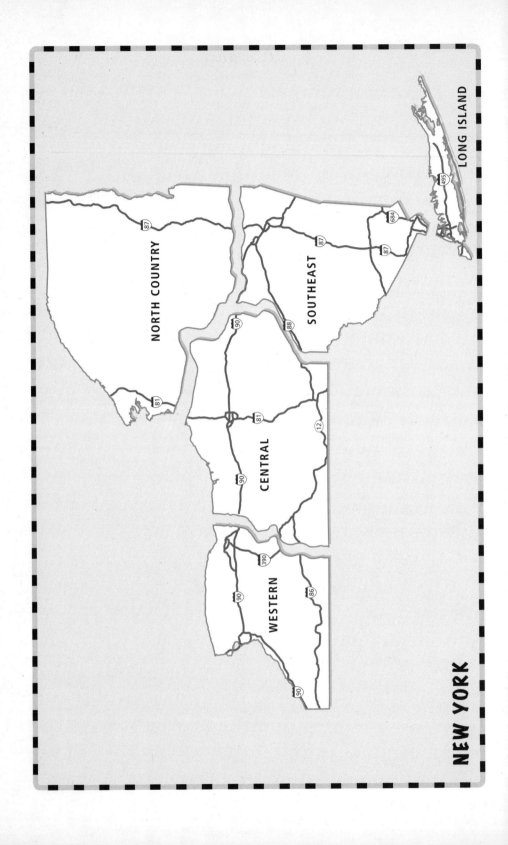

contents

✶ ✶

acknowledgments

An enormous thank-you goes to my mom for always believing in me—
even when I was betting on the other guy—and for supporting me in
every imaginable way. And to my husband, Imran, for providing tech
support, a twenty-four-hour emotional hotline, and countless hugs. This
book wouldn't have been possible without both of you.

My deepest gratitude to all the people I met in my travels, for letting
me sit in your office, your kitchen, and on the front porch. Thank you
for sharing your stories and trusting me to tell them in this book.

This has been an amazing journey. I am truly grateful to every person who has handed me a cup of Gatorade or a shot of espresso along
the way.

introduction

★ ★

WHAT IS A CURIOSITY?

Great question. I like you already!

A curiosity is anything you wouldn't find in a typical guidebook. So, if you're searching these pages for a good hotel room in Niagara Falls, you've bought the wrong book. If you want to know the scientific reason why they call Niagara Falls the "Honeymoon Capital of the World," keep reading. If you want to know how to get to the Statue of Liberty . . . um . . . do you still have your receipt? But if you're curious about who's waving back to Lady Liberty from the Brooklyn side, congratulations! You're gonna love this book.

It includes everything from a house shaped like a group of mushrooms in Rochester and a jailhouse-turned-restaurant in Owego to the Loch Ness Monster's long-lost cousin in the Adirondacks and a man who built his own castle with found objects in the Hudson Valley.

It's meant to be part guidebook, so, where possible, I'll tell you where you can go to see some of these cool things. Other stories are about private people doing cool things, such as the guy in Brooklyn who missed his home country so much that he built a replica of the Greek island he came from in his backyard. Please use your discretion with those stories; don't stand in the yard and gawk!

I'm going to give you a ton of material for your next cocktail party or watercooler show, and perhaps a few more reasons to get out there and see New York State. So, sit back in your coziest armchair and come along for the ride. Then, get in your car and drive.

WELCOME TO NEW YORK

Before we hop in the car and start meeting people, I thought we could take a little helicopter ride to get you acquainted with the state.

Ready? Headphones on, seatbelts fastened.

New York is the nation's twenty-seventh-largest state, clocking in at 54,471 square miles. I fear you won't be able to concentrate if I don't tell you the top three largest states, so here goes: Alaska is number one, at more than 650,000 square miles, followed by Texas, which is half that size, and California.

★ ★

OK, back to New York.

You see over there in the west? That's Niagara Falls, which pumps out 40 million gallons of water per minute! Over here, in central New York, are the Finger Lakes; despite the name, there are actually eleven. *The Wonderful Wizard of Oz* author L. Frank Baum was born here in Chittenango, and some say, central New York *is* Oz. Up there are the Thousand Islands. Not to split hairs, but there are, um . . ., 1,864 of them. We've got four mountain ranges, including the famous Adirondacks and the Catskills. And down there are the bright lights of New York City, one of the largest cities in the world.

Nearly half of the state's 19.3 million people live in New York City. On the other side of the state, Wyoming County has more cows than people, and in the Adirondacks' Lewis County, there are *twice* as many cows as people.

Not only are there more cows here than you realized, but there are also more castles than you may have expected. You'll read about five of them in this book.

The state flower is the rose and the state insect is the ladybug. Our official bird is the bluebird; our fish is the trout. The state animal is the beaver, a shout out to our European fur-trader founders.

Milk is the official state beverage, as New York is the third-largest dairy-producing state. (Ah ha! That explains all the cows.) The state fruit is the apple, introduced by European settlers in the 1600s, and, thanks to some elementary schoolkids in Syracuse, the state muffin is also apple.

Our state motto is *Excelsior,* Latin for "Ever upward." And, of course, the state song is "I Love New York."

So, grab an apple muffin and splash some milk in your coffee. Make a wish on a ladybug and get ready because . . . you're gonna love New York, too!

1

Western New York
Land of Talking to the Dead and Chicken Wings

When you think of western New York, you think: Kodak. Niagara Falls. Buffalo wings. But there's so much more to learn—and eat! In this chapter, we'll sample the region's other culinary delicacies, including bread made by monks and Rochester's famous garbage plate. (Hey, if my mom tried it, so can you!)

Once you've had a chance to digest all that, we'll visit with some avant-garde artists, including Surapa, the elephant who paints at the Buffalo Zoo! We'll tour museums devoted to everything from tractors to kazoos. We'll have tea in a storybook house in Forestville, do some ropin' and shootin' at a wild-west show in Sinclairville and attempt to communicate with the dead in Lily Dale.

Oh, and I almost forgot! Bring an extra pair of old shoes. Writing your name on the bathroom stall is so 1984—we're going to leave our mark on western New York by flinging our old footwear up in the Shoe Tree!

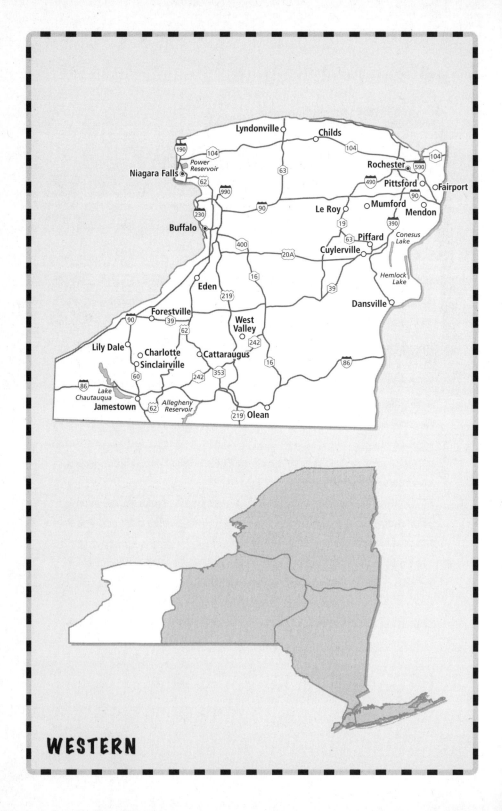

Lyndonville
Childs
190
104
104
Power
Reservoir
Rochester
590
Niagara Falls
62
490
Pittsford
63
990
90
Fairport
Buffalo
230
90
Le Roy
Mumford
Mendon
19
390
63
Piffard
Conesus
Lake
400
20A
Cuylerville
Hemlock
Lake
16
39
Eden
219
Dansville
Forestville
90
39
West
Valley
62
242
Lily Dale
Charlotte
Cattaraugus
16
Sinclairville
60
353
86
242
86
Lake
Chautauqua
62
Allegheny
Reservoir
Jamestown
219
Olean

WESTERN

THE SAUCE BENEATH THEIR WINGS
Buffalo

For years, cooking chicken meant breasts, thighs, and drumsticks, with the wings tossed aside as scraps for soup.

But in 1964, something magical happened at the Anchor Bar in Buffalo. Some of Domenic Bellissimo's friends stopped by late one Friday night to visit the bartender. They were ravenously hungry, so Bellissimo asked his mother Teressa, who was back in the kitchen, to whip up something for his friends. Ever the improviser, Teressa fried up a bunch of those chicken-wing scraps, smothered them with a secret sauce, and served them with blue cheese and celery.

And with that, the buffalo wing was born.

Fast-forward to 2001 and the debut of *Osmosis Jones,* starring Bill Murray as a compulsive junk-food eater who dreams of attending the fictitious National Buffalo Wing Festival. After seeing the movie, local newspaper columnist Donn Esmonde asked readers, "Yeah, why don't we have a Buffalo Wing Festival?" Well, entrepreneur Drew Cerza heeded the call and in 2002 launched the annual Buffalo Wing Festival.

The event opens with a running of the chickens, though you may be surprised to learn that it doesn't involve actual chickens—it's people dressed as chickens. There's an International Federation of Competitive Eating–sanctioned chicken wing eating contest, as well as a Miss Buffalo Wing pageant. Contestants are judged on their reading of Shakespeare and their knowledge of the wing, identifying correctly if a wing is mild, medium, or hot. It certainly doesn't hurt if the woman is hot as well, but at the 2006 event, Wisconsin's Dan Higgins, hamming it up in a size-eight bridal gown with the back blown out, strutted off with the title.

More than 50,000 people attended the festival that year and consumed nearly 300,000 wings—that's fifteen tons of wings! The vendors, who take the competition for best sauce very seriously, serve up wings in all kinds of creative flavors, including Jamaican jerk, garlic

★ ★

Is that a drumstick on your head or are you just happy to see wings?!

Parmesan, and, for the adventurous, suicidal and atomic. There's also a variety of other wing-inspired foods, including wing-flavored pretzels, chicken-wing sausage, and even chicken-wing soup.

The people of Buffalo take such pride in their winged heritage that one couple even married at the 2006 event, appropriately between the Miss Wing pageant and the wing-eating contest.

For more information visit www.buffalowing.com or call (716) 565-4141.

A WING A WECK, A WING A WECK
Buffalo

Are you done with those Buffalo wings? Good. Now wipe your fingers while I tell you what some foodies say is the *real* reason to visit western New York.

It's called beef on weck. Sure, other cities have roast beef sandwiches, but what sets this sandwich apart is the "weck," short for *kummelweck,* which is a crusty roll topped with rock salt and caraway seeds. Inside is a heaping pile of thinly sliced, juicy, rare roast beef with a dollop of freshly grated horseradish.

This local delicacy has been served in Buffalo-area restaurants and bars for more than one hundred years and is thought to have been brought to the region by German immigrants. Apparently, the reason why it hasn't taken flight outside of Buffalo the way the wing has

Aw, what the weck. Try the roast beef!

is—not for lack of an aerodynamic structure, but—because the weck is hard to bake and it doesn't have a long shelf life.

One of the best places to try beef on weck is Schwabl's, a 150-year-old family-owned business in West Seneca. The cozy, tavern-style restaurant is packed, yet the host doesn't take names—he remembers everyone. Behind the bar, you can actually see the thirty- or forty-pound hunk of beef roasting. Be sure to stick around for the show at the end of the bar as one of the restaurant's six carvers, the Edward Scissorhands of the meat world, slices the beef with masterful precision. Expert carver Nick Caparella explains why patrons can't request how their beef is cooked: Only the top two inches are well done and the rest is rare. We're talking watch-or-it-might-just-walk-away rare!

Among the restaurant's other charms are its warm German potato salad and, for the faint of heart when it comes to rare meat, Hungarian goulash over a bread dumpling. There is a vast array of beverage choices, including twenty beers, a dozen wines, ten classic cocktails, and birch beer on tap.

Schwabl's is located at 789 Center Road in West Seneca (716-674-9821).

A WING, A WECK, A WIPE
Buffalo

Buffalo has solidified its place in the culinary history books with the buffalo wing and the beef on weck. But there is another invention from Buffalo that is, dare I say, more important than the wing or weck.

It's the windshield wiper.

It was a dark, rainy night in 1917. Buffalo theater owner J.R. Oishei was driving his car when he collided with a bicyclist. Both lived, and the cyclist wasn't seriously injured. But Oishei was so shaken up that he vowed to figure out a way to improve visibility when driving in bad weather.

In 1920 he formed the Tri-Continental Corporation, which introduced the world's first windshield wiper, called the Rain Rubber. You know, for safe, um . . . driving.

The Rain Rubber was basically a handheld squeegee, a rubber blade on a wooden handle, so drivers could clean their two-piece windshields, popular on cars at that time. There was an opening between the upper and lower sections that drivers could stick the squeegee through to remove the water from the windshield.

World War I put windshield and wiper technology on hold for a few years, but thankfully, when the war ended, automakers were back on the case and finally developed a one-piece windshield. Trico, as the company later called itself, followed suit and made the first automatic windshield wiper.

After wooing Henry Ford, Trico had enough money to gobble up the competition. It came out with the first dual windshield wiper in 1929, and windshield-wiper fluid debuted in 1936.

So, the next time you're choking on your own road rage about the pouring rain or that truck in front of you that just kicked up a tsunami on your windshield, remember it could've been a lot worse if you had to squeegee it off by hand.

Go home, order a bucket of wings, and forget about the whole thing.

THE DA VINCI OF DA ZOO
Buffalo

You know the saying "An elephant never forgets"? It's true. Elephants are really smart and can do much more than hold each other's tails and stand on each other's backs.

The elephant minders at the Buffalo Zoo try to keep their girls intellectually stimulated with activities and challenges. They have tried a bunch of different things to help each girl find her individual strengths.

All three elephants, for example, play instruments. Surapa plays the cymbal, Jothi plays the tambourine, and Buki plays the harmonica.

Now, I'm just pushing the brush into the canvas to create mountains over the blue sky.

They also have scavenger hunts and watermelon-eating contests, where each one shows off her own competitive-eating style.

Buki does a "Bath Time with Buki" show during the summer, using material she picked up in the circus (seriously, they never forget!) and holiday photos in the winter. She's also kind of a kleptomaniac—er, trunkomaniac—as she always has something in her trunk, be it a stick or a blade of grass. "If we lose something in the yard—tools, or whatever—we know she's probably got it and we'll trade her for it!" says Kelly, one of the elephant keepers.

Jothi, whose nickname is "The Master of Disaster," isn't so much about doing tricks or picking things up with her trunk as she is about destroying things. Her appetite for destruction proves useful for watermelon eating.

The elephant keepers tried to get all three girls to take up painting. Buki, being the trunko that she is, just stood there with the paintbrush in her trunk. Jothi tried to eat the paintbrush. It was Surapa who proved to be the Picasso of pachyderms and the Da Vinci of da zoo. (Well, her style may be closer to messy Matisse.)

Each painting takes about five minutes, using four different colors. Kelly says "Paint! Back up! Give it!" Each time, Surapa takes a brush loaded with a different color and heads over to the easel to work on her masterpiece. "If she's in a blobby mood, we won't push her," Kelly says. "Other days, she's more inspired. If she's feeling swirly, she'll do five or six paintings in a row."

I'm not sure where an elephant gets her inspiration from as an artist, but I'll bet you one thing: She never forgets it!

You can see Surapa painting four days a week during the summer, or buy one of her paintings in the gift shop for about $40. (But be warned, they go fast.) One of the best times to visit is for Elephantastic Weekend in June, when all the girls show off their mad elephant skillz.

For more information visit www.buffalozoo.org or call (716) 837-3900.

SHARP OBJECTS ARE CLOSER THAN THEY APPEAR
Cattaraugus and Olean

Western New York is home to not one, but two cutlery museums: Cutco Ka-Bar and the American Cutlery Museum.

What's with the knife obsession? Are western New Yorkers a violent people?

Actually, the region has a rich history of cutlery manufacturing because of its proximity to Pennsylvania steelmakers. In the past 200 years, the area has been home to more than 150 companies that make axes, knives, and other sharp objects.

★ ★

The Cutco Ka-Bar Visitors Center is a corporate-based museum. Cutco makes everything from flatware to fishermen's knives and Ka-Bar makes military and sporting knives. Here, you'll learn about the ergonomics of knife handles and see a 7-foot Cutco knife that offers an up-close look at blade design.

You may not have absorbed a word I said in the last paragraph, being distracted by how odd the name Ka-Bar is. Well, it seems that one fur trader was so delighted with his knife that he sent the company a letter saying he used it to "kill a b'ar." The company, clearly touched by the letter, promptly changed its name to Ka-Bar.

The American Cutlery Museum is a small grassroots operation aimed at preserving the region's history of cutlery manufacturing and use. The curator is the president of the Bank of Cattaraugus, located across the street. In the museum you'll find the hunting knife John D. Merritt's parents sent him during World War II, and the machete he carried in case he was shot down over a tropical location. There's also a knife W. Larry Barr made from the leaf spring of his Chevy pickup, along with the sheath he made by tanning the hide of a deer he shot. A mounted buffalo head protrudes from one wall, accompanied by an 1870 buffalo-skinning knife. If you're sharp, you'll check 'em out.

Cutco Ka-Bar is located at 1040 East

I'll bet you think this whole buffalo over the buffalo-skinning knife is hilarious, don't you?

State Street in Olean; call (716) 790-7000 or visit www.cutco.com/
company/visitorsCenter.jsp. The American Cutlery Museum is located
at 9 Main Street in Cattaraugus; call (716) 257-9813 or visit www
.amcut.org.

THE SECRET SIDEWALK

Charlotte

Most of us don't have a million dollars to shell out for a waterfront
mansion on Lake Ontario's Beach Avenue. But there *is* a way we can
step into the fairy tale of lakeside luxury. It's called the Secret Sidewalk.

Once upon a time, a trolley ran through here, curving around the
resort community between the houses and the lake. When it was
removed, the city put a sidewalk in its place. It's called the Secret

Leave the glass slippers at home and take a stroll on the Secret
Sidewalk. But make sure you're back before midnight!

★ ★

Sidewalk because not too many people know about it, and just by looking at this stretch of Beach Avenue, you wouldn't even know it was there. There are six entrances to the sidewalk between the houses, some camouflaged with hedges, others running so close to the driveways, you'd think you were trespassing.

The mansions were built in a variety of styles, with gigantic porches, well-manicured lawns, and charming gardens that line the sidewalk. Between the sidewalk and the lake, resident-owned decks feature rows of pristine Adirondack chairs and even dining-room sets. Now *that* is dining on the lake—you can't get much closer than that!

My mom and I enjoyed an afternoon stroll along the sidewalk, chattering like a couple of little girls at a tea party about which house we'd want and why. Once we'd made our final selections, we picked out our favorite outdoor dining set. You know, for our first sunset dinner at the manse.

And they lived happily ever after. ~ The End. ~

The Secret Sidewalk runs from 490 to 720 Beach Avenue in Charlotte, but the best starting point is between nos. 490 and 510, near the intersection of Clematis Street.

THIS PLACE IS COBBLE-IVABLE!
Childs

Most Rochesterians know Ridge Road, part of State Route 104, as the road that Wegman's grocery store and the mall are on. But it used to be the shoreline of a glacial lake, Lake Iroquois, which receded 10,000 years ago.

The glacial activity left an abundant supply of smooth, rounded cobblestones. The architectural merit of cobblestones went largely unnoticed until about 1825, when masons in the Rochester area began using them as decorative facades. Between the 1840s and 1850s, approximately 1,200 cobblestone structures were erected in North America; nine hundred of them are in New York State. You'll

A young cobblestone ponders his best side before "entering" the building.

find them dotted throughout western and central New York, and most are private residences.

But Childs, New York, is home to the only cobblestone museum in the world. Of course, it's located on that historic State Route 104. You can take a tour of the complex, which includes three cobblestone structures: the oldest cobblestone church in America (built in 1834); a parsonage for the head of the church and his family; and, a one-room schoolhouse.

I'll give you a few Cobblestone 101 tidbits, just to wet your whistle.

First, what *is* a cobblestone? A cobblestone, Museum Director and Historian Bill Latin explains, is a stone you can pick up with one hand. It can be a smooth, oval lake-washed stone, or a rougher, but still flattish, field stone. How is a cobblestone structure built? Most of us would probably guess that the small, smooth stones are glued to the facade of a building, then grouted like mosaic—and most of us would've gotten that question wrong on *Jeopardy!* In fact, these stones are much longer than they appear, so they're stacked like bricks. That smooth, egg-like shape you see is merely a fraction of the overall stone. Some of the really flat ones are even set at a forty-five-degree angle, with each row alternating the angle, like herringbone.

Cobblestone wasn't more architecturally sound than brick, but it sure was prettier. Many of the homes were built by wealthy farmers who prospered after the Erie Canal was built. "People felt a certain amount of status to have a home that was so aesthetically pleasing," Latin explains.

Today, mortar in cobblestone buildings looks beige, thanks to erosion, but it used to be bright white. In the 1840s and 1950s, people took the "Thou Shall Make No Graven Images" commandment pretty seriously. In an attempt to make their homes less flashy, they used ox blood as a stain over the cobblestone and mortar.

Ox blood, less flashy? I think the flies alone would make me forget about church!

Alas, the cobblestone fad of the late nineteenth century faded as labor became more expensive. But, thanks to the museum, you can see cobblestone up close and personal, without getting arrested for trespassing.

For more information visit www.cobblestonesocietymuseum.org.

LIFE AFTER THE FARM
Cuylerville

Like a Hollywood starlet, there comes a time in every tractor's life when the work starts to dry up and neither Botox nor another stint in rehab is going to jump-start its career.

So, where does old farm equipment go when it's past its prime?

★ ★

Sometimes it's discarded on the side of the road. Sometimes it's abandoned in a field. But if it's lucky, it goes to the Tired Iron Tractor Museum in Cuylerville.

The museum houses the lifelong collection of Wayne "Bump" Hamilton (the guy was always bumping into stuff). Bump started collecting and restoring antique tractors—that's right, they're called antiques—in the 1960s.

Today, the museum features more than one hundred antique tractors (it's a pretty big museum), including a complete collection of pre-World War II John Deere tractors, and some names you might not expect to find on a tractor, such as Greyhound, Fiat, and Porsche.

There are other antique gems, including an 1810 apple butter kettle, an 1886 grain-thrashing machine, and a 1917 cherry pitter. There's even a set of antique dumbbells and an 1850 doggie treadmill. (Before they got their own spas, they had to work, too!)

Lining the museum's high windows are more than one hundred cast-iron tractor seats. (They're really quite beautiful. I'm thinking of getting one to use as an end table.) On a shelf between the rows of tractors are Bump's toy tractors.

But Bump's collecting habit went beyond farm equipment. He also collected old signs, antique gas pumps, oilcans, and wrenches (there are more

Can you believe the price of gas? Tell me about it! Too bad we're retired!

★ ★

than four hundred). Every time a salesman came a-callin', he would leave a pen—so Bump started collectin' them, too.

Bump passed away a few years ago, but his sense of humor is present throughout the museum, along with his passion for collecting. There's a CLEAN REST ROOMS sign near one doorway, but no restrooms in the building. Another sign explains: COWS MAY COME AND COWS MAY GO, BUT THE BULL IN THIS PLACE GOES ON FOREVER!

As you leave, a 4-foot saw hangs over the doorway, informing you that YOU "SAW" THE TIRED IRON MUSEUM.

It's a lot more fun than you ever thought you'd have at a tractor museum.

For more information visit www.antiquetractormuseum.com or call (585) 382-9736.

MADE IN THE KAZOO.S.A.
Eden

So, you go to New York, you buy a souvenir. You flip it over, and it's made in China. Welcome to the twenty-first century.

Today, so many things—especially small trinkets—are made in China. But don't go outsourcing your next vacation just yet. Good news, America! The metal kazoo is still made in the good ol' U.S.A., right here in Eden, just a few miles southeast of Buffalo.

There are eighteen parts to a metal kazoo, made by an assembly line of human-operated die-press machines, the same way they were made in 1916. You can actually watch this fascinating process at the Kazoo Museum & Factory in Eden. Or, you can try your hand at making one yourself. (Don't worry, you won't need seventeen friends.)

Also on display is a collection of historical kazoos (yes, there is such a thing), including wooden kazoos; kazoos in the shape of various instruments such as trumpets and saxophones; kazoos in the shape of planes, trains, and tractors; and even liquor-bottle-shaped kazoos (to "kazelebrate" the end of Prohibition in 1934).

THE CRUNCH STARTS HERE

I've got news for you, California. Granola was ours!

James Caleb Jackson co-owned an abolitionist newspaper and lectured on the cause, but poor health forced him into early retirement. He was near death when he decided to visit a spa for a "water cure," a popular alternative-medicine treatment in the mid-19th century. His miraculous recovery made him a believer in the healing power of water—so much so that he went to medical school and then bought a spa of his own in 1858.

The Dansville Water Cure, which Jackson renamed Our Home on the Hillside, became one of the largest spas in the world under Jackson's management. Of course, the first step of any water program is to drink more water, but there were also baths, wet-sheet wrappings, and yes, even water douches. Jackson, whom you might call a historical health nut, took it a step further, encouraging his patients to eat healthier. He had them cut out the bad stuff—red meat, sugar, coffee, alcohol, and tobacco—and eat more fruits, vegetables, and unprocessed grains.

In 1863, Jackson made his most lasting contribution to society, one that lives on in almost every American household today: He invented the first cold breakfast cereal, and the predecessor of granola. It was called "granula."

So, how did we get to granola?

Well, Kellogg caught wind of this new breakfast fad, and crunched out a knockoff of granula, one that was tastier and easier to make. The company changed the name to "granola," to avoid being sued by Jackson.

Dude, are you listening?

★ ★

Ready! Aim! Kazoo-er! Doo doo dee doo dee doo!

At the museum, you'll learn about Kazoophony, once an eighty-piece orchestra, which prompted *Playboy* magazine to declare: "If you ain't heard Mozart on the kazoo, you ain't heard nothing yet." In the gift shop, you can buy everything you'll need to start your own kazoo band.

If you're worried that maybe you don't have the gift of music, never fear: The museum touts the kazoo as "the most democratic of instruments because anyone can play."

Now if that's not all-American, I don't know what is.

For more information visit www.edenkazoo.com or call (716) 992-3960.

LANA'S THE LITTLE HOUSE

Forestville

There once was a lady named Lana.
Lana lives in the Little House.
The house has lots of nooks and crooks,
Even some painted-on books!
The shutters go clickety-clack.
There are fresh scones on the baker's rack.
The teapot goes woo! woo!
The piano upstairs will play a tune for you.
The garden is full of flowers,
And some milkweed for the butterflies.
Berries are ripe for the picking—
Strawberries, raspberries, and blueberries for pies.
There's a cat named Barney,
And a bullfrog named Charley.
Charley lives in a pond the shape of a heart.
Look closer, it's the turtle, George Burns, in that part!
They croak and they plop and they swish—
Oh, look! Here come Frank Sinatra and Dean Martin,
    the koi fish!
There's Milton Berle the bumble bee.
I'll see you all soon, I'm heading inside for a spot of tea!

The Little House isn't a fairy tale, though it feels like it what with all those characters on your trail. (OK, that's enough with the rhyming.) It's a real place, built in 1980 in Forestville by a couple of guys who wanted to create a real-life storybook house. Buffalo native Lana Lewis bought it in 2001, and before long, there were knocks at the door from curious neighbors.

Well, Lana knew how special the place was, and she decided to open it for tours and teas. As you wander around the gardens and

★ ★

This is Lana. Lana lives in the Little House.

through the house, she'll tell you the charming story of the place, while calling out hello to all of the animals she's named.

The price per person is $20 for a tour or $30 for the tour and afternoon tea. Lana tries to make it a truly special experience, with scones, butter tarts, and "world-class tea." She adds: "I don't make any of it, which is why I know it's good!"

I can't vouch for her baking skills, but I can tell you that she's a wonderful host to guide you through this fairy tale of an afternoon. For more information visit www.lanasthelittlehouse.com or call (716) 965-2798.

I LOVE LUCYTOWN
Jamestown

Do you love Lucy?

From the minute she entered America's living room in 1951, there was a lotta love for Lucille Ball. There was something very real about her and her relationship with real-life husband Desi Arnaz in the *I Love Lucy* show. She wasn't trying to present a perfect image like so many icons of that time. She took situations everyone could relate to and showed us the absurdity of it all.

So many people loved *I Love Lucy* in the 1950s that telephone companies reported a "substantial reduction" in calls when the show was on and department stores changed their late shopping night to Thursday from Monday, so it wouldn't conflict with the broadcast. It was only produced until 1957, but by the time of Lucille Ball's death in 1989, the show was airing in syndication in more than eighty countries.

Nowhere else is she more popular than in Jamestown, the hometown of Lucille Ball as well as her Lucy character. Here, you'll find the Luci-Desi Museum and the Desilu Playhouse featuring costumes, personal items, television clips, and recreated sets from the show. You can visit a replica of the Tropicana nightclub, where Arnaz's Ricky character performed, and try your hand at Lucy's famous Vita-meatavegamin commercial. (It's got vitamins, meat, vegetables, and minerals!)

You can visit her childhood home and the cemetery where her ashes are interred. The local theater is named after her, as is the local park. Sprinkled along 3rd Street in downtown Jamestown are three murals of scenes from the show. And, in one of the museum's three gift shops, you can buy every imaginable *I Love Lucy* product ever made, including a *Lucy*-themed Monopoly game, a *Lucy* bingo dabber, and a reproduction of her famous pink

Lucy! You got some mailing to do!

candy-factory chef's hat. You can even apply for a Lucy-Desi Visa card.

Twice a year, Jamestown hosts festivals in her honor: the Lucy-Desi Days in May and a Lucille Ball birthday celebration in August. The events feature Lucy and Ethel impersonators; Lucytown tours by Wanda Clark, Ball's personal secretary for more than twenty-five years; a Lucy Pizza-Toss Contest; and more. Writers and actors from the show as well as other famous stars come to Jamestown for the events.

So, head over to Jamestown and say, "Lucy, I'm home!" If you don't, you got some 'splaining to do.

For more information visit www.lucy-desi.com or call (877) LUCY-FAN.

JELL-O AND WELCOME TO AMERICA
Le Roy

Did you know that Jell-O and the human brain register exactly the same on an EEG machine? Did you also know that there is such a thing as a gelometer, a device used to measure the "jiggliness" of gelatin?

These are just a couple of the fascinating facts that you'll learn at the Jell-O Gallery in Le Roy, which is a half hour southwest of Rochester, toward Buffalo.

Jell-O was invented in Le Roy in 1897 by a carpenter who also made cough medicine. After a few false starts and one well-placed ad in *Ladies' Home Journal,* Jell-O finally caught on, and today we can all claim to have watched it wiggle and, yes, see it jiggle.

The Jell-O Gallery was created in 1997 for the jiggly dessert's one-hundredth anniversary. A museum devoted to gelatin might have the potential to be a small-town "eh," but this one is worth the trip. It's chock-full of fun Jell-O trivia such as which fruits float or sink in Jell-O, as well as great Jell-O paraphernalia including old advertisements by well-known illustrators such as Maxfield Parrish and Norman Rockwell. You haven't really lived until you've seen a Norman Rockwell

This is your brain. This is your brain and Jell-O.
Any questions?

painting incorporating Jell-O, or, for that matter, a still-life portrait of Jell-O.

You'll also learn about Jell-O geography. In the U.S., red is always the favorite flavor, but in Japan, it's coffee. From 1910 to 1920, Jell-O was served to immigrants at Ellis Island to welcome them to America. Utah, sometimes called "the Jell-O State," even made the jiggly treat its state snack. (There was apparently a countermotion for ice cream, but it was declared "unsexy" because it wasn't "wiggly and jiggly.") FYI: If you're ever attending a party in Utah and are asked to bring a "green salad," that means lime Jell-O with shredded carrots.

Oh, and in case you're wondering (you were, right?), fresh fruits such as apples and bananas float in Jell-O, while seedless grapes and canned fruits in syrup sink.

★ ★

I could go on, but I don't want to take all the fun out of it for you. For more information visit www.jellomuseum.com or call (585) 768-7433. While you're there, be sure to pick up a brain mold for your Jell-O!

LIVING WITH THE DEAD

Lily Dale

A woman walks down the street, past the small sherbet-colored Victorian homes, dragging one foot behind her and announcing to the air that she just got off the mother ship. Dracula jumps out from behind a tree.

This is what most people expect from Lily Dale, a small, gated community of Spiritualists in southwestern New York. "A strange little village . . . " one guidebook entry starts. "You have to be a psychic to live there!" a friend advised with a gleam of the bizarre in her eye.

Ms. Mother Ship and Count Dracula did indeed visit Lily Dale, but they were freaks there just as they would be in your town, giving all the residents a good laugh. They aren't what Lily Dale is about.

Lily Dale is an idyllic community one hour south of Buffalo, tucked between the placid Lake Cassadaga and the Leolyn Woods, a rich, old-growth forest. You have to be a Spiritualist to live there, but the community's gate is always open to visitors.

So, what is Spiritualism? The basic tenet of the religion, which was founded in western New York more than one hundred years ago, is the continuity of life after death. You can believe in God, Allah, Buddha, or no god, but the common thread is that you don't believe that life stops when you die; the spirit continues on infinitely. Spiritualist practice hinges on communicating with the spirit world.

Susan Glasier, the executive director of the town's governing body, the Lily Dale Assembly, once described Spiritualists this way: "We're just like everyone else, except we talk to dead people!" (That's an explanation for us laymen, because Spiritualists don't think of it as death, rather a transition of the spirit to the next level.)

How do you find a medium in Lily Dale? Just look in the garden!

It may sound somewhat fantastical, but if you go to Lily Dale, the one thing you'll notice is how completely normal it seems—and, how open-minded the people are. They welcome skeptics and the most devout believers with the same hospitality.

There are more than thirty registered mediums in Lily Dale, but not all Spiritualists are mediums. And, to clear up the psychic issue, Lily Dale medium Donna Riegel explains, "Every medium is a psychic, but not every psychic is a medium."

In the summer months, you'll pay a gate fee of $10 per person to enter Lily Dale, and there are plenty of free events such as meditation, healing, and "message" (as in, from the other side) services, but

Burnt Offerings

Spiritualism started in Hydesville, New York, in 1848, when the famous Fox sisters, Kate and Margaret, allegedly made contact with the spirit of a peddler who'd been murdered in their house years earlier. The spirit would knock to answer their questions.

Spiritualism was one of a whopping seven religions founded in New York State around that time. The religious wave was so immense that western New York was later dubbed the "Burned Over District," meaning there was no one left to convert.

Praise Jesus!

The seven religions are: the Free Methodist Church, Millerism, Mormonism, Perfectionism, Spiritualism, Universal Friends, and the Wesleyan Church.

The Wesleyan Church was founded in 1843 in Utica by Reverend Orange Scott as a splinter of the Methodist Church on the principles of abolition of slavery and women's rights. The Free Methodist Church, founded in Pekin, New York, in 1860 by Benjamin T. Roberts, took equality a step further, believing that the church shouldn't discriminate against the poor by charging for prime pew seats. (Hence, the "free" part.)

Speaking of "free" thinking, that brings us to Mormonism, founded in 1827 in Palmyra, New York, when then-fourteen-year-old Joseph Smith found a set of golden plates from an ancient civilization on a hill and became a modern-day prophet. Smith wrote the book of Mormon and, in his spare time, started the whole polygamy thing, personally taking on thirty-three wives.

Way to go, Joe.

Perfectionism took creative marriage to a whole new level. John Humphrey Noyes, who founded the religion in Oneida, New York, in 1848, decided that every member of the congregation should be married to every other member of the opposite sex. Well, the idea never quite caught on in the broader community, so the group said, what the heck—let's make silverware.

Now, it's going to get a little crazy. Can I get a hallelujah?

Millerism, which was the precursor to the Seventh-day Adventist Church, was founded by William Miller in Low Hampton, New York, in the 1840s. It was based on the notion that Jesus Christ would return to earth in 1844. You can imagine that Millerism sort of fizzled when 1844 came and went with nary a Jesus spotting.

In the 1700s, Jemima Wilkinson had a near-death experience and decided that—no, not that she was waiting for Jesus Christ—she WAS the incarnation of Jesus Christ. And so, in the town of Penn Yann, New York, the religion known as Universal Friends was born. Another key tenet was abstinence. (That makes sense. I mean, who has time for recreational activities, when you've got Jesus Christ in front of you?) When Wilkinson actually died, her body wasn't buried for years because everyone was standing around waiting for her to rise from the dead, like J.C. the First. Needless to say, this religion fizzled, too.

And now, for the awards. I'm going to give the award for "Least Likely to Win a Following on Wall Street" to the Free Methodists. Mormonism wins for "Most Likely to Get Divorced," and Perfectionism takes home the coveted "Most Likely to Succeed (at Something Else)" award.

Congratulations to everyone. Can I get an Amen?

Amen!

you'll have to share the mediums with everyone else. You can have a private reading with a medium, starting at around $40. There is also a library, a museum, and a hotel that offer no shortage of fascinating Spiritualist artifacts and books. Not to be missed is the charming pet cemetery; it's worth the gate fee to just wander around.

For more information visit www.lilydaleassembly.com or call (716) 595-8721.

A TREE FOR LOST SOLES

Lyndonville

Ever wonder what to do with that favorite pair of shoes that's past its prime? You hate to throw them away, but the Smithsonian won't return your calls.

Well, if you live in the village of Lyndonville, the answer is simple: You toss them up in a tree, where they will be immortalized until the next strong wind.

Locals call it "the Shoe Tree," but it's actually five trees, with hundreds of shoes dangling from the branches, lounging in the surrounding field, and crawling up the tree trunk, as if making a break for higher ground. They come in all shapes, colors, and sizes—sneakers, soccer cleats, work boots, cowboy boots, moccasins, and sandals.

There are many local myths about how the Shoe Tree started. One story goes that a man didn't like his wife's shoes and tossed them up in the tree. Another suggests it was a high school prank.

One online poster reports that nailing shoes to trees is a tradition among the cottage community in Canada, just across the lake from Lyndonville.

We're getting warmer.

The tree was started by Diane Bane, a local factory worker, in October 1986. She saw something on TV about those shoe trees in Canada and thought it would be neat to make one in Lyndonville. She was cleaning out her closet and had a bagful of shoes. She told then-boyfriend Earl Baun to find her a tree so they could start one.

A retirement community for elderly footwear.
Hey, anyone up for a game of shuffleboard?!

They hopped in Bane's truck with about eight to ten pairs of shoes. Bane kept watch while Baun tossed the shoes up in the tree. "Then, we went around begging neighbors, relatives, and friends—'Hey, you got any shoes?' They'd say, 'What are you going to do with them?' We'd say, 'Oh, throw them up in a tree!'" Bane says, giggling.

Several newspapers and TV stations have reported on the tree over the years but only once, in a 1995 *Rochester Democrat & Chronicle* article, has Bane been mentioned. Meanwhile, she lives right around the corner.

Why the mystery?

"We kept it quiet for a long, long time because we had a conservation officer that didn't like Earl," Bane says. "He said he was going to find out who started it and arrest him for littering!" Like a real-life Rosco P. Coltrane, that conservation officer was bound and determined

★ ★

to find out who did it. ("A gu gu gu!") Bane says he'd even harass the local hunters who gathered near the tree. "He'd say, 'I know you guys know who did this!'" Bane says, "but nobody would ever tell him!"

Now, the tree has become such a landmark, Bane says, even the sheriffs use it to give directions.

For the record, Bane, now a grandmother, has never thrown a pair of shoes in the tree. She admits it was her idea, but Baun, who passed away last year, did all the shoe flinging. Now, twenty years later, she's thinking about it. "I'm going to have to find a pair of shoes," Bane says. "I'll go over there and just wing one up there!"

The great thing about the Shoe Tree is that anyone can toss shoes up there and become part of a local landmark. The Orleans County tourism board says local custom is to make a wish as you toss your shoes in the tree.

I know what I'm going to wish for: a new pair of shoes! Well, that, and that I don't get busted by Rosco and Flash. Yeeeeeeehaw!

The Shoe Tree is located at the T intersection of Lake Shore and Foss Roads in the village of Lyndonville, town of Yates.

SOCIAL STUDIES IN THE OUTHOUSE
Mumford

Living history museums make for a wonderful class field trip. Inside of beautiful old buildings, people in period costumes show you how to churn butter, resole shoes, and stamp your own wallpaper.

Mumford is home to the largest living history museum in the state, and one of the largest in the U.S. The Genesee Country Village & Museum is a lovely historic village, with trellises draped with purple wisteria, a trolley that runs around it, and a couple of ox lounging back in the oxbow.

It may not be as big as Colonial Williamsburg, but the Genesee Country Village & Museum has a national distinction all its own: It has the most outhouses of any living history museum in the U.S.!

The thirteen outhouses aren't clustered in one place, nor are they noted on the village map. (Perhaps so you don't get them confused

Something in the Air

There's a scientific reason why they call Niagara Falls the "Honeymoon Capital of the World."

No, I didn't say physiological reason, so get your mind out of the gutter, OK?!

Niagara Falls is known in the scientific community as the "Negative Ion Capital of the World." Negative ions—which you can't see, taste, or touch—clean the air, dragging dust and other pollutants to the ground. When they reach your bloodstream, they boost the chemical serotonin your body produces, relieving stress, boosting energy, and even creating a feeling of euphoria.

Mass marketers have picked up on the negative-ion effect, which is why you're increasingly seeing products with ionizers—everything from air purifiers to hair dryers. The idea is that they alleviate allergens in the air and keep dust particles out of your hair, but hey, if you feel euphoric about drying your hair, who's a marketer to stop you?!

The average household has dozens or hundreds of negative ions, while a beach, a forest, or a mountain may have tens of thousands of them. So, while the view may be spectacular, that breathtaking feeling you get just may be the negative ions talking! You'll also feel the effects after a good rainfall. Ions get their charge when molecules are broken apart by catalysts such as sunlight or moving water. That refreshed, awake feeling you get in the shower? It's not psychological; it's the negative ions created by the falling water.

If your shower is dispensing a few gallons of water per minute and you feel that good, imagine how that feeling is amplified at Niagara Falls, which pumps out 37.4 million gallons of water per minute. Some people say the falls' effect is more than euphoria, it's an aphrodisiac!

So, the next time you hear about some crazy guy trying to go over Niagara Falls in a barrel or your best friend went there for a vacation and came back married, you know what to blame: negative ions!

All I want to know is: How can something so negative feel so good?

with the modern-day facilities.) But, as you wander around the village, they pop up here and there, offering insight into the people who once used these now-historic holes in the ground.

Each one is distinct and is often trimmed to match the house or building it belongs to. The outhouse tucked between the bushes near the Brooks Grave Methodist Church is a modest white four-seater with a wood-shingled roof. An outhouse between the schoolhouse and land office has separate privies for men and women.

Out by the oxbow and nearby garden, there's a humble two-seat shack, the wood showing the wear of time. A blue two-seater in the corner of a white picket fence on the Foster-Tufts property screams middle class.

The Cadillac of outhouses.

James Livingston, a wealthy entrepreneur, had an in-house outhouse, meaning the three-seat outhouse was attached to his white Greek Revival mansion, which had giant columns and wide porches on both floors.

The octagonal-shaped Hyde House has one of the classiest commodes I've ever seen. It's not octagonal, but still pretty fancy. It's lime green, to match the house, with teal stripes and lime-colored scalloped trim on the roof and matching cupola. Built for a farmer-turned-doctor, it had four seats.

Now that's outhaute couture!

For more information on the Genesee Country Village, visit www .gcv.org or call (585) 538-6822.

TAKE A WALK ON THE OCEAN FLOOR

Olean

Imagine hiking through giant rock formations that were once part of the ocean floor, without getting wet.

Imagine doing it in western New York, more than 300 miles from the Atlantic Ocean.

Rock City Park, located just this side of the Pennsylvania border, is the world's largest formation of quartz conglomerate. It's like cement with small white pebbles mixed in, just the way the ocean jumbles everything up. The formations are massive—some three or four stories tall—creating canyons with nooks, crannies, and gaps where the rocks overlap. The formation resembles a bunch of giant aquarium rocks, just waiting for a fish—or a human—to swim through.

The rock was created 320 million years ago, and the formation was the result of the tectonic plate shift that pushed up the Appalachian Mountain chain. "Remember, much of the continent used to be covered in ocean," explains Dale Smith, who co-owns Rock City Park with his wife, Cindy. As the ocean receded and the earth eroded, it exposed these stunning rock canyons.

★ ★

You might've guessed that glaciers played a part in the rock formation, but here's another *Jeopardy!* question you and I would've gotten wrong. "The glaciers passed as close as 75 miles away, but not here," Dale says.

Once you've completed your walk on the ocean floor, take some time to enjoy the breathtaking 35-mile view from the tops of the rocks.

I think I'm still going to need some time to get my head around the fact that the ocean was once in western New York, and that I just went deep-sea diving without an oxygen tank! But, that's to be expected, I guess. As Cindy Smith explains, this was all a very long time ago, B.C. (Before Cindy!)

Is it just me? Or do you feel like doing an air breast stroke through that opening, too?!

Rock City Park is located at 505A Rock City Road off of Route 16, a few miles south of Olean. For more information visit www.rockcitypark.com or call (866) 404-ROCK.

SECRET INGREDIENT: MONKS

Piffard

You go to the grocery store and pick up a loaf of bread without giving it much thought. But have you ever had bread made by a monk?

The monks at the Abbey of the Genesee, tucked in the rolling hills of the Genesee River Valley, have been baking bread for more than fifty years.

★ ★

It started with a recipe one of the monks, Brother Sylvester, picked up while he was in the Navy, stationed in the Mediterranean, during World War II. He would bake the bread for the other monks at meal-time, but guests enjoyed it so much, they started asking for an extra loaf to take home.

This is where it comes in handy to be quiet and listen to what God is telling you to do. Brother Sylvester got himself a patent on that bread recipe, the monks built a bakery, and, like the bread in the oven, the business rose from there.

Today, the monks crank out about 40,000 loaves of Monks' Bread a week, sold at an on-site store; grocery stores in Buffalo, Rochester, and Syracuse; and the abbey's Web site.

So, does Monks' Bread taste different? Absolutely. It's fresh, yet hearty, with a yeast-y twang. Brother Sylvester tweaked the recipe to make it richer, since eight months out of the year, the monks aren't allowed to put butter or anything on their bread. However, butter isn't the key ingredient—or even *an* ingredient. The monks are a peace-loving people and refuse to engage Enemy No. 1: trans fats. They use soy oil.

Every monk takes a shift in the bakery, from the abbot on down. "Some of our ingredients are more quality ingredients than other companies because their overhead is more expensive than ours," says Father Stephen, the bakery's production manager. "Monks don't cost much for upkeep!"

Michael Rizk, who used to help out in the bakery when visiting on retreat, says working with monks was very different from your aver-age nine-to-five job. "Monks aren't competing," Rizk says, "they're cooperating." And even though they're not getting paid, they work with a smile on their faces.

Rizk adds that the monastic environment helps to make the work more like a meditation. "You focus on the present moment," he explains. "It's God's work."

In the calm center of my bread-loving place, the secret ingredient has become apparent to me—monks!

Photo by Father Stephen Muller

Five-six-seven-eight some yeast . . . some soy oil . . .
Monks and bread incorporated! We're gonna do it! Give
us any bread we'll make it . . .

I think I have the recipe now: Mix a bushel of wheat, a cup of
sugar, a pinch of yeast, and a splash of soy. Stir in three dozen mind-
ful monks, a handful of smiles and cooperation, to God's taste. For
more information on Monks' Bread, visit www.geneseeabbey.org.

THE HOUSE THAT GREW FROM A BOTTLE
Pittsford

Everyone calls it the "Mushroom House" because it looks like a group
of mushrooms to scale. But here's a little secret: It was never meant
to look like mushrooms at all.

The house was built in 1970 for lawyer Robert Antell and his wife Marguerite, a sculptor. They told architect James Johnson that they wanted him to "surprise them" with something really unusual.

So, Johnson, who also designed Rochester's famous Temple Sinai, started looking for inspiration. He knew the house had to be raised because it was on a ravine. "I went into the shop where [the model] was being built—really, just our garage," Johnson recalls. "A fellow working on it had gone into the field next to the house and picked some wildflowers. I saw the Queen Anne plant and said, 'Whoa!' and pulled it out of the Coke bottle."

The stem of the Queen Anne plant became the basis for Johnson's design. It's not clear who started calling it the "Mushroom House," but I guess it was just easier than saying the "Stem of the Queen Anne's Lace Plant House."

Photo by Steve Whitman

Man, they grow 'em big here!

The three-bedroom, three-bath house consists of five interconnected pods: four are enclosed for the main house, including one "kids' pod"; the fifth is an open-top deck. The pod floors are covered in 9,000 earth-tone ceramic tiles made—literally made and fired—by Marge Antell. The walls are stucco. Tentacle-like stems sprout from columns up into the ceiling.

"We're 25 feet up off the ground," says Chris Whitman, who bought the house with her husband Steve in 1999. "Because you're up high, you're living with the birds." Another nice feature, she says, is that, with all the windows, "when the seasons change, it's like the house is full of paintings. And they change every season."

The Whitmans, who are cousins of the original owners, recruited Johnson to design an addition when they bought the house. It was tricky because the house's landmark status meant they couldn't alter the exterior. So, Johnson and his team chose the obvious solution: An underground pod!

To access the underground pod, or as the Whitmans call it, "the cave," you take a stairwell that descends from the middle of the living-room floor, where a fireplace used to be. There's a tunnel, which Johnson calls a "time tunnel," with mosaic on the floor that creeps up the cave-like walls. "My idea was to connect the old with the new, since there was a time warp of thirty years or so" between the two projects, Johnson says.

The Mushroom House is off Park Road in Powder Mill Park.

NEVER PUT A HORSE IN REVERSE
Rochester

You know George Eastman for his contributions to photography. Frankly, if it weren't for him, your camera might still be the size of a microwave.

Eastman quit school at the age of fourteen to help support his family. When he was in his early twenties, Eastman became obsessed with making photography simpler, and he started mixing chemicals in his mom's kitchen after work. From those cauldrons sprang the Eastman Kodak Company.

That's all tremendously impressive, but while you were busy trying to figure out what to point your nano-camera at next, here are a few things you might've missed about the man behind the camera.

Eastman created the name Kodak because he wanted a distinctive word that didn't violate any foreign trademarks. The less scientific reason was that his mother's maiden name was Kilbourn, and the guy just really liked the letter *K*.

Eastman's obsession with convenience wasn't limited to photography. In the garage of his dream home, built in 1902, he had a giant lazy Susan–type device installed so that he never had to drive his horse and carriage—and later, his car—out backwards. (Maybe the neighbors complained when he pulled the horse out you-know-what side first.)

In the conservatory of his home, a 9x11-foot replica of an elephant head—one of his African safari conquests—towers overhead. That same room contains an organ that once had 7,200 pipes. Each morning, an organist would play while Eastman, a lifelong bachelor, ate breakfast.

Sure, we all have organists for our Cheerios, but here's one thing you probably can't top: After one performer complained of poor acoustics in the conservatory, in 1919 Eastman invented a hydraulic-lift system to literally slice the house in half and extend that room by 9 feet without disturbing any of his precious gardens.

Soon after his African safari, Eastman was diagnosed with an irreversible spinal disease. He took his own life in 1932. But true to form, he left this note: "To my friends: My work is done. Why wait?—GE."

Today, Kodak is one of the most recognizable brand names in the world. Eastman's mansion is a landmark, and the attached museum contains cameras the size of a doghouse, more than 400,000 photos and negatives, and more than 25,000 film titles—including the personal collections of Ken Burns, Spike Lee, and Martin Scorsese.

★ ★

Whether you're interested in a master's degree in photo preservation or just want a peek at that elephant head, check out the George Eastman House at 900 East Avenue in Rochester. For more information call (585) 271-3361 or visit www.eastmanhouse.org.

TONY ECKMAIER'S BOWL-Y GRAIL
Rochester

Tony Eckmaier's motto is: "All materials are art materials and all projects are art projects." He's the kind of guy who goes to the kitchen to get a sandwich and leaves a trail of art in his wake.

He has a deep appreciation for famous works like the *Mona Lisa,* but he doesn't appreciate when they're put behind velvet ropes and glass cases. "They lock up the really good art because it's dangerous!" Eckmaier declares.

As a result, Eckmaier's chosen gallery is his front yard in downtown Rochester. Here, large, metal birds are suspended from trees. Toy carousel horses scale the fence as if fleeing a merry band of children demanding one more bounce on the horsey. There's a pile of flat rocks in the shape of a man, which Eckmaier explains is an *inukshuk,* a man-made landmark used by the Inuit people in the Canadian arctic tundra, where there are few natural landmarks. (That's not a problem here on Eckmaier's lawn.) Nearby is a tree made of blue glass, a giant hand protruding from the ground, and what appears to be a collection of bowling balls.

Bowling balls?

Eckmaier says he's actually become somewhat of a bowling-ball magnet after creating a bowling-ball machine along his fence. The ball travels down a wire alley overhead, hits a lever, drops down, winds around, and somewhere along the way it crushes fresh herbs such as mint, thyme, and sage.

People are always looking to unload their stuff—and their guilt for simply throwing it away. So, if you haven't bowled in fifteen years and it's time to send the ball on its way, you go, "I know, the bowling ball guy!" Eckmaier estimates that, thanks to such donations, his inadvertent bowling-ball collection is eighty and counting. And it's not just bowling balls: Eckmaier finds all kinds of things dropped on his doorstep. He calls it the "inanimate-object breeding program," which has provided a lot of raw materials for his art.

When he's not in the garage—I mean, "Secret Lab"—creating art, you might find him off jousting with other members of his medieval fight club, the Society for Creative Anachronism. ("We dress up in armor and hit each other with sticks," Eckmaier explains.) He even makes his own armor in the Secret Lab. One of his favorite self-made

Bowling balls, this way. Secret Lab, thattaway.

★ ★

toys is a "jousting machine" comprised of two knight dolls on horses rigged to garage-door openers.

Now, if you could just stand right there and clack these coconut halves together for me . . .

THE GARBAGE PLATE
Rochester

It all started with two hot dogs, cold beans, and french fries. That was the main dish served at Alex Tahou's restaurant when the Greek immigrant opened it in 1918 in a former train station in downtown Rochester.

Nick Tahou took over his father's restaurant in the 1940s, and it still carries his name today. Ask anyone from Rochester—they know Nick Tahou Hots. And it's all because of the "garbage plate," which is to Rochester what the cheesesteak is to Philadelphia.

The origin of the name "garbage plate" dates back to the 1980s, when Nick's became popular with college students—especially those sobering up after a night of heavy drinking—since it was open twenty-four hours. Nick's offered comfort food at its finest: Meat, potatoes, beans, and macaroni all piled up on one plate and smothered in a deliciously spicy, greasy concoction infused with ground beef.

The students, in an act of either fatigue or rebellion, snubbed the standard—"I'd like two hot dogs, cold beans, and french fries, please"—in favor of "Gimme one of those plates with all the garbage on it!"

"We hated that!" said Nick's son—also named Alex—who now runs the family business. "We would say, 'Don't call it that! It's hots and potatoes, or a cheeseburger plate.'"

But every good businessman knows when to cash in his chips—or his hot-dog plate—and while the Tahous didn't like those kids calling their food garbage, this is the dish they were coming for and telling

Gimme one of those plates with all the garbage on it!

all of their friends about. In fact, the word-of-mouth buzz drove so much traffic to the restaurant that it made advertising unnecessary. By the late 1980s, Nick's embraced the crude nickname-turned-phenomenon, tacking on a sign out front that read HOME OF THE GARBAGE PLATE, and trademarking the "garbage plate" name.

You can get your own garbage plate—with your choice of meat and up to four different side items—for about $6 at two Nick's locations: 320 West Main Street in downtown Rochester and 2260 Lyell Avenue in the town of Gates. The Gates location is still open twenty-four hours but the downtown restaurant, which is in a grittier area, closes at 8:00 p.m.

PLEASE, DON'T FEED THE ARTISTS

Rochester

Their tagline is: "You know where art hangs, where art shows . . . and even where art sells . . . but where does art live?"

Look, if you're having cold feet, there are less dramatic ways to tell me.

From the minute you walk into Artisan Works in downtown Rochester, you get the sense that if art was an animate object and could purchase real estate, this is where it would choose to live. Huge open space. Tons of display space. Art-y roommates that totally "get" it. Lots of outside-the-box thinking. It's a painting's paradise.

Artisan Works functions like a museum or gallery—but without the pretense—as well as an artists' cooperative, an event venue, and a community outreach center. Housed in the former Farrell factory, which made cannons during World War II, nearly every inch of the 40,000-square-foot space is covered in art.

A sculpted wooden motorcycle greets you at the door and a bridal dress flies on a white bicycle overhead, while in the showroom next door, two bears rumble high on a ledge next to a giant wooden Swiss Army knife. In another alley, a chair shaped like giant lips sasses it up next to a jukebox. Long hallways and high ceilings give visitors tons of breathing room for their artistic interpretations, while all sorts of nooks and crannies allow for intimate contemplation.

Artisan Works is the brainchild of entrepreneur Louis Perticone, who has an eye for art and a nose for business.

There is a large showroom, used for weddings or other large events, and themed rooms for dinner parties or other small gatherings. Among the small rooms is a Frank Lloyd Wright dining room, a Japanese tatami dining room, a Marilyn Monroe room (where you can do your best dress-blowing impression—ooh!), and a 1950s retro lounge. There's the Boulevard Geribaldi, a corridor of artists' studios that you can peek into, observing artists in their natural habitat! (Though, please, don't feed the artists.)

And then, just when you thought the tour was over, you discover an art garden on the roof. It's as if there's so much art with so much energy that some of the pieces—which include a giant gorilla—just busted out the top! You can have your wedding up there or just pack a brown bag lunch and take it all in.

For more information visit www.artisanworks.net or call (585) 288-7170.

THE LADY WITH THE ALLIGATOR PURSE

Rochester

> Miss Susie had a baby.
> She named him Tiny Tim.
> She put him in the bathtub to see if he could swim.
> He drank up all the water.
> He ate up all the soap.
> He tried to eat the bathtub,
> but it wouldn't go down his throat!
> Someone call the doctor.
> Someone call the nurse.
> Someone call the lady with the alligator purse!

Do you remember this children's rhyme? Maybe you sang it starring a Miss Lulu. Maybe you jumped rope to it. Maybe you paddy-caked it.

★ ★

(Hey, kids are fickle. They can't be trusted to precisely relate oral history.) One thing we can all agree on: It was a solid parenting decision to call for the doctor. Ditto the nurse. But, have you ever wondered who that lady was with the alligator purse? No matter how that rhyme has changed, she always seems to be in there.

Well, the people at the Susan B. Anthony House in Rochester claim that that lady was, in fact, Miss Anthony, who was known for carrying a large alligator purse in her suffragist travels during the second half of the 19th century.

So, wait. Let me get this straight. Your kid just tried to eat the bathtub, is currently digesting soap, and you need a suffragist?!

Apparently, it wasn't so much that they needed a suffragist as it was the suffragist being in the right place at the right time. That

Next time your kid eats the soap, stop the first person you see with one of these!

rhyme traces its origins to California, where Miss Anthony spent several months lobbying for women's right to vote. So, while the kids were jumping rope and making up their rhyme, they saw this woman, day after day, hurrying past with an alligator purse . . . purse rhymed with nurse . . . and there you have it!

A hop, skip, and a vote later, you can buy a jump rope with a copy of that rhyme for $3 at the Susan B. Anthony House (www.susanb anthonyhouse.org/giftshop-cd.shtml). If you go there, you can also see the purse—in person!

THE ABANDONED SUBWAY
Rochester

Looking at downtown Rochester, it's hard to remember that this recovering casualty of suburban sprawl was once America's first boomtown. But all you have to do is look beneath the surface.

Along Broad Street and South Avenue, below Nick Tahou's restaurant, the Gannett Building, and the Rundell Library, are a series of decrepit tunnels. This was once the Rochester subway system.

It was the 1920s and Rochester was booming. But the townsfolk were grumbling that the part of the Erie Canal that ran through downtown had become a giant cesspool and they wanted that smelly thing the heck out of their city! So, the canal was rerouted to go around the city. Rochester, meanwhile, had been doing a bit of navel-gazing and realized that it was missing one thing that all the other cool cities had: rapid transit.

So, out went the water and in went the tracks! Rochester converted that old canal bed into a subway tunnel, and the Rochester Subway opened for business in 1927. "This was one of the biggest public works projects outside of New York City or Boston," explains Tom Hack, chief structural engineer for the city of Rochester. But two years later, the Great Depression hit and ridership never picked up after that. "It was a great idea, but bad timing," Hack says. The subway was shut down in 1956.

★ ★

A few parts were filled in, others claimed by the homeless. The part beneath the library was flooded and used as an early air-cooling system. From the outside, you can still see the water rush through the crescent-shaped windows and into the Genesee River below.

Next to the library entrance, as the light begins to fade, a crumbling stairwell descends from the ceiling to a platform that slips off to nowhere. Deeper into the tunnel, a small building sits crumpled in the darkness. In another corner is the "elephant door," used to bring elephants up into the War Memorial (now the Blue Cross Arena) for the circus. A waterfall beneath the library breaks the eerie silence.

Light reappears in the part known as the Broad Street Aqueduct, between the library and the Gannett building, revealing stunning graffiti on the crash walls between the tracks. It's not your run-of-

Next stop, underground art. Please watch your step.

the-mill, profanity-laced thug art. Brightly colored and painstakingly detailed, it looks to be the work of high-end graffiti artists.

"Most of the graffiti runs in 10-foot sections, and it changes almost weekly," Hack says incredulously. "If you came back next week, this would all be different!" The artists, Hack says, never leave a trail. There are no spray-paint cans littered about, and in twelve years, he's never seen a single artist down there.

The decaying tunnels are dangerous, and trespassing is strictly forbidden. But the city is working on a redevelopment plan for the former subway tunnels, and one day soon you might be able to go down there.

What you can do now—legally—is check out one of the original Rochester subway cars at the New York Museum of Transportation in the Rochester suburb of Rush. Visit www.nymtmuseum.org or call (585) 533-1113.

AMERICA'S FIRST DAREDEVIL AND DARE BEAR
Rochester

Da da da da! Ladieeeees and gentlemen! I present to you . . . the very first American daredevil . . . Sa-aaaaam, Paaaaaaaaatch!

(Hey, look. This was before television got you all razzled and dazzled. That sort of thing used to work to get a crowd going.)

Now, you know about Harry Houdini and Evel Knievel and that time Fonzie jumped the shark. You may not know the name Sam Patch. But you should—he's the guy who first blazed the trail of daredevilism.

Patch's dare of choice was simple but dangerous: He jumped over waterfalls. It started when he was just a boy working in a Rhode Island textile mill and he would jump off the mill dam to entertain the other boys. His first big jump, which catapulted him to fame, was in 1827, when he successfully jumped the 80-foot Passaic Falls in New Jersey.

Rochester Images: From the Collection of the
Rochester Public Library Local History Division

Darnit, Chester! Didn't I tell you Friday the 13th was an unlucky day?

Patch, who earned the nickname "The Yankee Leaper," successfully jumped Niagara Falls—twice, no less!—but alas, the life expectancy of a falls jumper isn't very long.

Patch decided to take on the 96-foot High Falls in downtown Rochester. He successfully made the jump during a practice session. For the big show, on Friday, November 13, 1829, there was great fanfare. Patch was said to have a pet bear cub, Chester, who often "jumped" with him. I say this with air quotes because in the case of the Rochester show, Patch got caught up in the pre-show excitement

572

and tossed Chester off the 25-foot tower built for the jump. So, whether he really jumped—or was pushed—who knows?!

In any case, you probably know where this is going. That Friday the 13th jump would be Patch's last, at the ripe old falls-jumping age of thirty. He apparently dislocated both shoulders in the impact and drowned. His body was recovered the following spring. (Chester lived, by the way.) Patch was buried in Rochester's Charlotte Cemetery with a wooden board that said simply: SAM PATCH—SUCH IS FAME.

Rochester holds the famous daredevil and his buddy Chester dear to its historic heart. There's even a sightseeing boat named the *Sam Patch* that does tours on the Erie Canal.

You can take a stroll around High Falls, but please, no jumping. Instead, head over to the High Falls Visitors' Center, which features some cool interactive exhibits, including a replica of a Rochester city street and a mini–High Falls, as well as unique exhibits from local artists. For more information visit www.centerathighfalls.org or call (585) 325-2030.

A ROOTIN' TOOTIN' GOOD TIME!
Sinclairville

Wild Bill Frost bellies up to the bar and says, "I need some raw gut!"

It's been a tough day up here in Sinclairville. What with all that ropin' and shootin'. Then, all heck broke loose when that horse thief snuck in and made off with some a them there horses! Thank goodness they caught the bugger and threw his sorry bee-hind in jail! I'll tell you, this town ain't big enough for the both of us.

That's a day in the life of a New York cowboy.

It's all part of the rootin' tootin' good time that Bill Frost and his friends, the Wild Bunch, put on four times a summer at Frost's farm in Sinclairville. The show includes trick roping, whip cracking, comedy skits, a bank-robbery shootout, and mounted cowboy balloon shooting. For you city folk, that means actually firing a gun at a target while you're on a horse, a great cowboy sport that Frost introduced

Rattlesnake Pete Rochester

His name was Pete Gruber, but everyone called him Rattlesnake Pete. When he was a boy growing up in Oil City, Pennsylvania, his Native American friends taught him how to catch snakes. And he was pretty darn good at it.

Most boys outgrow their creepy-crawly phase at some point. Not Pete. He grew up to be a snake-oil salesman and the northeast's go-to guy for any sort of snake emergency. When Pete moved to Rochester in 1893, he opened a saloon that doubled as a museum for his collection of live snakes. He decorated the walls in snakeskin.

Billed as "The Greatest Curiosity in the City," Rattlesnake Pete claimed other oddities in his collection, including a four-legged chicken, the first electric chair, and "the stony corpse of a petrified female." Many of the bizarre exhibits, along with more common items such as saddles, guns, and ropes, hung from the ceiling like a butcher shop. All the bric-a-brac around the saloon is probably why he has been mistaken as the founder of the Cracker Barrel restaurant chain. (He wasn't, but that little historical blooper should make your next visit to a Cracker Barrel that much more entertaining.)

Pete provided the townsfolk with snake oil, thought at the time to be a pain reliever for arthritis and other joint problems. He also took some of the locals out with him when he went on a snake hunt, wearing his rattlesnake-skin vest and driving a Rambler with two brass snakes for a hood ornament.

But perhaps Rattlesnake Pete's most curious use of snakes was in treating goiters, which are caused by a swollen thyroid gland. Instead of simply applying snake oil to the goiter or developing some sort of cream as you might expect, Pete would actually wrap the entire snake around the victim's—I mean, patient's—neck! The

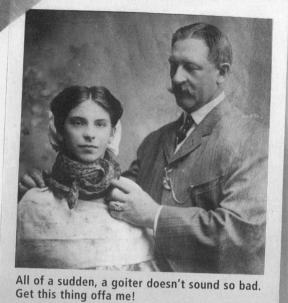

All of a sudden, a goiter doesn't sound so bad.
Get this thing offa me!

snake didn't cure the goiter per se, but the constricting process
apparently brought some relief.

No word on what he used to treat the anxiety caused by having a
snake around one's neck.

Wild Bill Frost "can" really rustle 'em up with that soda-can lasso!

to New York State about ten years ago. Why, if it weren't for him, the rest of us would still be sitting there in our big, floppy hats, offering a soft glove clap for jockeys in tight pants hopping over fences!

Frost travels around the region doing one-man shows, but a few years ago, he and his wife Lucile were traveling through Arizona on the famous Route 66 when they came across an old Wild West town. Frost decided right then and there that he was going to bring the Wild West to western New York. He bought the whole town, brought it home, and set it up on his farm.

The Wild West town includes the Wild Bunch Saloon, a jail, a bank, and a town store. There's also a noose—"For shoplifters!" Frost declares—and what they call a "Hollywood Outhouse." Frost explains: "A cowboy might use it during the show, but if he doesn't come out fast enough, another cowboy throws a stick a dynamite in there. Blows 'em to bits!"

Frost also runs a saddle and gun shop on the farm and what the tourism folks call "the best saddle museum east of the Mississippi!"

Stop by and see Wild Bill, Butch Cassidy, Billy the Kid, Jack Diamond, Black Bart, and the rest of the Wild Bunch. You'll steer clear of the town marshals, if you know what's good for you, and tip your hat when you pass by one a them pretty saloon girls.

For more information call (716) 962-5168.

DEER DAD, YOU WERE RIGHT!
West Valley

When Lenny Nagel was ten years old, his father gave him a set of deer antlers and said, "These are nature's art and, just like snowflakes, you will never find two alike. Take good care of them."

Like most boys, young Lenny took that as a challenge and set out to prove his father wrong. He picked up deer antlers every chance he got, whether it was in the woods or at a garage sale.

Does Sigourney Weaver know about this?!

Forty years later, Nagel has more than 4,500 sets of antlers. And you know what? His father was right—no two are alike!

★ ★

Nagel and his wife Barb, both avid hunters, have opened the collection to the public in a museum called the Antler Shed that they set up in a barn behind their house.

The first thing you notice when you walk into the barn are the support pillars, covered in hundreds of antlers. Spaced less than an inch apart, the poles look like a dinosaur spine or a creature from the movie *Alien*. Each pole, Nagel explains, represents the lifetime collection of one person. The poles are surrounded by mounted deer heads and antlers tacked all over the walls—even on the ceiling!

"What I really enjoy doing is, if it's an older person's collection—and the kids have no interest in keeping it—getting all of their information and writing a story about it and putting it in the museum," Nagel says.

For example, there's the story of Carl W. Hey. Hey's favorite venue to hunt deer was in a place called the Muck Farms, swamps that were drained and converted to potato farms. The deer "love swamps and they love taters," Hey used to say, "makes 'em grow big horns!" He also admitted, "I missed my wedding by one hour, I missed two of my kids' births. I missed lots of bank payments and always missed my mother-in-law's birthday. But never an opening day of deer season!"

And while the price of antlers has increased significantly—Nagel used to be able to buy an entire box of antlers at a yard sale for $5 to $10, but now antlers sell for anywhere from $20 to $400 on eBay—he's not in it for the money. "Once something goes up there, it's in the collection," Nagel says.

In addition to the antlers, the museum has a collection of knives and other household objects, such as a manicure set and a curling iron, with deer-antler handles. Some of the utensils date back to the 1700s.

The museum has many taxidermy trophies, some part of personal collections, some mounted by Nagel himself. On the second floor is a black bear standing on its hind legs, which Nagel shot in Minnesota. In the corner, Nagel built a small hunting cabin, complete with a mannequin dressed as a hunter. "That's my taxidermied brother!" Nagel exclaims.

You gotta love taxidermy humor.

The Antler Shed Taxidermy and Whitetail Museum is located at 8558 Hebdon Road in West Valley. For more information call (716) 699-4427.

THE ELECTRIC COW-PANY
Wyoming County

New York State is home to New York City, one of the most densely populated cities in the world.

On the other side of the state, life is pretty different. In Wyoming County, there are more cows than people. By the numbers, that's about 52,000 cows and 43,000 people.

Most of the pop-moo-lation consists of Holsteins, those iconic black-and-white dairy cows. New York is, after all, the third-largest dairy-producing state in the nation.

So, what's it like living in a place where there are more cows than people?

Diane Johnson-Jaeckel of the Wyoming County Tourism Agency says you have to be pretty resourceful to live in a place this rural. "People here are multitalented. They can take care of livestock, fix machinery, make repairs, do electricity, and even pull cars out of ditches in the winter!"

Sounds like a pretty great place to build life skills. But I know what you're thinking: What about the smell?

I'm not gonna lie to you. Cows are adorable, but they do stink. Though, if you live around them long enough, you don't notice it. During an interview on the Emerling family farm, Mike Emerling said matter-of-factly: "I don't smell anything right now."

Fortunately for those of us passing through who *do* smell something, Emerling and three other farms have teamed up to test new

So, did you hear about Mabel? Girl, that man milked her for all she was worth!

technology called a manure digester. Essentially, it extracts methane gas (the stinky part) from the manure and converts it to electricity used to power the farm.

Emerling said his annual electric bill used to be about $92,000. The manure digester pumps out twice that amount of electricity, which might impress you more if you realize it's enough to light up seventy-five homes!

You can take a tour of Emerling and other farms in Wyoming County, but consider yourself warned: They haven't quite worked out the stink yet. Hey, things just don't become ex-stinked overnight! For more information on tours, visit www.wyomingcountyny.com.

GOING FOR THE GOLD IN NEW YORK

Western and Central New York

Just about everything west of Albany in this state is snow country, thanks to weather-meddling Lake Ontario. Shoveling is a way of life. Here, you're just as likely to overhear odds-making on a white Easter as you are a green Christmas.

You would think that if you're the city that gets the most snow, you lose. But in 1970, a former meteorologist for the National Weather Service in Rochester decided to turn that around and started the Golden Snowball Awards. Each year, the snow is tallied in the regions' largest cities and the *winner* is the city with the most snow.

City of Syracuse, Media Center

And the winner is . . . Syracuse! (Try to act surprised.)

The cities that compete are Albany, Binghamton, Buffalo, Rochester, and Syracuse, but it hasn't been much of a competition—Syracuse has won each of the last five years. And, since 1950, Syracuse has recorded the most snow of the five cities 70 percent of the time.

In the 2006–2007 season, Syracuse logged more than 140 inches of snow. That's about 12 feet, which is enough to cover you and all of your friends, even if you're sitting on each other's shoulders having a chicken fight. Rochester came in second with more than 107 inches; that's nearly 9 feet, which would bury even Andre the Giant, who was 7 feet, 4 inches tall.

The awards focus on the regions' biggest cities, but some smaller communities such as Oswego scoff at all the attention their urban counterparts get for snowfall. Oswego averages about 180 inches per season. These people eat a foot of snow for breakfast. Oswego has been known to get 300 inches in a single season; that's 25 feet, which would cover you and your friends, even if you were all having a chicken fight on the shoulders of Andre the Giant.

If you're wondering why the state's largest city, New York, isn't on the list, that's because it gets an average of just 2 to 3 feet of snow per season.

And so, while the ladies on Fifth Avenue are wearing their full-length fur coats as winter armor, and the Orange men and women of Syracuse are getting all the glory, the people of Oswego shovel smugly, knowing that they are New York's true winter Olympians.

2

Central New York
Digging for Diamonds and Dinner in Jail

Central New York *is home to the Finger Lakes, which are perfect for summer getaways and fall leaf peeping. But, did you know that Oz, the magical land Dorothy visited, is said to be right here in Central New York? (Quick, check the bushes for Munchkins!) There's also cause to believe that the real Bedford Falls, from* It's a Wonderful Life, *is here, too!*

Not to be missed is the two-story outhouse in Phelps. (That should give you plenty of material for your car jokes.) You might want to try your hand—well, not your hand, exactly—at Cohocton's tree-sitting contest or spend your day digging for diamonds in Herkimer.

You know what they say, "When in Naples," . . . you do as the Naplese and order up a slice of grape pie because this is the self-proclaimed "Grape Pie Capital of the World!" Hang on to the fork, though, because we're headed to Oneida, where we're going to investigate cutlery's sexy past.

Finally, I don't want to force you against your will, but you must stop by the former jailhouse in Owego for dinner. Be nice, though, or I'll tell them to close the cell doors after the salad!

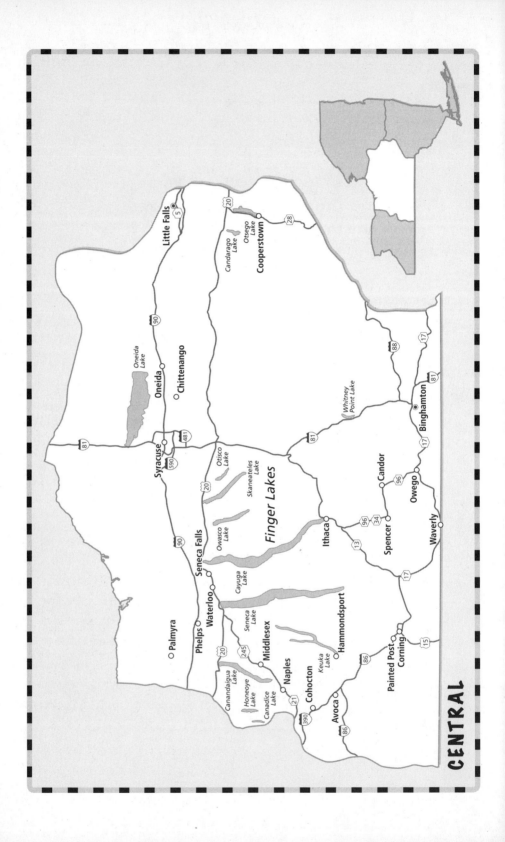

WOO! WOO! YES, I NEED A ROOM, PLEASE.

Avoca

Sick of the standard-issue hotel room? Looking, maybe, for a few more bells and whistles?

At the Caboose Motel in Avoca, you can rent a caboose for the night. Built in 1916, the now-retired cabooses were overhauled with a fresh coat of red paint and each was branded for a different U.S. rail line: Nickel Plate Road (short for the New York, Chicago & St. Louis Railroad), New York Central System, Great Western, Pennsylvania Railroad, and Erie Railroad.

Inside, the cabooses were renovated and equipped with a shower, bathroom, seating area, heat and air-conditioning, cable

Grab your jammies and hop aboard!

TV, telephone, and sink. Each caboose sleeps five or six people: Two upper bunks are part of the original sleeping area, and on the main floor, there's one single and one double bed. One caboose even has some of the original lime-green train seats.

You thought I was kidding about the bells and whistles, but each caboose also has a speaker that pumps out train sounds. Woo woo! But don't worry, you can control the volume, so you won't actually feel like you're sleeping on the tracks.

The motel also offers standard hotel rooms and welcomes curious passersby who just want to come in for a tour. I'm holding you to the honor system—don't go buying the "I slept in a caboose!" trucker hat, unless you actually did.

If you do spend the night, don't forget to walk through the aisle and demand tickets from your family members.

All aboard! Please watch your step and stand clear of the closing bathroom door!

For more information on the Caboose Motel, visit www.caboose motel.net or call (607) 566-2216.

YOU ARE NOW . . . ENTERING . . . THE HORSEY ZONE
Binghamton

Touring Binghamton can be a little dizzying. That's because the area is home to not one, not two, but *six* carousels! The region even refers to itself as the "Carousel Capital of the World."

The carousels were gifts from local shoe manufacturer George F. Johnson, donated between 1919 and 1934. "George F," as they called him, was big on incentives to improve the quality of life of his workers and the community. He felt that the carousels made for a happier life and would contribute to young people becoming more productive citizens.

Johnson also felt strongly that there should be no charge for admission to the carousels, a policy that stands today. However, the city likes to say that the price is one piece of litter—that is, please find and dispose of one piece of litter in exchange for the free ride!

The carousels were all manufactured by Allan Herschell, another famous New Yorker, and two even have the original Wurlitzer band organs. If you ride all six, you get a commemorative button.

I feel like someone's following me. Anyone there? Doo dee doo doo . . .

A fun bit of trivia: The carousel at Binghamton's Recreation Park was featured in an episode of the *Twilight Zone.* (Doo dee doo doo . . .) That's because *Zone* creator Rod Serling grew up here and used to ride this carousel as a child. The episode is called "Walking Distance."

As you lock the door to your rental car . . . unlock your imagination . . . Beyond it is another dimension . . . a dimension of bright lights, bouncing animals, and tinkling organ music . . . You've just crossed over into . . .

The Horsey Zone.

For more information visit www.binghamtoncvb.com/visitors/carousels.aspx and www.rodserling.com/binghamton.htm.

MAKE IT SPIEDIE, I'M HUNGRY!

Binghamton

Buffalo's got the wing and Rochester has the garbage plate, but when you're in Binghamton, make it spiedie!

Hahhhhhh. Smell My Breath!

I'll make you a deal. On the count of three, we both eat the garlic, OK? That way no one gets accused of dragon breath. Ready? One . . . two . . .

One festival devoted to garlic is curious enough. As it turns out, there are at least eight garlic festivals right here in New York State!

The largest is the Hudson Valley Garlic Festival (www.hvgf.org) in Saugerties, where nearly 50,000 people come to eat garlic steak sandwiches, garlic mashed potatoes, garlic ice cream, and chocolate-covered garlic cloves. There's also the Mohawk Valley Garlic and Herb Festival in Little Falls (www.littlefallsny.com) featuring a garlic cook-off and the Garlic Queen Pageant; and the Cuba Garlic Festival in Cuba (www.cubanewyork.us), which kicks off with a little dancin' in the streets, followed by a coronation of a Garlic Queen *and* King.

There's also the Multi-Ethnic Garlic Festival in Binghamton; the Susquehanna Valley Garlic Fest in Milford; the Fox Run Vineyards Garlic Festival in Penn Yan; the Long Island Garlic Festival in Riverhead; and the Sharon Springs Garlic Festival.

Some people are drawn to garlic for the taste; some eat it because it helps you stay healthy, especially if you feel a cold coming on. But the reason they come to the garlic festivals is for the variety.

Do you know what kind of garlic you buy in the grocery store? Probably not. That's because there's one choice and it's labeled "garlic." In fact, there are more than 200 varieties of garlic!

"There are different types of heat—mild to very hot," Bill Ziese, a garlic grower and organizer of the Sharon Springs Garlic Festival, explains. "Some creep up on you, some burn immediately. There are some where heat forms in the back of your tongue. There's also garlic that's nutty and earthy," Ziese says.

Bavarian garlic, for example, is mild. Music garlic (how cute is that?) is zesty.

Transylvanian garlic (oh yeah, there is such a thing!) is a little hot, and German White garlic is hot with a capital "H!" One grower called it "garlic with attitude."

For all you garlic lovers out there, Ziese has some advice: "If you keep eating garlic every day, your body stops smelling like garlic!"

Hhhhhhey, honey? Good news!

For a full listing of garlic festivals, visit www.garlicseedfoundation .info/festivals.htm.

Some like it hot. Do you?

(I'm going as fast as I can—stop rushing me!)

The spiedie is Binghamton's local delicacy, likely brought over by Italian immigrants in the 1920s. It consists of cubed chicken, lamb, or other meat, marinated overnight or longer in a concoction of olive oil, vinegar, Italian spices, and mint. It's then grilled on skewers and served on Italian bread or a roll, which you use like an oven mitt to pull the meat off the skewer!

The name spiedie comes from the Italian *spiedo,* which means "kitchen cooking spit." (Not a semi-pornographic men's bathing suit.)

In 1983 a couple of local families got to talking about who had the best spiedie recipe. So, they decided to put their spits to the test and held a cook-off. After a couple of years, the cook-off ballooned into the Spiedie Fest and Balloon Rally.

David Pessagno, the festival's coordinator, fondly recalls his grandfather talking about how he and his friends would leave the Endicott Johnson Factory and head to Augie's after work to help their friends sell lamb spiedies on the corner for five cents.

Pessagno, who has been with the festival for twenty-three years, has a friend who is a hot-air balloonist, which is how the balloons got involved.

Today, the August festival features all kinds of food, music, arts and crafts, plus thirty or more hot-air balloons. There are even a few tethered balloons in fun shapes. Some call it the Macy's Thanksgiving Day Parade in the Sky. Past events have featured a dog, an eagle, a dragon, and even a monster truck balloon.

So, get spit-fired up and head over to Binghamton—and make it spiedie! For more information visit www.spiediefest.com.

THE NIGHT WATCHMAN IS A DONKEY
Candor

The Fallow Hollow Deer Farm in Candor is the second-largest fallow deer farm in the U.S. (The first is in Texas.) For the uninitiated, fallow deer don't guide Santa's sleigh (those are reindeer); they are raised primarily for venison.

The venison from this farm has been served at some of New York City's finest restaurants, including the Four Seasons, and to some pretty famous people, from the governor to Martha Stewart.

There are 425 hilly acres for the deer to roam, with an 8-foot-high steel fence, in case any of the deer had any ideas of running off to New York City to pursue acting instead of dinner!

Martha and Brian Goodsell are the humans who run the farm, but they can't possibly walk around all 425 acres to guard their herd. So, when they started interviewing for the position of night watchman, they considered guard dogs, but dogs are small enough to run the risk of getting hurt by the deer's antlers.

Then, they found the applicant with the perfect skill set: the donkey.

Donkeys are herding animals, so you can't have too many or else they just protect the other donkeys, Martha explains. But if you have only one or two, they'll adopt the deer as their social circle and pro-tect the herd, she says. One way to tell if a donkey feels safe: You'll find him lying down, burping up grass balls!

So, what are the big, tough bucks doing while the donkey's keep-ing an eye on the herd? The bucks usually hang back and send out the ladies to test the waters for danger! The donkey, not one treat a woman like a canary in a coal mine, partners with the lead doe to keep a lookout. And when a predator such as a coyote or fox approaches, the donkey will bite, chase, and stomp it to get it away from the herd.

So, ladies, the next time your man isn't standing up for you and you call him another name for a donkey, be careful! You may be insulting the donkey.

For more information visit www.fallowhollow.com or call (607) 659-4635.

★ ★

Trivia

That's Ms. Rudolph, to You!

OK, fellas. The buck stops here.

I've just received this dispatch from Candor, and I'm taking it all the way to the North Pole.

Martha Goodsell of the Fallow Hollow Deer Farm explains that, in the winter, male reindeer shed their antlers first; the ladies keep their antlers longer to protect the winter food supply.

So, while we've all been dazzled by Rudolph's bright nose and brawn and the antler-clad machismo of Dasher, Dancer, Prancer, Vixen, Comet, Cupid, Donner, and Blitzen (we should've known by the names), they were frauds!

"At Christmas, when you see the [antlered] reindeer pulling Santa's sleigh, they couldn't have been males," Martha says, with an enlightened smile. "At that time of year, they're all ladies!"

I demand a remake of the movie. I was robbed of some of Christianity's most famous female role models!

In the meantime, please join me in song: "Rudolph the red-nosed reindeer / had a very shiny nose. And if you ever saw HER / you would even say it glows. . . ."

GETTING TO THE POINT
Candor

When Robert Berg makes a point, people pay attention.

That's because Berg makes atlatls.

Of course. Wait, atla—WHO?

An atlatl is a spear-throwing device. It is "essentially, a stick with a handle on one end and a hook or socket that engages a light spear or dart on the other," according to the World Atlatl Association.

"It was the weapon of choice in North America prior to . . . the bow and arrow," Berg explains. (The bow and arrow, incidentally, came on the scene around the same time that Jesus Christ was born.)

"It was used by every ancient culture in the world at one time or another," Berg says. It was used by hunters during the last Ice Age and, some say, was a contributing factor to the extinction of the woolly mammoth. When Columbus arrived in America, he was greeted by the natives, who were—you guessed it—armed with atlatls.

The atlatl was such a powerful weapon, in fact, that it was "the only weapon Cortez and his Conquistadors feared because it easily pierced Spanish armor," Bob Perkins writes on his website (http://atlatl.com).

Today, the atlatl is still used by some tribes in Australia, Papua New Guinea, and South America, but in North America, it is used only for sport and competition.

Berg, who owns Thunderbird Atlatls in Owego, doesn't just make atlatls; he also uses them for hunting and fishing. Manning his booth at a Native American Pow Wow in Owego, Berg flashes pictures of wild boars he shot with atlatls in upstate New York and Georgia.

Why not just use a gun?

"I'm a primitivist," Berg explains. "If everyone's goin' that way, I go this way—it's easier goin'!"

And, for all you techno-elitists, Berg says, "It's not unsophisticated. . . . It's all the same technology, brought forward. I twist the cordage to make the atlatl in the exact same ways they twisted the cables to hold up the Brooklyn Bridge!"

If you're looking to beef up your survival skills (you know, should you find yourself stranded on a desert island or on a reality TV show), Berg teaches a primitive survival class as well as atlatl making. Leave

★ ★

I can shoot this spear with an atlatl tied behind my back!

the apron at home, though, because this isn't a pottery class—after you learn to make an atlatl, you'll learn to shoot it as well!

Anyone have any good boar recipes?

For more information visit www.thunderbirdatlatl.com or call (800) 836-4520.

THE WONDERFUL WIZARD OF CHITTENANGO
Chittenango

L. Frank Baum had many jobs, from reporter to fancy-poultry breeder, but he was always a great storyteller.

One day, when he was living in Chicago, Baum was telling a story to some neighborhood kids in his living room. One little girl looked up and said: "Mr. Baum? What's the name of the place where Dorothy and her friends live?"

Baum hadn't yet given it a name, but he didn't want to disappoint the little girl. His eyes raced around the room before settling on a filing cabinet. The bottom drawer was labeled O-Z. He turned to the little girl and replied, "Oz."

His wife, Maud, "thought it was an absurd word," says Kathleen Sorbello Di Scenna, an L. Frank Baum historian. "The children thought it was magical."

Baum, author of *The Wonderful Wizard of Oz* and more than a dozen other Oz-based books, was born in Chittenango, a small village about 15 miles east of Syracuse.

Every summer, thousands flock to Chittenango for a four-day Oz festival, featuring everything from the Emerald City Classic golf tournament to a spaghetti dinner with some of the original Munchkins; a Wizard of Oz ballet; a parade featuring a slew of Dorothys, Tin Men, Lions, and Scarecrows; a costume contest; and a Wizard's balloon launch. In 2007, the name of the festival was changed to Oz-stravaganza from OzFest so as not to be confused with the (Ozzie) Ozzfest heavy-metal music festival.

Those who have studied Baum's life and writing suggest that, in the *Wizard of Oz,* "Kansas is based on his experience living in

Toto, I've got a feeling we're not in Kansas!

Fall Person Peeping

Cohocton

The Finger Lakes region is one of the best places for fall leaf peeping, with rolling hills painted in vibrant shades of red, orange, and gold, and lakes in every direction to reflect the autumnal art.

If you're visiting Cohocton, southwest of Canandaigua Lake, you're likely to peep something else besides leaves up in those trees: people!

For more than forty years, the village of Cohocton has held a Fall Foliage Festival. One of the signature events is the annual Tree Sitting Contest.

The contest used to involve individuals sitting in trees for forty-eight hours, but the event is now a relay team sport and there are no overnight shifts. The designated sitter sits 5 feet off the ground in an Air Chair, which is "like a hammock, only you sit in it rather than lie in it," says Tom Cox, president of the Cohocton Development Corporation.

In addition to sitting, contestants compete in athletic and trivia events, making it something like *Survivor* meets *Jeopardy!*—in a tree!

About half of the contestants are teenagers, but they've had competitors of all ages. "The first year, we had a lady eighty-seven years old sit!" Cox says.

The winning team is the one that logs the most tree time over the course of the weekend and the one that wins the most challenges. Teams are docked three minutes for each bathroom break and are automatically disqualified if a member drops something from the tree.

"There are people who've competed for many years who are like professional tree sitters," Cox adds. "They do training . . . to have no ground time." (I don't even want to know!)

Photo by Melissa Cox

Ready for the battle of the sittest?

Mind you, the contestants aren't just battling each other; they're also battling the elements. Temperatures can drop into the twenties at that time of year and anything is possible—wind, rain, or even snow. So, in addition to snacks, books, cell phones, and Game Boys, they also take tarps and snowsuits!

The contest has gained such notoriety it even spawned a Trivial Pursuit question, which is about the type of trees the sitters sit in. The answer (hey, you bought the book, you earned it) is Sugar Maple.

The winning team receives a $300 cash prize, bragging rights as Tree-Top Champions, and most importantly, a bathroom break!

★ ★

drought-ridden South Dakota, while Oz is based on his boyhood in central New York.

"I believe that central New York *is* the Land of Oz," Di Scenna says.

She points out that, in one of his less-famous works, *Dot and Tot in Merryland,* Baum describes his boyhood home in central New York, called Rose Lawn, and it sounds and awful lot like Oz. "In my opinion . . . Dorothy is actually walking onto Rose Lawn," Di Scenna explains.

This may not be heavy metal, but man, this is heavy!

Chittenango boasts that it "transforms into Oz" during Oz-stravaganza, but you can visit some of Baum's personal landmarks any time of year to see if you can find little bits of Oz in central New York.

First, there's the yellow brick road Chittenango installed down its Main Street to get you into the Oz spirit. In nearby Mattydale, on Route 11 (formerly Plank Road) is where Rose Lawn used to be; the former family property is now home to an action-sports center. There's the Matilda Joslyn Gage house in Fayetteville, where Baum's mother-in-law lived, and the Stanton house, 10 miles south, where his mother lived. There's also an old-growth forest near the North Syracuse Junior High School that the keepers swear was Baum's inspiration for Oz's enchanted forest!

Use your brain. Have a heart. Have courage! And, as you stroll down the Yellow Brick Road, the local shopkeepers would like to remind you, "There's no place like Chittenango!"

For more information visit www.landofozpres.net and www.chittenango.org.

YOU'RE A GIANT FAKER. NO, *YOU* ARE!
Cooperstown

Some people go to war for their religious beliefs. George Hull had other ideas.

Hull, an atheist, thought that the (largely Christian) American public would be gullible enough to believe in giants just because it said so in the Bible. So, in 1868, Hull and a partner secretly commissioned a sculpture of a "petrified man," more than 10 feet long, made out of gypsum. To get the statue to look old and authentic, they did everything from hammering the "skin" with a block of wood with hundreds of sewing needles to create pores to dousing it with a gallon of sulfuric acid.

Hull buried the gypsum giant in a shallow, 5-foot grave on a farm in Cardiff, New York, that was owned by a relative. Then, he went back to work as a cigar manufacturer in Binghamton and waited.

A fake giant is classic. Never goes out of style!

Sure enough, about a year later, workers who'd been hired to dig a well on the farm discovered the giant.

Hull wasted no time, quickly pitching a tent over the site and charging 50 cents admission per person to see the great Cardiff Giant!

Within a few months, people began questioning the authenticity of this petrified giant. That didn't really matter, though, because the discovery was provoking something much bigger: a debate about religion versus science that forced people to question their fundamental beliefs.

Visitors flocked to see the giant when it was thought to be a great scientific discovery and even later when it was proved to be a great

Round and Round the State

Cooperstown

If you're not sold on paying admission to the Farmers' Museum just to see a fake giant, here's another reason to visit this rural-history museum.

In addition to living-history demonstrations such as wallpaper making and cow milking, the museum is home to the Empire State Carousel.

Photo by Richard Walker

Get a little crazy and ride a loon on the Empire State Carousel!

The carousel was built over two decades by more than 1,000 artisans—from carvers to quilters, painters, and woodworkers—and assembled on Long Island. It was started in 1982 and found a permanent home at the Farmers' Museum in 2006.

The museum calls it "the museum you can ride on," but I like to think of it as a cheat sheet to New York State. There are twenty-three hand-carved animals—all indigenous and famous in various parts of the state—that you can ride on. There's Bucky Beaver, representing our state animal and fur-trading roots; Benny Brook Trout, representing our state fish; Daphne Duck, a shout-out to the duck farmers of Long Island; and Louie Loon, a nod to the bird that has captured the imagination—and poetic license—of the Adirondacks.

If you're not an animal person, you can ride in a scallop shell (the state shellfish) or an Erie Canal boat.

There are also paintings of famous New Yorkers from all corners of the state, from Susan B. Anthony and Uncle Sam to P.T. Barnum and daredevil Sam Patch. There's even a little (oh, the irony) Cardiff Giant painted in the P.T. Barnum panel!

Go ahead. Give it a whirl!

hoax. It was such as success that P.T. Barnum tried to buy it. When he could not, he created a copy . . . of the fake giant! In fact, both fakes were on display in New York City—2 blocks apart—at the same time. In a testament to Barnum's showmanship, his fake actually drew more visitors.

The Cardiff Giant was acquired by the New York State Historical Association in 1947, and is currently on display at the Farmers' Museum in Cooperstown.

So, why are people still paying money to see this fake giant, more than one hundred years later? Barbara Franco explains in "The Cardiff Giant: A Hundred-Year-Old Hoax": "Despite the fact that hoaxes were a common occurrence of the nineteenth century, the Cardiff Giant's extraordinary success sets it apart as a classic in the art of hoaxing."

Oh, man. That *is* classic.

Finally, Franco writes: "Everyone goes away satisfied that they have seen the great American hoax."

To get in on the hoax, visit www.farmersmuseum.org or call (888) 547-1450.

NO BASEBALL EXPERIENCE NECESSARY
Cooperstown

Did you know that, even if you've never played baseball in your life, *you* could be in the Baseball Hall of Fame?

The Cooperstown museum has an exhibit called "Sacred Ground," which honors some of the sport's most beloved ballparks. At the entrance are fabric mâché statues honoring some of the game's most famous fans!

There's Pearl Sandow, who cheered for the Atlanta Crackers—and later the Braves—while attending more than 5,000 games in her sixty-six-year fan career! You couldn't miss her, with a pile of white hair that she described as a "snow-cone style." On her 100th birthday, the Braves even brought the Cooperstown statue to join her at the stadium, where she was named team captain for a day.

The stats of these superfans are pretty impressive!

Dancing his way to superfan fame was Yoyo, who wore a suit, fedora, and sunglasses, and did the "Mummers Strut" through stadium aisles during Philadelphia Phillies games for more than thirty years! Mummers.com describes the strut this way: "Spread your arms, supporting an invisible cape; pumping your elbows, rocking and bobbing your body, you strut forward and back, sideways and in circles."

And, how can we tawk about supa fans and nawt tawk about Hilda Chesta? A die-hard Brooklyn Dodgers fan, Hilda Chester attended nearly as many games as the players did from the 1920s until the Dodgers left Brooklyn in 1957. After a heart attack in 1941, she couldn't yell anymore, so she brought a frying pan and iron ladle to the games to keep making a ruckus for her boys!

And so, my fame-loving friends, you don't have to hit 500 home runs to be in the Baseball Hall of Fame. All it takes is dedication. Cheer, strut, or bang your frying pan until they retire your ladle!

For more information visit www.baseballhalloffame.org or call (888) HALL-OF-FAME.

FROM GLASS SLIPPERS TO ATOMIC ART
Corning

Great news, Cinderella: We've got your glass slipper right here! Now, here's the bad news: It's not very comfortable. Ooh, hey, watch yourself. Look out for that lightning!

Hey, if the shoe fits!

The Corning Museum of Glass has a lot of what you might expect—vases, bowls, glass-blowing demonstrations, and glass in technology exhibits— but the museum also has a slew of glass objects you probably didn't even know existed.

In addition to the glass slipper, there's a glass glove and—taking Cinderella to a whole new level—a glass evening gown! There's a set of colored lenses, attached like measuring spoons, which were used by Victorian tourists to view the landscapes through rose-colored glass . . . or yellow or blue . . . (Ooh, wicked stepsister, you're looking a little green today!)

There's a Barbie-sized, 3-D glass portrait of an Egyptian pharaoh. It's the oldest known glass portrait, dating back to the 1400s . . . B.C.!

★ ★

There's a household iron made of glass, a short-lived design aimed at conserving metal during World War II. The museum also has World War II–era bullets tipped in glass, for the same reason.

The museum has some glass that will bend your definition of glass. There's glass created in 1945 by the test explosion of an atomic bomb in White Sands, New Mexico, as well as glass created by the impact of meteorites (which looks like drumsticks left on the grill too long) and glass created by lightning (which looks like a hollowed-out log).

For all of you "world's largest" lovers—get your checklist ready— the museum is also home to the world's largest paperweight, clocking in at a whopping 100 pounds!

With the world's largest collection of glass—more than 45,000 objects—there's definitely something that'll make you go "Hmmm" at the Corning Museum of Glass.

Was that glass eye looking at me?

For more information visit www.cmog.org or call (800) 732-6845.

HOW MANY FINGERS AM I HOLDING UP?

The Finger Lakes

Given the name, you might guess that there are five Finger Lakes, but in fact, there are eleven. (Though, the large ones do look like fingers.) And, while it's fun to think of their creation as God making His own Hollywood Walk of Fame handprint, the lakes were actually formed by glaciers during the last Ice Age, more than 100 million years ago.

Can you name at least three of the lakes?

I didn't think so.

Allow me. The lakes are, from west to east: Conesus, Hemlock, Canadice, Honeoye, Canandaigua, Keuka, Seneca, Cayuga, Owasco, Skaneateles, and Otisco.

It's hard to stand out in a family of eleven, but here are a few fast facts to help you tell them apart:

Keuka Lake is one of the few Y-shaped lakes in the world, and its water flows both north and south.

This Lake's Got Flare

Canandaigua Lake

The Finger Lake known as Canandaigua has some of the most expensive lakefront property in the U.S. It's a popular summer-home spot 40 miles southeast of Rochester.

You'd think that, with all the golfing, boating and other activities of the affluent—not to mention, learning to spell Canandaigua—that residents wouldn't have much time for historical appreciation. But they've managed to preserve a pretty spectacular Seneca Indian tradition known as the "Ring of Fire."

Every year, in early September, the Seneca elders would light a fire on top of Bare Hill, located on the southeastern side of the lake in what is now Middlesex, in order to give thanks for a good harvest. As a symbol of unity, members of the tribe would light smaller fires all along the shore, creating a ring of fire around the lake. They chose Canandaigua for the sacred event because it's where they believe their ancestors first emerged from the earth. In fact, *Canandaigua* means "the chosen spot."

Photo courtesy VisitFingerLakes.com | Valerie Knoblauch

Today, the event is held on the Saturday of Labor Day weekend. A bonfire is lit on Bare Hill— probably not by children, but let's not call them elderly—at dusk. Residents who live on the shores of the 16-mile-long lake take that as their cue to light red flares, recreating the Senecas' ring of fire.

Two of the other western Finger Lakes, Keuka and Honeoye, also host rings of fire.

In case you're wondering how you coordinate hundreds of people with flares, local shops, including Wegmans grocery stores, begin selling them in early summer for $1 so residents have plenty of time to get their flares by Labor Day. However, it's not clear how they remember where they put them!

* *

The St. Lawrence River must've hogged all the islands (you know, that little place called the Thousand Islands) because there are only two islands in all of the eleven Finger Lakes! The smallest (145 feet long) is Squaw Island in Canandaigua Lake. The 11,000-year-old island is said to be where Seneca women and children hid during the 1779 Sullivan Expedition, an American offensive against the Iroquois. The other is Frontenac Island in Cayuga Lake, and is thought to have been an Algonquin burial ground.

The two deepest lakes are Seneca and Cayuga (618 feet and 435 feet, respectively); their deepest points are below sea level. The deepest part of Honeoye Lake, by contrast, is 30 feet.

All but one of the lakes (Hemlock) were named by Native Americans. Canadice Lake means "long lake," but it's actually the smallest of the Finger Lakes at just under 4 miles long. Cayuga, the longest of the lakes (nearly 40 miles), means "boat landing." Seneca means "place of stone." Conesus translates to "always beautiful," which, I'm sure, caused quite a fuss among the other lakes at the time.

Why is it always Conesus, Conesus, Conesus?!

IT'S NOT ABOUT BEING WRIGHT
Hammondsport

> If I say, "Ford," you think automobile, right?
> If I say, "Wright brothers," you think airplanes, right?
> Now, what if I say, "Glenn Curtiss"? Anything?
> Right.

In 1907 Glenn Hammond Curtiss was dubbed "The Fastest Man on Earth," clocking in at more than 136 miles per hour on a V-8-powered motorcycle he built himself. At the urging of early flight enthusiasts such as Alexander Graham Bell (yes, he of telephone fame), Curtiss took his speedy talents to the skies, where he soared to the titles of "founder of the American aircraft industry" and the "Father of Naval Aviation."

★ ★

It's not Wright, I tell you. It was Curtiss who was issued the first U.S. pilot's license! (The Wright brothers were actually nos. 4 and 5 in the pilot's license pecking order.)

So, why do we know the name Wright, but not Curtiss?

Simple: It's easier to have one name on a multiple-choice test! Well, that and the fact that the Wrights, who worked secretively, spent much of their time suing other aviation pioneers like Curtiss to ensure that it was their name that would forever be the answer to that multiple-choice question. "It was this mentality that they could control aviation by patent," says Trafford Doherty, executive director of the Glenn H. Curtiss Museum in Hammondsport.

Curtiss, meanwhile, was working out in the open—like the Wikipedia of his time—with Bell and others to build better flying machines and find practical applications. He also got help from Henry Ford, who loaned Curtiss his best lawyer to help fend off the legal advances of the self-righteous Wrights.

While the Wrights were off working in secret, it was Curtiss who made the first preannounced public flight. For those of you keeping score at home, that's "Fastest Man on Earth" in 1907, and first public flight in 1908. Man, time really flies!

Another fun fact: Curtiss was also responsible for early development of the RV. "Curtiss loved to camp, but he hated to sleep on the ground!" Doherty explains.

Take a plane, train, or automobile to the Glenn H. Curtiss Museum in Hammondsport, located at the southern tip of Keuka Lake. For more information visit www.glennhcurtissmuseum.org or call (607) 569-2160.

ANCIENT NEW YORK BLING
Herkimer

Did you know there was a diamond mine right here in New York?

OK, it's not the kind of diamonds you're thinking of. They're actually quartz-like objects called Herkimer Diamonds. They look a lot like diamonds in the rough. The big difference is that they're not as faceted as their more expensive counterparts, and they're not quite as hard. Diamonds are a 10 on the hardness scale; Herkimer Diamonds are about 7.5.

Herkimer Diamonds, the mine says, are "doubly terminated quartz crystals already faceted by nature." They are unique to the area and—gemistorians, prepare to be dazzled—they're believed to be more than 500 million years old. That was when a shallow, prehistoric sea used to cover much of New York and the east coast.

The diamonds, which can grow up to 6 inches but are typically less than an inch in diameter, are tucked in elliptical-shaped pockets in dolomite limestone bedrock. Sometimes excavation can turn up a few, sometimes it can pop open a whole pocket!

Look at the size of that rock!

The mine opened to the public in 1955 and, for a small fee, you can spend the day digging for diamonds. Here's the best part: You get to keep everything you find!

So, let's see, that's more than fifty years and thousands of people who've been digging up these diamonds. Isn't the supply about to run out?

Not anytime soon. The mine consists of 400 acres, less than five of which have been used up in the last fifty years. So, keep digging!

Now, I'm definitely drawn to shiny objects, but I've got to be honest here, when I saw couples and families out there all day, toiling away with their hammers, baking in the summer sun, it seemed more like prison than a vacation. Still, everyone I spoke with absolutely loved digging for diamonds.

What am I missing? Maybe it's all in the marketing. Say "diamonds" and we're there.

Renee Scialdo Shevat, president and owner of the Herkimer Diamond Mines, puts it this way: "When you find a pocket, it piques your interest that you'll find more. It's like the lottery—you might win that million dollars!"

Plus, some people think the crystals have mystical properties—that they "activate the third eye," boost psychic abilities, and aid in general well-being.

They also make a very pretty pendant.

To check out your prospects, visit www.herkimerdiamond.com or call (315) 891-7355.

EIGHT BRAINS IN JARS
Ithaca

Does having a larger brain make you smarter? Is my brain different from your brain?

These were the questions of Burt Green Wilder, a Civil War surgeon and founder of Cornell University's anatomy department. Well, this was the late 1800s, so his questions were just a smidge less polit-

The murderer, he's right behind me, isn't he?

ically correct. What Dr. Wilder really wanted to know was: Were the brains of "educated and orderly persons" (i.e., white men) different in size, shape, or weight from those of women, murderers, blacks, and the mentally ill?

In order to find out the answer to this loaded question, in 1889 Dr. Wilder started a brain collection, the first of its kind in the U.S. At its peak, the collection consisted of at least 600 brains (all donated, by the way); today, the collection has dwindled to seventy, though only eight are on display at Cornell because those are the only ones still matched up to their bios.

★ ★

In case you're wondering how Dr. Wilder got women and African Americans to donate their brains after that introduction, it was to prove Wilder wrong—that their brains were, in fact, no different.

And, you know what? They were right! Six hundred brains later, Dr. Wilder had absolutely no evidence that the brains were any different among races, genders, or varied mental capacities.

The brain collection today is exciting because it contains the brain of Wilder himself, as well as the brain of a convicted murder, Edward Rulloff, who was executed in 1871.

The first thing your critical eye will sleuth up is that Rulloff's brain appears to be slightly greener than the rest. Ah ha! A difference! Well, yes. But, Barbara Finlay, a psychology professor at Cornell and the curator of the brain exhibit, explains that it's "slightly green due to the fixative that we're using, not anything to do with being a murderer."

The truth is, once you get over being dazzled by seeing actual human brains in jars and inspecting them closely to see if you will be *the chosen one* who finds the differences among them, you will begin to realize that "There's nothing particularly interesting about any of these brains . . . or unusual," Prof. Finlay says. "That was kind of the point."

Still, Prof. Finlay asserts that their presence is significant. "This is a very important first step in understanding ourselves as material beings and our minds as material," she says.

Did she lose you? Still hoping to find that bloated "murderer lobe" behind Rulloff's cerebral cortex?

Try to work past it. The idea is to use *your* brain to ponder the physical brains before you. Is this the tangible, physical place where thinking and reasoning occur?

Prof. Finlay asks: "Is it the case that these things [brains] do the thinking and not some disembodied spirit or soul?"

And that, right there, is the power of eight brains in jars.

The Wilder Brain Collection is on display on the second floor of Uris Hall at Cornell University.

★ ★

IS THAT CAR WEARING A TUTU?

Ithaca

Artists mingle with farmers. Monks mix with belly dancers. And here comes a man on stilts, riding a bike!

A family brandishes window screens, slathers them with soap, and waves them around to make a breeze of bubbles.

The ladies from the Red Hat Society sit on bales of hay on the back of a red pickup truck as the He-Man Chainsaw Marching Band revs up a tune and the Geek Squad performs its rendition of *Stomp!* using computer keyboards.

Honk! Honk! Hey, buddy, it's the Volvo ballet! Wearing giant tutus, the cars accelerate in and out of formation, while men in leotards and tutus sashay through for the big finale—a dramatic pose across the hood! It's like *Swan Lake* meets "Greased Lightning." Oh wella, wella, wella, well . . . Tell me more! Tell me more!

This isn't your average small-town parade, with high-school marching bands and the local legion; this is how they do a parade in Ithaca.

Ithaca?

You wouldn't know it to look at this college/industrial city of 30,000, surrounded by farmland, gorges, and waterfalls, but Ithaca is brimming with artistic, cultural, and intellectual diversity. The city, just south of Cayuga Lake, has repeatedly earned itself a spot on nationwide lists,

Coupe, jete, turn, and . . . drive!

★ ★

from "Most Enlightened City" to "Great Places You've Never Heard About."

The parade is part of a four-day artistic extravaganza, called the Ithaca Festival, which, it should be noted, defies its plain vanilla name. Everyone gets involved, from babies to seniors—even the neighborhood dogs!

The festival includes music, arts and crafts, a food court to show off some of Ithaca's finest cuisine (did you know that Ithaca has more restaurants per capita than New York City?), and a Sustainability Fair, aimed at increasing green awareness, from solar-powered popcorn to vegetable-oil-fueled parade floats.

The Ithaca Festival is held every year on the first weekend after Memorial Day. For more information, visit www.ithacafestival.org.

Then strap on your stilts, pop out the window screens, and grab the dog's hybrid unicycle because we're having a parade—Ithaca style!

HEY, BUDDY, CAN YOU SPARE AN HOUR?
Ithaca

While you're in Ithaca, you might notice a little funny money changing hands.

No, it's not Monopoly money, it's Ithaca Hours! Haven't you heard of it?

Ever the socially progressive city, Ithaca was one of the first U.S. cities (in modern times) to develop its own currency. Called Ithaca Hours, the local currency is aimed at helping out small businesses and keeping money in the local economy. One Ithaca Hour is worth $10. A tenth of an hour is worth $1. There's also one-eighth, one-quarter, one-half, and two-hour increments, but I'll let you do the math on those!

Here's how it works: Local businesses pay $10 a year for membership in the Ithaca Hours network. In return, they get their business listed in a directory of businesses that accept Ithaca Hours as well as

Don't wait until the eleventh hour to spend your tenth of an hour ($1) in Ithaca!

two Ithaca Hours, the equivalent of $20, to spend at each other's businesses.

There are about 600 businesses in the network. You can whittle away the Hours on everything from a cup of coffee to dance lessons. And, when you consider that all those businesses get two Hours per year, this initiative alone is pumping $12,000 into the local economy every single year—and keeping it there!

"We're taking the barter system a step further," says Stephen Burke, president of Ithaca Hours, the organization that runs the currency system. "Some people think they're like coupons. They're not. It's exactly like cash. It *is* cash."

Why is it called an Hour? It's meant to remind you that the currency represents someone's labor. It's also a political statement on the minimum wage. "No matter what kind of work you do, you should be making at least $10 an hour," Burke says.

One of the most amazing aspects of the currency system is that Ithaca Hours offers business loans—in Hours, of course—with 0% interest! "We're here to help small businesses," Burke explains. Plus, say a business takes out a loan worth $2,000. Because it's in Hours, that money is guaranteed to stay in the local economy. "It's putting it into circulation faster," Burke says.

Hours are also offered as grants to community projects and non-profit organizations. Some employers even offer their employees partial wages paid in Hours.

If you're just passing through and want to get a few Hours in, you can trade your U.S. dollars for Ithaca Hours at the Autumn Leaves Bookstore on the Commons, or at Small World Music, owned by Burke, on West State Street.

Honestly, do you know how many Hours I spent on that?!

To read more about Ithaca Hours and find out which businesses accept the currency, visit www.ithacahours.org.

TAKE THE TOILET SEAT, KISS THE FISH
Keuka Lake

When you hire an outdoor guide, you want someone who knows what he's doing and, should it come to that, could help you survive in the wilderness.

You want a guide like Dave Durkee.

Durkee was a first-grade teacher for seven years. He loved the kids, but he was getting burned out. "I wanted to live sanely and simply," Durkee says. So, he quit his teaching job and opened a small guide service for hunting and fishing on Keuka Lake.

But his quest to scale back didn't stop there.

Durkee decided to build himself a log cabin. "I cut the trees out of the forest. Peeled the bark off by hand. Stacked and stickered [to dry out] the wood for a year. Then I built my cabin," he says, matter-of-factly, the way you or I might say, "I had chicken for dinner last night."

I'm serious. Take the toilet seat.

While he was building the log cabin, Durkee lived in . . . a tepee! (You were gonna say tepee, right?) For the first five years of tepee, then cabin, living, Durkee didn't have electricity or running water. He insists that he still wouldn't have them today, if the growth of his business didn't demand it.

So, what do you serve for dinner in a tepee?

"Everything I shoot, I eat," Durkee says. "I eat a lot of fish and venison." He also has a garden on the side of the house, with at least a dozen vegetables.

What about a refrigerator? Did he, um, have an outhouse?

There's a cold spring near the cabin, so Durkee dug a hole in there and put the, uh, refrigerables in there.

And yes, he had an outhouse. It's a subject that prompts some of the best advice you'll probably ever get on the outdoors. "In the wintertime . . . the trick is to keep the toilet seat right next to the wood stove. So, when you take it out and sit down on it, it's nice and toasty warm!"

Durkee's now on his second log cabin (his daughter lives in the first one), which is decorated with old traps, pelts, deer-head mounts, and fishing spears. "It's definitely not a girly-girl cabin!" he says.

Durkee runs the Finger Lakes Guide Service, offering something for everyone from kids to hunters and even the girly girls. He runs hunting and fishing expeditions, children's charters, dinner cruises, and booze cruises.

He may be a mountain man, but Durkee is a wild child at heart. He's well known on Keuka Lake as "Captain Dave," but he quickly adds: "I'm like the crazy pirate of Keuka Lake!"

When Durkee takes out a group of kids, he tells them about a made-up Native American tradition he calls "Kiss the Fish." "I tell them that they have to kiss a fish in order to thank the lake for providing for us. Sometimes it takes a while, but once you get one kid to do it, all the others want to do it, too!"

For more information visit http://flguideservice.com or call (315) 730-8333. Please, no e-mails. It's bad enough he has to have a phone. Don't push Captain Dave further onto the grid than he already is!

WINE, BEER, AND SPIRITS IN THE DUNGEON
Little Falls

From the outside, it looks like the "Cousin It" of castles, covered in a dense mane of trumpet vines.

Inside, it's an elegant dining room with superb food. Eat, laugh, enjoy. Head down to the dungeon for a drink or a game of pool. But check your photos carefully when you get home; you never know what unexpected foggy swirl of a guest might jump in there!

(Cue Vincent Price laugh track.)

This is Beardslee Castle, a 19th-century estate-turned-restaurant. Yes, it's a castle, but it's not one of those frou-frou castles that makes you afraid to move for fear you'll break something. It's the kind of castle you want to explore, from first nook to last cranny, hoping that something gives you a reason to stop in your tracks!

The castle was built by Augustus Beardslee in 1860. Beardslee's son, Guy, ran the estate for a while. A subsequent owner, Anton "Pop" Christensen, turned the property into a restaurant in the 1940s. After grappling with a terminal illness, Pop hung himself in what is now the side entrance foyer.

Psychics say the place has a lot of "restless energy," and the restaurant has a collection of stunning photos, taken by employees or patrons, that show ghostly figures. Some say the castle is haunted by Native Americans (this is Mohawk country, after all); some say it's the ghost of Pop. Some say they've seen Mr. Beardslee carrying a lantern out back looking for a lost child. Some say it's a woman in a white nightgown.

Cause this is din-ner! Din-ner tonight. You're fighting your appetite inside of dinner, dinner . . . to-night!

The current owner, Randy Brown, says, "I don't believe in clanking chains or anything like that," but adds that he gets about five to six really good photos a year from patrons or employees that have inexplicable human-like images in them. "That's enough to make me wonder."

If you're thinking of coming to the castle with your Ouija board or séance circle, don't bother. Brown doesn't permit ghost rustling on the premises. His theory is: "If something's there, don't go poking on it!"

In jest, he says, when local kids are bad, sometimes their parents will threaten to "bring them to Old Man Beardslee's place!"

After all, isn't that what a castle's for? To scare small children into behaving? Well, that and the amazing food. Have I mentioned the food? Let's just say, Beardslee Castle, you had me at hello, oregano and rosemary rolls with olive tapenade!

Beardslee Castle is 6 miles east of Little Falls at 123 Old State Road. For more information visit www.beardsleecastle.com or call (315) 823-3000.

UPHILL, BOTH WAYS
Middlesex

The next time your parents or grandparents haul out one of those "In my day, we used to walk to school uphill . . . both ways!" stories, try this one on them.

There's a place in the town of Middlesex, on the east side of Canandaigua Lake, that the locals call Spook Hill. Heading north on Newell Road, if you drive to the dip between a slight hill and the steeper Spook Hill and put your car in neutral, it will appear that your car is being pulled backward . . . uphill.

It works both ways. If you're driving south on Newell, just as you descend Spook Hill, it will appear that your car is being pulled forward, up the hill.

★ ★

This isn't one of those feelings you get on a stationary train when a moving train passes and you just feel like you're moving. Your car will *actually* be moving.

Is it an optical illusion, or the work of something sinister?

It depends on whom you ask.

Legend has it that an Indian chief killed in battle was once buried on the hill and his spirit still lingers there, causing the freaky occurrence. Another local tale tells of a man named Silas Pratt, who lived nearby and was said to practice black magic. One day, he vanished. He liked to walk his dog on that road, and some say, more than one hundred years later, his ghost still does.

The more pragmatic explanation is that it's an optical illusion. The two hills are merely bumps on a larger hill. So, gravity is pulling your car down the large hill, appearing to go upward when it hits the smaller bump on the hill.

Still, kids try it on their bikes, young men take their dates there to impress them, and for some local teens, it's a rite of passage as soon as they get their driver's license. Scientists are drawn to the site, out to prove, through detailed measurements, that it's merely an illusion.

Whatever you choose to believe, it works. And it's bizarre.

To try it for yourself, take Route 364 and turn west on South Vine Valley Road. (*Not* North Vine Valley Road.) The third left is Newell Road. The dip is between Woods Road and Spike Road. If you're iffy on the directions, call the Yates County Chamber of Commerce at (800) 868-9283.

These are local roads, and the traffic is light, but while your mouth is hanging open in amazement, please don't forget two very important things: 1) Steer. 2) Keep an eye on the rearview mirror for approaching traffic.

Boo!

★ ★

THE START OF SOMETHING GRAPE!

Naples

The village of Naples, 4 miles south of Canandaigua Lake, is among the smallest communities in New York State, but that hasn't stopped it from doing grape things: It's known as the "Grape Pie Capital of the World."

I know what you're thinking. Grape pie? Why have I never heard of this? Grapes aren't a rare ingredient like, say, the hair of a unicorn, so why isn't the grape pie right up there with apple, blueberry, and pumpkin?

The reason is because grape pies are labor intensive. You have to peel and de-seed each grape before you can make the filling. And really, who has time for that? Apparently, the people of Naples.

It all started in the early 1960s, when Al Hodges, owner of the Redwood Restaurant in Naples, wanted to come up with something new to draw more customers into his restaurant. When he came across a recipe for grape pies from a local German woman, he realized it was the perfect thing, given the abundance of grapes in the area. But, Hodges and his chefs didn't have the time. Meanwhile, Irene Bouchard, who lives across the street from the restaurant, had just quit her job at Widmer Wine Cellars and opened a bakery in her home. So, Hodges recruited her to churn out the grape pies, which were selling like hotcakes. (Well, hot pies.) That first year, she made fifty pies during the fall grape season. By the 1980s, she was making thousands of pies.

Bouchard, known as "The Grape Pie Queen," inspired other local bakers to grape-ness, and today, it's estimated that 70,000 grape pies are sold in Naples each year. Most bakers only make the pies during the fall grape-harvest season, but some, such as Monica's Pies, freeze the grapes so they can sell the pies year-round and even online (www.monicaspies.com).

A good time to visit is for the Naples Grape Festival in September, which features all kinds of grape things, including grape pies, tarts, cookies, jellies, and ice cream, and a pie contest to crown the "World Champion Grape Pie Baker."

Isn't that grape?

SMALL ON SPACE, BIG ON GOD
Oneida

There are at least a dozen tiny churches from New York to California, but the World's Smallest Church just may be in Oneida.

The Cross Island Chapel is 4x7 feet and seats two. It's built on a man-made island in the middle of a pond, so you'll need a boat to get there.

For weddings, the chapel can fit the happy couple, two witnesses, and a minister if they're standing, but if you're inviting more than two people, you might want to bring a few extra seats. (Might I suggest canoes?) Better yet, just have everybody else watch from shore.

The chapel, which is nondenominational, was built by Chandler Mason and his daughter Beth in 1989. Chandler, a Baptist, had already built another tiny island on the pond and pitched a small, wooden cross on it as a symbol of God. His wife, Kay, recalls that, when neighbors saw the cross, they said to Chandler, "You need a church to go with it!" Taking the dare, Chandler looked up "smallest church" in *The Guinness Book of World Records* and made sure his was even smaller.

The interior has two chairs and a pulpit. There are two stained-glass windows to let the light in, but, amazingly, there's also electricity inside. There's one overhead light and an outlet so you can plug in your boom box to play the wedding march. Of course, the walk down the aisle would probably be more like an aerobics-style march in place, but hey, you're getting married in the World's Smallest Church! And, five-six-seven-eight . . .

A hand-painted sign on the shore says the chapel was "Dedicated as a witness to God," which Kay says, was intended just as the cross was, to "remind people of God." And, in case you haven't put it

★ ★

Photo by Chandler Mason

Row, row, row your bride gently to the chapel!

together yet, the Cross Island Chapel got its name from that island
with a cross on it that Chandler had built a few years earlier.

The church may be small, but getting it out to the middle of the
pond was no small feat. Kay says it was done in the winter, when
the pond was covered in a thick sheet of ice. About twenty of the
neighborhood guys brought their snowmobiles to help Chandler drag
it out across the ice!

The pond is on the Masons' property, off of Sconondoa Road in
Oneida (3 miles from the New York State Thruway), but visitors are

always welcome. There aren't regular services held at the church, but if you'd like to go inside, or even get married at the World's Smallest Church, just call Kay (315-363-4488) and she'll row you out there.

FREE LOVE AND FLATWARE
Oneida

Once you hear this next story, you'll never look at a spoon the same way again.

John Humphrey Noyes founded the religion known as Perfectionism in 1848. He was raised in a deeply religious household, and the idea for this "perfect" community sprang from his refusal to feel guilty for his sins.

Focusing on the community over the self, one of Perfectionism's core doctrines was that every member of the community was married to every other member of the opposite sex. And so, Noyes and his 300 followers lived in a 93,000-square-foot mansion as one big happy family!

OK, people, let's make some Noyes!

To be clear, Noyes believed that he was doing God's work. Once you converted to the religion, you were absolved of your sins and could focus on personal and social perfection.

The community disbanded in 1879 amid a failed leadership transition and persecution from the outside. Many members married quickly but, after more than thirty years, some had a hard time integrating into traditional society. So, the community reorganized in what was called a "joint-stock company," which later became Oneida Ltd.

One good thing about striving for perfection was that it created a strong work ethic in the community, which proved useful when they formed the company that went on to become one of the most recognized names in silverware.

Of course, the company doesn't like to talk about its free-love past. The only reference on its Web site (www.oneida.com) is: "The company originated in a utopian community established in the mid-19th century, and has had a strong reputation for quality since that time." Knowing the real story, I think we will all view their slogan, "Bring Life to the Table," in a whole new light!

Today, you can take a tour of the Oneida Community Mansion (www.oneidacommunity.org), which is run separately from the company, to learn more about the history of this utopian community-turned-silverware maker.

Did you ever think your tableware had such a provocative past? Fork, you sexy thing!

OH, ONE MORE THING BEFORE I R.I.P.—
Owego

Have you ever pondered your own epitaph? Are you happy with one of those stock engravings such as "In Memory of" or "Rest in Peace"? Or, do you feel it needs to say a little more?

Well, at Evergreen Cemetery in Owego, a couple of bombastic bards got a little carried away. They wrote one of the longest epitaphs in the U.S., clocking in at 135 words!

Here it is:

> *Well, we have got what was coming to us, and here in this burial plot we lie:—*
>
> *We fourteen skeletons of Gibsons, Tinkhams, Drakes, Pixleys, and Curtises, that once were clothed with flesh and lived and loved and laughed and danced and sang and suffered just like you till the God-created life-transmitting spark that had been passed down to us from its beginning died.*
>
> *But we were not animals, or insects, or plants, which likewise have their life-transmitting sparks, but beings into whom at our birth had been breathed a soul-entity that came directly from God.*

★ ★

And to him our soul-entities have gone to be dealt with by
Him as our treatment of others whom He had created deserves.
What think you of these beliefs?
                                      —Erected in 1935 by E. T. G.

Thanks for asking, you guys. Well, first, you probably didn't need to tell me you were once clothed with flesh. I got it. And you definitely didn't need to tell me what you were not—animals, insects, etc. Got that, too, thanks.

Second, you could've left it at lived and loved and laughed. By the time you tacked on dance and sang, it seemed a little desperate, like maybe God was paying you by the word or something.

In loving memory of the English language.

And, finally, it was just shameless to repeat—not to mention dilute—a powerful phrase such as "life-transmitting spark" twice!

To be fair, you made some excellent points. I liked the stuff about living life to the fullest and treating others fairly. But, all the sparks and repetition made it feel more like a cigarette that you couldn't quite get lit.

With all that literary flicking, I'm not so sure your neighbors will be able to rest in peace.

Lord knows it's going to keep me up tonight.

THE WHOLE FAMILY IS GOING TO JAIL
Owego

All right, wise guy, you're coming with me. I'm going to take you downtown and book you.

That is, book you a table at the Jail House Restaurant in downtown Owego!

This isn't just a gimmick: It really was the county lockup from 1910 to 1998, when a new jail was built and this one was converted into a restaurant. The bars are still on the windows and there are still jail cells inside—you know, to preserve that prison charm. The only difference is, now, instead of serving jail time, they serve dinnertime!

"It's a historic landmark and it's cool," says Chris Nowak, who took ownership of the restaurant in 2007. "You're literally eating in jailhouse cells!"

Indeed, the tables, which are refurbished jail cots with a glass top, are right inside the cells. On the second floor, you can even request to have the cell doors closed while you dine. There's also one cell left intact, complete with rickety cot, chipped sink, and toilet for that perfect I-spent-the-evening-in-jail photo op!

Nowak was careful to keep the bar crowd and family dining areas separate. (It's smart to keep prison gangs apart.) The first floor houses the bar area, which has a Hard Rock Cafe feel to it and a motorcycle on display that was built out of recycled jail metal by the guys downstairs at Jail-house Choppers. The second floor is a more contemporary family-dining area, with sheers and candles instead of choppers for decor. (Martha and Paris would love it.) Though, remember, you're still in jail, so if anyone gives you lip at the table, ask the waitress to close the cell doors!

C'mon in. We've got a cell—I mean, table—waiting for you.

The food is reasonably priced and, in the summer, there's low-key live entertainment—everything from country to jazz—in the gazebo across the street.

Hmmm. I had no idea that jail could be such a pleasant experience!

Adding to its intrigue, legend has it that a ghost, perhaps a former inmate, still occasionally roams through the jail. Maybe he's trying to spring one of his friends, or maybe it's just that your chicken smelled so darn good!

If you're curious about the jail and its history, you can ask one of the waitstaff to give you a tour.

The Jail House Restaurant is located at 176 Main Street in Owego. For more information call (607) 223-4210.

★ ★

SLEEPING IN THE SELF-HELP SECTION

Owego

A typical day in the life of John Spencer is just like yours or mine: He goes to work. Cooks supper. Has some wine. Does some reading. Goes to bed.

But Spencer's lifestyle is as extraordinary as the rare books he sells. Did you notice that "goes to work" wasn't followed by "comes home?" That's because Spencer lives in Riverow Bookshop, the four-story bookstore he owns and runs in downtown Owego!

No, I'm not talking about an apartment on the third floor. I'm talking about an apartment of rooms sprinkled here and there throughout the bookstore.

Near the front entrance is a landing that leads to the bargain basement. That's Spencer's kitchen. The basement doubles as his garage.

Welcome to my living room. Care to buy something?

There, you'll find cheap books as well as power tools. In between bookcases on the second floor is a door leading to a college-dorm-sized room. It has a twin bed, small closet, and shower stall. A sign over the door reads SELF-IMPROVEMENT section.

"I always tell people that I live in the science section, but I'm thinking of moving to psychology!" Spencer jokes.

The dorm-like room may seem a little small for a grown man, but it's definitely an improvement when you consider that he was sleeping on the bottom row of a bookshelf when he first moved in seven years ago!

Out among the books on the second floor is Spencer's office and living room, complete with an antique couch and a refrigerated wine cooler. Get the Mystery Machine revved up because there's also a trick bookcase that moves to reveal a secret room! That's where Spencer keeps his private stash of rare items. (But you meddling kids stay out of it!)

On the third floor are a closet and an open-air pantry, as well as a stereo system and a sauna. He also uses this floor to dry out old books in kitty litter and store rare books, including a collection of Bibles, some dating back to the 18th century.

"I'm an atheist, but I probably have one of the largest collections of Bibles!" Spencer says.

On a nice day, you might catch Spencer up on the roof, making dinner in his solar-powered oven.

Some of Spencer's belongings may be in the fiction section (is that a hot pot?), but you can file this story under nonfiction!

Visit www.riverow.com or call (607) 687-4094.

JESUS GOES HOLLYWOOD
Palmyra

When you think of Mormonism, you probably think of Utah. Well, thank your latter-day saints you bought this book. I'm here to tell you what you *should* be thinking: Palmyra.

★ ★

Hollywood on the Hill known as Cumorah.

I'll give you three reasons: 1) Mormonism was founded in Palmyra.
2) Only 14 percent of the world's Mormons live in Utah. 3) In
Palmyra, you can watch Jesus *fly*.

The divine aerial display is part of the annual Hill Cumorah Pageant,
a dazzling Hollywood-like production that tells the Mormon story. It's
put on by the Church of Jesus Christ of Latter-Day Saints in Palmyra.

The *Rochester City Newspaper* described it this way: "If Heaven
isn't as spectacular as this [show], some of us will be very disappointed."

If you don't believe that Hollywood can come to a town of about
8,000, let me give it to you by the numbers:

There are more than 600 cast members, from all over the country, in the epic show. The outdoor stage is the size of half a football field, spread over ten levels. There are more than 2,000 costumes and 400 wigs. There's free seating for 9,000 people at each of seven shows held each year. The pageant has been performed for more than seventy years.

Impressed yet? Wait. There's more.

You also get techno-tacular Hollywood effects, including waterfalls, an earthquake, and a ship caught in a storm of thunder, lightning, and rain. Plus, pillars of fire and the flight of Jesus Christ as he descends 30 feet to Earth.

Man, his career has really taken off since he went Hollywood!

You don't have to be a Mormon to attend, but you do have to be a Mormon to be in the show. So, if you have dreams of being Jesus Christ, skip the Shakespeare and brush up on your Joseph Smith. (You know, the guy who wrote the *Book of Mormon.* Seriously, you're going to have to know this stuff if you want to be Jesus.)

For more information visit www.hillcumorah.org.

ALL STEEPLED TOGETHER
Palmyra

At the intersection of Main, Church, and Canandaigua streets in Palmyra, there's a church on every corner, all built in the 1800s! Hey, Ripley, can you believe it?

The "Four Corners" churches represent four branches of Christianity: the Western Presbyterian Church (built in 1832), the First United Methodist Church (1867), the First Baptist Church (1870), and the Zion Episcopal Church (1873).

Why are they all at the same intersection? Wasn't land wide open in the 1800s?

Maybe it was one of those Ingalls-Olsen rivalries like in *Little House on the Prairie,* and they were all jockeying for positioning and parishioners. Hey, everybody, come to *my* church!

★ ★

"I know you'd like to think that, that there was some sort of competition," says Bonnie Hays, executive director of Historic Palmyra. "But I don't think it was any kind of plan. I think what happened was simply that those were the lots available."

Remember, this was just after the wave of religious fervor spread across western and central New York. At the same time, Palmyra was becoming a hub, with the installation of major north-south and east-west roads, plus the Erie Canal and the railroad. "All the denominations were trying to get a foothold out here in the new western lands," says Wayne County Historian Peter Evans.

At the time, the Presbyterians were meeting in East Palmyra, but as Palmyra got hip, they thought it was silly to keep schlepping out to East Palmyra, and so, set up shop—er, steeple—in downtown Palmyra as the Western Presbyterians.

There wasn't much parishioner-stealing going on among the churches, Hays says, but she notes that several Presbyterians opted to change teams to Episcopalian after their preacher began pushing temperance and abolition.

Hays says that, today, all the congregations remain friendly and even attend holiday events or early masses at each other's churches. "Sometimes they'll have a joint mass, like for Easter," Hays says. "One church will have it and everybody comes. They work very well together." The churches have also combined their annual fund-raising bazaars so that people can hop from one to the next.

That's all fine and good, but what about the parking?

"Parking is probably one of the biggest foes that history has!" Hays declares unexpectedly. "We need more parking, let's tear down another building!"

Alas, that is the casualty of a church on every corner. Two of the churches tore down nearby houses to build parking lots. The others use street parking or municipal lots. You might even on occasion catch a parishioner parked in another church's lot. "Just don't tell the pastor!" Hays jokes.

★ ★

Two of the church bells still work, and yes, they ring at the same time! They toll at mass times, as well as at noon and dinnertime. Isn't that a bit of a cacophony?

"No, it's cool!" Hays says. "It's more like a round, like 'Row, row, row your boat.' It's kind of melodic."

If you'd like a tour of the churches, visit www.historicpalmyrany .com or call (315) 597-6981.

LOOK OUT BELOW!
Phelps

The village of Phelps, in the Finger Lakes region, has a unique historical bragging right: It has a two-story outhouse.

(I'll give you a minute to let that sink in.)

There are, if you can imagine, other two-story outhouses in the U.S., though more than a few of them are gags. The two-story outhouse in Phelps is no joke. It was functional—both upstairs and downstairs—for about thirty years until running water came along. It is thought to be the only two-story *brick* outhouse in the U.S. (Yes, it's a brick . . . house. I'm not going to make any vulgar jokes. You go on ahead without me.)

It's really the minivan of outhouses, with a-commode-ations for three upstairs and three downstairs. The seats are spaced a few inches apart. Who, you ask, would want to take care of their business so close to another person? Well, if you look closely, you'll see that the holes are three different sizes: One for papa, one for mama, and one for baby! (Goldilocks would've loved it.)

The outhouse is actually attached to the main house, which was built in 1869 for Dr. John Quincy Howe. However, you can't access the outhouse from inside the house for . . . um . . . aromatic reasons. You have to go outside. In the case of the upstairs outhouse, you have to walk across the kitchen roof. (Imagine that in the middle of a cold winter night!)

The Ghost Stays in the Picture

Palmyra

Not only does this small town have four churches on four corners, it also has four museums.

There's the Alling Coverlet Museum, which has the largest collection of handwoven coverlets in the country. It makes me feel a little guilty now that I just throw my quilt carelessly on the bed!

There's also the Print Shop Museum, which features a collection of 19th-century printing presses made in Palmyra; and the Palmyra Historical Museum, a former boardinghouse hotel that houses a variety of historical artifacts. There's an entire room devoted to religion, featuring everything from history on the four churches to the adorable "Catholic Corner."

Perhaps the most intriguing is the William Phelps General Store. It's a three-story building, with a store on the bottom floor and a house on the upper floors where the Phelps family lived. Everything is left intact from 1905—from dirt on the front door to the eggs in the cooler!

Apparently, Julius Phelps, who inherited the store that year, was a bit of a slacker. He made not one change to the place after his father died, not even electricity. When World War I broke out, he didn't want to deal with ration coupons. So, one day, he walked out, locked the front door, and never came back. Just left everything inside.

You'd never suspect that it would be the slacker son to make the biggest contribution to history, would you?

Adding to its intrigue, the place is haunted by at least five ghosts, according to Bonnie Hays, executive director of Historic Palmyra. One of the ghosts, Julius's daughter Sibyl, had run off to New York

City to become an actress. When she ran out of money, her father made her come back home.

Well, Sibyl may have been a little resentful about that dream deferred, because she used to be a pretty ornery ghost. "Chairs would rock. Things would fly from one spot to the other," Hays says. "We lost some visitors one day because they just got too scared. Oh well!" she says, laughing.

Sibyl was a Spiritualist, so recently, they started bringing in mediums on her birthday to do readings. They even put on a little show for bus tours, where Hays plays the Sibyl character. That seems to have settled her down.

"I think she has really come to enjoy her fame now," Hays says of Sibyl. "I call her the star of her own show!"

★ ★

And now, the part you've been waiting for: How does the two-story part work?

"The people downstairs just had to lean forward!" Don Tiffany, of the Phelps Community Historical Society, likes to joke with visitors.

Then he demonstrates, with arms outstretched wall-to-wall, that the downstairs is a few feet narrower than the "penthouse privy," as he likes to call it. All of the . . . ahem . . . deposits, are going to the same place, but they're being dropped a few feet apart. So, while it's great fun to imagine all of the "Look out below!" scenarios, there was never any risk to the people downstairs.

Just to be on the safe side—I call top!

This isn't bathroom humor, it's a real two-story outhouse!

You can take a tour of the Howe House, now owned by the historical society, and if you ask nicely, they just might show you the outhouse. But please, don't leave anything behind.

The Howe House is located at 66 Main Street in Phelps. For more information visit www.phelpsny.com/history/ or call (315) 548-4940.

TRY THE KRAUT CAKE
Phelps

The village of Phelps is famous for something besides its two-story outhouse: It was once known as the Sauerkraut Capital of the World.

Phelps used to be one of the major processing centers for sauerkraut, and that's because Ontario County is the biggest cabbage-farming area in the world.

So, you've got all that cabbage, then all that sauerkraut—what do you do? Of course, you hold an annual Sauerkraut Festival! All the sauerkraut factories have long left the village of Phelps, but the festival has kept going for more than forty years, earning it the added distinction of being one of the oldest festivals in the state.

The four-day festival includes a parade, with catchy slogans such as "Sauerkraut and More in 2004!" and "We're 41 and still having fun!" There's also a cook-off, a decorate-your-own-cabbage-head contest, and a Phelps Sauerkraut 20K race.

And, of course, there are the food vendors, who've managed to tuck kraut into every food imaginable, from salsa to fudge. Most people opt for the traditional kraut and hot dogs, but a festival specialty is the chocolate sauerkraut cake. It might sound gross at first, but I'm told that you don't even notice the kraut—it just makes the cake moist.

There are so many possibilities for sauerkraut that the festival organizers sell a book called *Cookin' with Kraut,* featuring sixty kraut-infused recipes. It's got everything from spicy sauerkraut pizza to key lime cheesecake (with a cup of kraut) and my personal favorite, Phelps Phajitas (with 1½ pounds of kraut).

★ ★

The mayor once described Phelps as a "quaint, historic village" that will soon be "its own version of Mayberry." But I'm telling you, these people know how to kick it with kraut. If you're going to make a fajita, that's phajita with a "ph"!

Stop by the gift shop at the Howe House (of two-story outhouse fame) and pick up a copy of *Cookin' with Kraut* for $5. For more information on the festival, visit www.phelpssauerkrautfestival.com.

A TOWN GETS ITS WINGS
Seneca Falls

Fans of the film *It's a Wonderful Life* have often speculated whether or not the town of Bedford Falls, where the Frank Capra holiday classic takes place, really exists.

Well, the town of Seneca Falls, tucked between two Finger Lakes—Seneca and Cayuga—claims that it is, in fact, the real Bedford Falls.

Just a minute. Just a minute. Now, hold on, Mr. Potter. First Oz in central New York, now Bedford Falls?!

That's right. Consider this: Both places, the fictitious Bedford Falls and the real Seneca Falls, were mill towns with a canal, steel-truss bridge, Victorian homes, and large Italian population. Why, even the Main Streets, with their grassy medians and globe street lamps, look identical! Capra's even been to Seneca Falls; a local barber will testify to having cut the director's hair on numerous occasions. There was even a real-life character in Seneca Falls who sounds an awful lot like Mr. Potter!

So, every year, Seneca Falls hosts an *It's a Wonderful Life* weekend in early December. Of course, there's a screening of the film. There's also a parade, a tree lighting, pictures with Santa, and the town is decked out in replicas of the Christmas lights from Bedford Falls!

Karolyn Grimes, who played George Bailey's (Jimmy Stewart's) youngest daughter, Zuzu, attends the festival every year. On her Web site, www.zuzu.net, she describes her first visit to Seneca Falls. "While

★ ★

I stood there, I watched the halo of air that came from my mouth . . . and then I saw it—the bridge. It was lit with beautiful, white lights and provided a path over a canal to the other side of town," Grimes writes. "Was I in Bedford Falls or was I in a New York town called Seneca Falls? I felt like I was in both! . . . In a sense, I was 'home.'"

Clarence! Clarence! Get me back to Seneca Falls!

For more information visit www.therealbedfordfalls.com.

EXCUSE YOU, LAKE!
Seneca Lake

It is said that the Finger Lakes are shaped like fingers because the Great Hand of the Father touched the land, making it fertile for growing crops.

The lakes even appear at times as if divine power is at work. Seneca Lake, the deepest of the Finger Lakes at more than 600 feet, can go from glass calm to a mighty storm in five minutes.

But sometimes, a funny noise comes out of the lake.

"It sounds like a big gawump!" says Bill Whitwell, a graphic artist who's lived on Seneca Lake his entire life.

The locals now refer to the noises, which sound like a cannon or sonic boom, as "Seneca drums," a term that references the area's Native American heritage. The Seneca Indians used to say that this was the sound of the drums of their ancestors, perhaps an indication of evil spirits, or maybe a grumble from the God of Thunder.

But in the past, the noises have been called everything from "Seneca guns" to the more illustrative "lake farts."

One scientific explanation is that the drums/guns/farts are caused by natural gas being released from the cracks in the bottom of the lake. No one has actually seen a lake bubble to support this theory—they've only heard the sounds—but it's still pretty plausible, since the area is rich in natural gas.

That explanation would lend itself most fittingly to the term lake fart, but let's face it, that's not good for tourism or real-estate prices.

Imagine the classified ad: "Five-bedroom, two-bath restored Victorian home, big porch, breathtaking views of Seneca Lake. Hear the wind rustle through the trees, the birds chirp, and the lake fart!"

The booms are usually pretty benign; most Seneca-area residents barely notice them anymore, though some believe that the noises are loudest just before a natural disaster.

This phenomenon isn't entirely unique to Seneca Lake; it can also be heard coming from nearby Cayuga Lake and bodies of water in Connecticut, North Carolina, and other parts of the world. The Dutch call them *mistpoeffers,* the Italians refer to them as *brontidi,* and the Japanese say *uminari.* But only in America, land of liberty and justice for all, will you hear the term "lake fart."

God bless America. This land is your land. From sea to shining, farting sea.

CHEWIE THE DANCING CAMEL
Spencer

Some people have dogs as pets. Others have cats. Some have horses.

Gail Fulkerson has a pet camel.

She named him Chewie because he looks like Chewbacca from the movie *Star Wars* and "he makes all the Chewbacca noises!" Fulk-erson says. "Whoever wrote that part *had* to be around camels."

Chewie is a Bactrian camel, which means he's got two humps. Well, he's got two, but one is flat and floppy. That usually means that a camel has been without food for a long period of time and had to cash in the fat (not water, that's a myth) stored in one hump to survive. However, it could also be genetic.

Fulkerson, who runs the Heaven Llama Farm, has a soft spot for animals that nobody wants. When she saw Chewie and that adorable flat hump, she knew she had to have him.

Now that he's in Heaven, Chewie appears to be smiling all the time. "He loves snow!" Fulkerson says, as she prepares to feed Chewie a carrot from her mouth. One thing that's not on Chewie's

It's true. I've been known to bust a move every now and again.

schedule, however, is parades. "He gets too hyped up with the music and then he has to dance!" Fulkerson says. "He does the happy camel dance."

He makes Chewbacca noises *and* he dances? Oh my goodness. I'm in love!

Fulkerson explains why the farm is called Heaven: "When there's an animal no one wants, we say, no problem! We'll send him to Heaven." Last I checked, Heaven had nineteen llamas, seven alpacas, and two guanacos, which are cousins of the llama.

That's a lotta llamas.

No wonder: "Llamas are like potato chips," Fulkerson says, "you can't have just one!"

She takes some of the animals to visit the elderly, handicapped, and kids in juvenile detention centers. The animals "have to walk through the security gate and everything!" Fulkerson says.

When she's not dancing with Chewie or sending a llama through a security check, you'll find Fulkerson in her art studio, where she makes and sells pottery. One of her most popular creations is the "Mommy Pot," a small pot no taller than your thumb, for dandelions and other short-stemmed flowers that your kids bring home.

"That's what pays for my animal habit!" Fulkerson says.

If you'd like to visit Chewie and the gang, or buy a Mommy Pot, call Fulkerson at (607) 589-4886 or send an email to pots@lightlink .com.

A HOLIDAY IS BORN

Waterloo

The origin of most American holidays is pretty straightforward. Veterans Day is November 11, marking the end of World War I. The Fourth of July celebrates America's independence. And Valentine's Day, well, that's just an excuse to demand chocolate and flowers from your sweetie-pie schnookermuffin and boost retail sales during the post-Christmas slump.

Many of us lump in Memorial Day with the other military-honoring holidays, hearing a newscast of remembrance as we get ready to fire up the grill. But what you might not know about Memorial Day is that it has an actual birthplace: Waterloo.

It all started in 1865, when the Civil War ended. Amid all the hoopla, welcoming home local soldiers from the war, Waterloo pharmacist Henry Welles and his wife would watch through their street-front window as widows and orphans solemnly walked to the cemetery. As time went on, they felt as if those soldiers lost in battle were being forgotten by the community.

Welles did a little lobbying, and on May 5, 1866, his desire for a day of remembrance was realized. Businesses and banks closed. Flags were flown at half-mast. Residents marched to the cemeteries, placing flowers on the graves of fallen soldiers. Memorial Day was born.

"It was the first time a town had closed down and done nothing but commemorate the losses of soldiers," said Caren Cleaveland, owner of the Gridley Inn and chairwoman of Waterloo's Civil War Memorial and Ball.

One score and forty some years ago, our fathers brought forth on this continent a new holiday!

May 30, 1868 was the first national observance of the holiday, originally called "Decoration Day." In 1971, Congress passed an act to change the holiday to the "last Monday in May," ensuring a three-day weekend.

Dozens of other towns across the U.S. have claimed the distinction of holding the first Memorial Day, but Waterloo has the earliest documentation of such an event and, in 1966, President Lyndon Johnson issued a proclamation, recognizing it as the official birthplace of Memorial Day.

Waterloo lives up to its heritage, holding a parade on the actual Memorial Day, no matter what day of the week it falls on, and three days of celebrate/commemorate events over Memorial Day weekend. The festivities include a parade, a reenactment of the first Memorial Day, a Second Inaugural Address by an Abe Lincoln impersonator, a performance of the official Memorial Day song, and a good, old-fashioned Civil War Ball. Throughout the weekend, there are live cannon-firing demonstrations and tea times with Lincoln.

If you can't make it to Waterloo for Memorial Day, never fear because Waterloo is home to the National Memorial Day Museum, open May through December. For more information visit www.water loony.com.

GR8 PL8Z
Waverly

No matter where you live, Don Merrill's got your number.

That's because he's got one of the largest collections of license plates in the world. He keeps them neat and organized on 180 floor-to-ceiling panels that flip like a book. If you spent five minutes looking at each board, that would take you fifteen hours!

There are a *number* of things I could tell you about Don Merrill's license-plate collection . . .

There are license plates from U.S. presidents, including a 1937 Georgia plate that says simply, "FDR." There are plates from celebrities, including Jackie Gleason, and rare plates such as the first one ever issued in the state of Virginia. It is—you guessed it—numbered "1."

A former car dealer, Merrill is somewhat of a legend in the license-plate collecting biz. They call him "Uncle Don." He is revered as the first and only person to amass a collection of plates from every state for every year, a collection he later sold to a museum in Vermont.

When he was inducted into the Automobile License Plate Collectors Association Hall of Fame (oh, snap!), the tribute described Merrill's collection this way: "In the plate-collecting fraternity, a visit to Waverly was—and remains—a visit to Mecca."

Merrill is a serious collector but maintains a sense of humor. The bathroom near the plate collection is covered from floor to ceiling in license plates. Even the TP dispenser and overhead light fixture are made of license plates. "My Tiffany lamp!" Merrill calls it.

And Merrill's eclectic collecting doesn't stop at the bumper. He's got dozens of other collections—everything from vintage automobiles to oil cans (in an original display case); even vintage bubble gum!

He built two buildings behind his family home to house the collections, which are punctuated by some rare one-off items such as a full-bodied, taxidermied moose and a booth from the local soda fountain with about 200 pieces of chewing gum stuck under the table. "We cleaned the benches and left the gum intact as a part of history," Merrill explains.

Oh, so that's the vintage gum? Nope. "That's modern gum," Merrill explains. "But over here, I just bought this original gum from a gum collector in Czechoslovakia!"

His wife even caught the collecting bug; she's started a collection of toy sewing machines.

"I think she started collecting in self-defense!" Merrill says.

Is there anything this guy won't collect?

★ ★

"I threatened to collect blondes once, but my wife didn't go for it!" Merrill jokes.

The Merrill Collection is a private museum, but Merrill gives tours by appointment.

3

North Country
and the Adirondacks
Where Pirates Roam and
Raccoons Eat Crackerjacks

Welcome to the *Thousand Islands—all 1,864 of them! (What's a few islands among friends?!) While you're here, be sure to take a tour of two of New York's most fascinating castles—Boldt and Singer. One is a fairy-tale castle, and the other is straight out of a mystery novel— whatever you do, don't lean against the bookcases. And, if you time your visit to the Thousand Islands right, you just might meet some pirates!*

The Adirondacks may not have the highest peaks in the land but Adirondack Park is so large, it's the size of five other national parks combined, including the Grand Canyon!

Feeling strong? Head to Thendara, where you can test your Superman skills and race . . . a train! Oh, and great news, I found out that you've still got a shot at winning a gold medal in Lake Placid—no athletic ability required.

If you've ever wondered what Santa does the other 364 days of the year, stop by North Pole, NY, and ask him yourself.

One packing tip before you go: Bring your binoculars because legend has it that the Loch Ness Monster's American cousin lives in Lake Champlain!

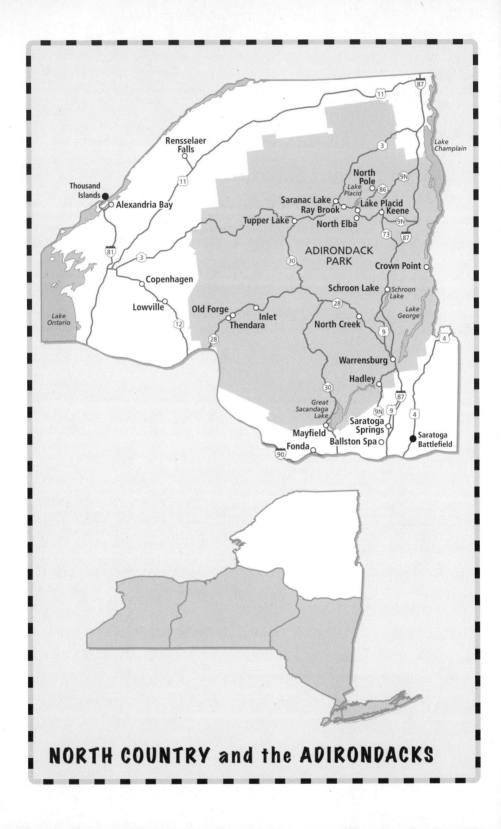

NORTH COUNTRY and the ADIRONDACKS

IT EATS THE GRAND CANYON FOR BREAKFAST
Adirondack Park

Adirondack Park may just be a dark green blotch on the map to you, but did you know it's the same size as Vermont? Maybe this will help put it in perspective: It's bigger than Yellowstone, the Grand Canyon, Yosemite, the Everglades, and Great Smoky national parks . . . combined!

Here are some more facts for you to chew on:

There are over one hundred villages and towns inside the massive park, but guess what? No cities!

Now, stop right there. Hamilton County, in the heart of the Adirondacks, is the third largest county in the state, but please drive carefully: There are no stoplights!

Lewis County, the westernmost county in the Adirondacks, has twice as many cows (53,000) as people. Why all the cows? This area has the largest concentration of milk producers in the state (New York *is* the third largest dairy-producing state), and they contribute to the world's largest cream-cheese factory, located in Lowville.

Not far from Inlet and Old Forge, on the southeast shore of the Stillwater Reservoir, there's a small hamlet called Beaver River. There used to be a road that went there, but it got washed out when they flooded the reservoir. The train stopped running in the late 1950s. The only way to get there now is by snowmobile in the winter and boat in the summer. A few families still live there year-round.

Beaver River is home to the Norridgewock Lodge (www.beaver river.com), a resort that capitalizes on its remote location, saying, "Getting here is half the fun!"

Of course, the lodge would like a new road put in to broaden its appeal to include those who want to get there, *then* have fun. But, you'll never believe it: Some of the residents are fighting it! They don't want a road. They like the solitude—and those low real-estate prices.

★ ★

"There's a real self-reliant spirit of people here," says Mitch Lee, a tourism official for the town of Inlet and a great Adirondack story-teller.

The rest of us like to act like we're accustomed to the wilderness when we visit in the summer, but you really have to have a hearty spirit to live in the Adirondacks year-round.

In the winter, "I commute with a chainsaw in my Jeep in case there's a stray tree in the road," Lee says matter-of-factly. "You can't wait for National Grid to show up two hours later. You just cut the tree and move on."

Check out www.visitadirondacks.com.

YAR, IT'S AN INVASION!
Alexandria Bay

Ahoy, maties! Me lookout up in the crow's nest just spotted him a boatload of pirates and those scurvy dogs are headed fer Alexandria Bay!

Every August, pirates invade the village of Alex Bay for the horn-swagglin' good time that is Bill Johnston's Pirate Days. Bill Johnston, also known as the "Pirate of the Thousand Islands," earned his pirate stripes by plundering and setting afire a British steamer during the Canadian Rebellion in 1838.

The ten-day festival kicks off with the pirate-scouting party landing ashore. They are confronted by soldiers in the street. Some hilarious one-liners are exchanged, and then it's a cacophony of clanging swords as the village attempts to defend itself from these ne'er-do-wells.

Round one goes to the village—hooray! The pirates are rounded up—even the kids in the crowd dressed as pirates—and marched down to a military encampment on the shore.

Down on the waterfront, the swordplay continues. There are chants of "Let the boy go!" for a young pirate, clad in chains, as the pirates toss gold coins into the crowd to win them over.

Well, shiver me timbers, it's a pirate ship!

Then, all of a sudden, a soldier yells, "Fire in the hole!" and the crowd goes silent as everyone sees it at the same time—a spectacular multi-sailed pirate ship is approaching. Why, it's Bill Johnston, the famous pirate of the Thousand Islands! Cannon and musket fire fill the air and the tension builds. If the pirates win, they'll to take over the town!

The crowd, always up for a good invasion, begins chanting: "Take the bay! Take the bay!" A woman shouts, "Treasure, here, Cap'n!" As more gold coins are flung into the crowd, a boy yells out, "Pirates rule!"

★ ★

And, of course, they do! The pirates win and a Mardi Gras–like celebration ensues, with pirates dangling from every level of the ship, tossing beads and coins.

The festival includes a weeklong treasure hunt in town, as well as a pirate magic show, pirate juggling, a children's pirate parade, daily "fight a pirate" events where kids can help battle pirates, and a Little Pirate Putt mini-golf tournament. There's also live music every night and other events for the adults.

Gangway, landlubbers! Get yer little buckos to Alex Bay for Pirate Days!

For more information visit www.alexbay.org or call (800) 541-2110.

OUTHOUSE ARCHEOLOGY
Ballston Spa

The last time you bought a bottle of water or soda, I'll bet you tossed it in the recycling bin or (gasp!) trash, without giving it a second thought, didn't you?

Bottles have been disposable for so many years, that we've forgotten they are historical artifacts—even the ones that come from former outhouse pits!

"Old outhouses are actually a main source of obtaining bottles for collectors," says Jan Rutland, director of the National Bottle Museum in Ballston Spa.

The museum has an exhibit called "The Privy Pit," which is a backlit illustration of all the different layers, from 2 feet (bottles from 1910 to 1915) to 9 feet (early 1860s).

Think about it: Before recycling and modern trash disposal, they used to burn garbage. But glass won't burn, Rutland says, and you wouldn't want to leave it above ground for someone to cut a foot on. "You already know where there's a hole dug!" Rutland explains, so you tossed medicine, whiskey, or poison bottles in the outhouse pit.

Bottles used to be handmade, which makes some of them extremely valuable. That might explain why someone would want to go digging through prehistoric poop to find them! (Apparently, it's no longer technically excrement after one hundred years—it's composted dirt—but still!)

The museum has a video of a Travel Channel *Cash and Treasures* episode in which host Becky Worley goes on an outhouse dig. She starts out skeptical but gets hooked after a few hours. "This toilet is a gold mine!" she exclaims.

Of course, in the biz, they don't call it prehistoric poop digging, but rather, "outhouse archeology." (I trust you will find a way to work this newfound knowledge into the conversation at your next cocktail party.)

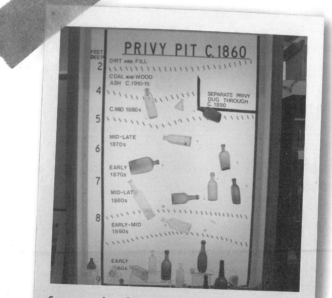

Someone dug through all these layers of one man's you-know-what to find another man's treasure!

★ ★

Beyond the novelty of the privy pit, the National Bottle Museum has an extraordinary collection of glass bottles. I highly recommend the poison bottles. (To view, not ingest.) They're cobalt blue, which was to warn people, but the color attracted children (whoops!) so bottle makers started putting skulls, coffins, and spikes on them to convey the danger. There are also some cool liquor bottles shaped like violins, and candy bottles in the shape of phones, ducks, and even guns.

I promise, you'll never look at a bottle—or outhouse—the same way again!

For more information visit www.nationalbottlemuseum.org or call (518) 885-7589.

PLEASE, NO JUMPING ON THE BANDWAGON
Copenhagen

How often do you hear the expression "jump on the bandwagon?" Well, in Copenhagen, they actually have one!

The Copenhagen bandwagon resides in a small, white-sided building with four square windows, so you can see it from the road. There's black lettering on top that says COPENHAGEN BANDWAGON.

The bandwagon was built around 1875 for the Copenhagen band and used for about twenty-five years. It spent some time on loan to a museum in Cooperstown, before being returned to Copenhagen in 1969 for the village's centennial. In the 1980s, a local legislator and a team of volunteers jumped on the bandwagon, so to speak, giving it a much-needed overhaul and a permanent home.

With 16-foot long scroll-y wooden sides, the bandwagon is a carnival-sleigh-like vehicle on wagon wheels. The undercarriage and wheels actually came from a circus. There are white swans painted on the front and it is inscribed for J.H. Raymond's Cornet band, so named for the band's second leader, John Raymond. It was used in the late 1800s for parades and political rallies, with the band all decked out in brass-trimmed uniforms and black chapeaus with a red ostrich feather!

★ ★

The band has long stopped playing, but the bandwagon, which seats about ten people, is still used for parades at Memorial Day and Christmas. This is how Santa rolls in Copenhagen!

Kate Fazio and Gertrude Horning were among the volunteers who helped with the restoration. Kate pulls out a photo of people in 19th-century costumes riding on the bandwagon during the 1969 centennial parade.

I inquire about who would've been riding in the bandwagon for its Copenhagen homecoming, to which Gert quickly replies: "Well, there's the mayor, and the rest are wealthy or influential people. Basically, people who are impressed with themselves." She sits up straight in her chair. "You know, they're from Pucker Street!" Gert says, pursing her lips like a haughty socialite.

Photo by Helen Jones

Just because other people jump on the bandwagon doesn't mean you have to, too.

Oh, and contrary to the popular expression, "jumping on the bandwagon" isn't as easy as it sounds. "It's hard to get into because it's pretty high up there," says Gert, who got to ride in it once as Mrs. Claus. Plus, there are no cushy seats, which can be a little rough on the posterior when you're bumping along on wooden wheels.

So, kids, let that be a lesson to you. Be yourselves. Don't go jumping on the bandwagon. It's not that comfortable anyway. But, if you want to see one, head over to Copenhagen. Look for the little white building across from the Family Medical Care practice on Route 12. Or, stop by when the Clauses are in town and see it in action!

BAKE TO THE FUTURE
Crown Point

Talking to Yannig Tanguy, you don't really get the sense that he's a Renaissance man so much as you feel like he's *actually from* the Renaissance period and stuck here because his time machine broke down.

Tanguy, a young entrepreneur who owns the Crown Point Bread Company, makes his own bread using local ingredients and flour he mills

Bonjour! Would you like some bread? I will get my horse!

himself. But it doesn't stop there. He also builds his own clay ovens! Some of them are at historic sites, and Tanguy actually uses them to bake bread for the troops during reenactments.

When he's not baking bread using 300-year-old recipes, or tending the counter of his cafe, which makes you feel as if you've been transported to the French countryside, you'll find him traveling through town with a horse and cart, selling his bread the old-fashioned way.

"Right now, there's no faster way to do delivery than with a horse and wagon," Tanguy says. (Notice he's vague about the time period in which he's speaking.) As if that's not enough, he also plays the fiddle!

Tanguy's father is from Brittany, in western France, and there's one thing that stands out from his visits there as a child. "I loved bread and butter," Tanguy says. "French bread was a real treat."

But isn't it hard doing everything by hand?

"It's a challenge doing everything the old-fashioned way," Tanguy admits. But, "it's about being a really good artisan," he says.

In a 2003 article, *Adirondack Life* magazine savored the artisanal quality: "A slice of his Swabien rye, a dense, grainy bread seasoned with fennel, anise, coriander and cumin, topped by a hunk of organic farmer's cheese . . . is a hearty meal in itself."

"Food is magic," Tanguy says. "Cooking is magic."

And so is that time machine you flew in on, buddy. More bread, please!

For more information visit www.crownpointbread.net or call (518) 597-4466.

I BELIEVE THIS BELONGS TO YOU
Fonda

Tom Porter, a Mohawk native, grew up in the Akwesasne community on the Canadian border. His people were driven there from the Mohawk Valley, 200 miles to the south, after the American Revolution.

The idea of getting some valley land back had been kicking around, but the issue came to a head in the late 1980s, when civil war broke out on the Akwesasne reservation over the proliferation of casinos. Porter and others who wanted to preserve traditional values raised $25,000 to buy land.

When news of their intentions spread, a friend wrote to Porter informing him that 300 acres were going to be auctioned. Then, a wealthy woman, who wished to remain anonymous (some locals say it was Jane Fonda because her ancestor settled the town of Fonda), gave him $250,000 to bid for the land.

Then, something even more extraordinary than Barbarella herself happened. "When the other potential bidders heard about what he was doing, they all stepped back" and let Porter win the bid, said Emily Tarbell, a fellow Akwesasne Mohawk.

When Tarbell, who now runs a bed-and-breakfast on the property, first arrived, she said to her cousin: "I've never been here before, but I know I'm home."

Today, the community, known as Kanatsiohareke (pronounced Gana-jo-*ha*-lay-gay), runs a farm on the property, hosts traditional Iroquois festivals, and offers college work programs and summer classes in Mohawk language. Next door to the B&B is an Iroquois gift shop.

Visiting Kanatsiohareke is amazing. They welcome everyone warmly, and I highly encourage non-Mohawk to visit. Tarbell will take you on a tour of the property; breakfast is particularly cool because Porter, Tarbell, and other Mohawk residents often join you at one big table for an intimate—often hilarious—conversation that you won't find in any textbook!

I'll never forget the story that Rob White—whom Tarbell calls the "MacGyver of the Mohawks" because he can fix everything from a car to a broken heart—told about the time they drove a bull an hour and a half to a slaughterhouse in the back of a pickup, only for it to escape from the facility.

Personally, I would've run from the building screaming, "Bull on the loose! Run! Run for your lives!" White, knowing they needed that meat for a festival, grabbed the bull by the neck and then chased it all over town!

But it's better if you hear the story from him. I can confirm that the Mohawk tradition of storytelling is alive and well in Fonda.

For more information visit www.mohawkcommunity.com or call (518) 673-5356.

THE TRUTH IS OUT THERE
Great Sacandaga Lake

Rumor has it that an Adirondack Atlantis sits at the bottom of the Great Sacandaga Lake.

One guy in Albany told me that he heard you can actually see the city below you when you're boating on the lake! Some say divers swim in and out of the houses. Others say there's a locomotive sitting at the bottom of that lake, as well as a Native American burial ground.

The tales are so prolific, they even spawned an *X-Files* episode!

Well, I did some digging and . . . the truth is out there.

In the mid-19th century, the Sacandaga River Valley was positioning itself as the "Coney Island of the North," with a large hotel, rustic theater, roller coaster, midway, boxing matches, baseball, and more. But every spring, the valley would flood, as would the upper Hudson River area around Albany and Troy. So, in 1930, they made it permanent by flooding the valley, including twelve communities, to create a reservoir today known as Great Sacandaga Lake.

The flooding displaced more than 1,000 residents, and nearly 4,000 graves from more than a dozen cemeteries had to be moved. But, I'm sorry to report, no Atlantis. Most of the buildings were either moved, dismantled, or burned.

However, when the water level is low, usually in the fall, you might see a few "islands" (hills from the former valley), including Sport Island, where the baseball diamond was, and foundations from former buildings.

So, how did all the rumors start?

"It flooded much faster than they had anticipated," says Bill Loveday, a former Fulton County historian, "which cut short removing some of the things."

Group Dynamics in the Graveyard

Hadley

There is a cemetery on Bruno LaVerdiere's property that wasn't there when he moved in.

What is—*gulp*—going on over there? Have there been any reports of disappearances in the past ten years?

No, no. Nothing like that. LaVerdiere is an artist. (Ah, should've seen that coming!)

"I get my inspiration from historic sites—shrines, graveyards, monuments," LaVerdiere says. He recalls that, when he first moved to the Adirondacks, one of the first things he noticed was all the old, charming cemeteries of thirty to fifty headstones, or stumbling upon a small family cemetery in the woods.

He started building these little monument-like sculptures. "I didn't really think of them as gravestones," LaVerdiere said.

One day, he decided to take a couple dozen of them out to the road leading up to his house and bury—I mean, display—them on the side of the road. Suddenly, it was a graveyard. "There's a different energy when you put all the pieces together," LaVerdiere says.

Looking at it, it's hard to remember that no one is buried there. It reminds me of family vacations as a kid. Whenever we'd drive past a cemetery, my dad would say, "Hey, do you know how many people are buried there?" No, Dad. How many? "All of 'em!" he'd reply, with that smug I-got-your-nose! look.

So, Dad, do you know how many people are buried in this cemetery? None of 'em!

"A lot of people think it's real," LaVerdiere said. "That was never my intention."

Perhaps some of LaVerdiere's reverence comes from the fact that he spent fifteen years in a monastery training to be a monk. Not surprisingly, he was the guy who cut all the gravestones for the monks.

Turns out, that wasn't his calling.

However, that sound you hear *is* him calling. Back on the porch, LaVerdiere, now in his seventies, runs over to a giant clay horn suspended from the ceiling and begins, well, tooting his own horn—another sculpture he's made.

"Blow in it, and they'll hear you across the river!" he says. "Dogs bark back!"

The minute LaVerdiere's lips purse, his brother Rome pops out of his seat on the porch and dashes to an even bigger horn set up in the yard like a swing set.

Aw, isn't that sweet. Two brothers having a horn-to-horn conversation!

The newest little old cemetery in the Adirondacks.

As for the train rumor, Loveday recalls a picture of a locomotive sitting in four or five inches of water. People assumed it was left to be flooded, but Loveday says it was actually removed. There are, however, still some train tracks on the bottom of the lake.

One strange-but-true tale is that, with all of the farmland in the valley, the stuff that made the crops grow washed into the lake during the flooding and the fish ate it.

"It created an atmosphere for the fish that made them huge!" Loveday says. Just a few years after the flooding, the reservoir/lake snagged the world record for the largest northern pike!

To learn more about the flooding of the Sacandaga River valley, visit the Fulton County Museum (www.fultoncountymuseum.org) at 237 Kingsboro Avenue in Gloversville.

PING-PONG INDEPENDENCE DAY
Inlet

If you spend your Fourth of July in the town of Inlet, you'll have a ball!

A couple thousand of them, actually.

Every Fourth of July, children gather in Fern Park, wearing little red bows in their hair, white-starred tops, red-hooded sweatshirts, navy shorts, and Uncle Sam hats. They run around for a while before it's time to line up behind the rope, their legs dancing in anticipation.

Ready! Aim! Fire the pillowcases!

Then, a father yells, "Here it comes!" Suddenly, a small plane emerges from behind the tree line. Thousands of ping-pong balls, in all different colors, rain on the field. The children dart out to scoop them up. Then, just as fast as they got out there, they're already on their way back, eager to cash in their ping-pong balls for prizes.

There are three drops, for different age groups, and each child can collect three balls. Prizes are awarded according to the color of the ping-pong ball. There are commemorative water bottles, glow sticks, temporary tattoos, and kaleidoscopes, as well as coupons for doughnuts, dinner, and other items from local businesses. Out of the roughly 9,000 balls dropped, there are nine golden balls (Daddy, I want a golden ticket!) that yield grand prizes such as a family cruise on nearby Raquette Lake.

Oh, and in case you're wondering how they do the drop, it's a bunch of guys leaning out of a seaplane with pillowcases full of ping-pong balls!

I think it's wonderful that somebody finally decided to give the ping-pong ball a proper Independence Day, liberating it from a mundane existence of being thwacked by a paddle a couple thousand times, only to be lost in a dusty hairball in the corner of the basement or garage.

> And the ping-pongs' red glare!
> The blues, greens, and yellows in air
> Gave proof on this day
> That our ping-pongs, we do care
> Oh say does that star-spangled child yet wave,
> Three ping-pong balls with glee—
> And the prize she will have!

For more information on Inlet's Fourth of July Ping Pong Ball Drop, call (688) GO-INLET or visit www.inletny.com.

WHERE RACCOONS EAT CRACKER JACKS

Keene

Man, is this place wild!

Deer, moose, antelope, and buffalo jut out of the walls. A couple of animals appear to be burrowing back *into* the walls. An otter leans over a branch to look for dinner in the pond below. One of the raccoons is having Cracker Jacks for dinner. (I guess he didn't feel like cooking tonight.) A couple of his friends are paddling in a tiny canoe as a fox lurks behind. A bear roams the floor as the king of the jungle shows his teeth. Overhead, mountain lions strut on a beam and a white peacock perches on a branch.

This is North Country Taxidermy and Adirondack Reflections, a virtual department store and fine-art gallery for taxidermy.

I'm not a fan of stuffed dead animals, but this is a must-see for anyone visiting the North Country. Surrounded by some of the highest peaks in New York State, this shop has something for everyone. There's traditional taxidermy—deer mounts and full-size bears for the hunting purists— and plenty of birds and antler candelabras for those looking to add a little hunting-lodge chic to their home.

It said there was a prize at the bottom!

Some of the whimsical poses show that taxidermy doesn't just have to be about a trophy, it can also be fine art—and hilarious! Who knew?

There are hundreds of taxidermied animals

on display—everything from mice to moose. (Seriously, they have taxidermied rodents!)

Prices range from $50 for a mouse to $1,200 for those paddling raccoons and more than $5,000 for a full-size bear.

If you've already got taxidermy but it's, um, on the geriatric side and in need of a replacement or two, the shop also offers feet and replacement parts.

For the man who has everything, might I suggest a deer rump?!

For more information visit www.northcountrytaxidermy.com or call (518) 576-4318.

CHAMP THE LAKE MONSTER
Lake Champlain

You've heard about the famous Loch Ness Monster in Scotland, but did you know he had an American cousin?

Legend has it that a similar, serpent-like creature lives in Lake Champlain. The locals call him "Champ."

Dee Carroll, who runs a restaurant and ship store at Westport Marina with her husband Bob, swears she's seen it. When they were driving once, Dee was looking out the window at the lake. "I turned to Bob and said, 'What's that post-like thing?' I looked back and all that was there were two concentric circles." Dee said. "Posts don't do that."

Bob, however, is a little more skeptical. A local group has been tracking head sightings versus body sightings for some time, Bob says. Body sightings can be more questionable, since it could easily be the way the light is hitting the waves. Well, that, and, Bob points out, "Most of the body sightings have been close to shore, between 4:00 and 6:00 p.m.—the cocktail hour!"

Still, he says, "There's something out there that people are seeing."

There was a wedding party of thirty to forty people on a boat, the Carrolls recall, and all of them came back convinced they'd seen it.

Love Those Loons

Aside from the Adirondack chair, the loon is probably the most popular icon of the Adirondacks.

So, what makes some people so crazy for loons?

"Loons are an enigma," says Mike Prescott, a guide for Adirondack Connections known as "The Loon Man."

Loons look like ducks decked out in contemporary formal dress, with black and white feathers and a red-eye accent. But they're not ducks. Ducks can actually walk on land; loons can't. Loons have prehistoric-like legs that make even getting into the air a chore. "They need at least 100 yards" of runway (runwater?) space in order to take off, Prescott explains. Once airborne, they can go up to 70 miles an hour!

Loons are perhaps best known for their diving abilities and poetic cry. "When loons are alarmed, they don't fly like most birds, they dive," Prescott explains.

Meanwhile, that cry may sound like an expression of loneliness, but, in fact, the loon is trying to tell you that you are too close to his family, so back it up, OK?!

That part cracks me up. You watch people get really close to them, then the wailing starts. The person is probably thinking or saying, "Wow! What a beautiful sound. How nice that he's singing for me!" Meanwhile, the loon is like—"What part of BACK IT UP don't you understand?!"

If you ever see a loon walking on water with its wings tucked tight (and I hope you only see it on the Discovery Channel), that's known as the "penguin dance," and it means "You have completely invaded my personal space and I am TOTALLY FREAKED OUT!"

Once you know the ground rules, you can paddle to your heart's content, watching them as Prescott does. "I'm sort of like the CIA of the

One step closer and I swear, I'll scream.

bird world!" he says proudly. But the loons haven't done anything wrong. Just the opposite: Prescott says they're an important indicator of environmental health and water quality.

If you ever notice a loon waggling her back foot, Prescott says, that's to help her cool off, "like when you're too hot in bed and need to stick your foot out of the covers!"

While we're on the pillow talk, loons are pretty territorial when it comes to their families, so the cruisin' loons go elsewhere. "We have a couple of lakes that we call singles bars," Prescott says, "because the loons haven't hooked up yet!"

Imagine the lines you'd hear in *that* place: Hey, hot foot. What are you drinking?

★ ★

The Carrolls' son was on a boat with his wife and thought he saw a giant log. "Then, the log started swimming!" Dee says.

I asked Dee if she was afraid to go out on the water. She said no. "If Champ were gonna be vicious, he would've done it by now!"

Lake Champlain, like Loch Ness, lends itself to tales of a creature living there, as it's a freshwater lake that doesn't freeze over in the winter because it's so deep.

But there are a few problems with the lake-monster story. Early Native Americans claimed they saw a "horned serpent" and European settlers first reported seeing the creature in 1609. Four hundred years is a long time. So, is there a Mrs. Champ, baby champs, and grand-champs? Or, is it the same monster with a really long life span?

If you want to swap theories, head to Port Henry's Bulwagga Bay on the first Saturday of August for the town's annual Champ Day. For more information visit www.lakechamplainregion.com.

THE SECRET MAP OF LAKE GEORGE

Lake George

I've come across a mystery and I think you should check it out.

Go to Beach Road, on the southwest corner of Lake George. Here, you'll find a row of shops and restaurants.

For darn's sake, put the GPS away! This is one of the busiest tourist spots in the northeast, and I'm pretty sure you can't get lost even if I blindfolded you. Now, pay attention.

On Beach Road, there's a restaurant called Adirondack Sandwich Works, formerly Big Bob's Burgers & More.

Did you find it?

Good.

Now, across the street . . .

Hey! Focus. Do *not* get distracted by the doughy, warm smell of panini. First rule of mystery club is always eat *before* mystery club. Do you want to check out this mystery, or not?

★ ★

OK, across the street are three wide, round steps. At the top, a map of the lake and a compass circle are etched in the sidewalk. I want you to stand exactly in the middle of the circle.

Now say something.

If you do it right, you'll hear an echo of your own voice as if you're standing in some sort of invisible chamber! No one else around you will be able to hear it; they'll hear your normal voice.

Some people, when they get to the middle of the circle, speak timidly, then get a funny look on their face as if they've just seen a ghost. Others sing.

"We just kept saying 'hello' over and over, and then started calling our son's name," said Laura Zamrok, who visited the spot with her

Step right up. Do you have something to say? (say . . . say . . .)

★ ★

husband, Brian, and infant son Christian. "It sounded as if we were standing on top of a hollow, metal tube!"

Once you get the hang of it, you might try: "I'm the king of the world!" or "Activate the cone of silence!" It's so fun and empowering to hear the boom of your own voice, you just might surprise yourself and announce a run for the presidency!

May I have . . . your attention . . . PLEASE! (please . . . please . . .)

Well, in any case, you'll have your own attention!

DO IT FOR YOUR COUNTRY!
Lake Placid

The winter Olympics were held in Lake Placid more than twenty years ago, but did you know that you still have a shot at winning a gold medal?

It's part of an environmentally-conscious program called "Gold for Green." If you drive a hybrid car to Lake Placid, they'll give you a gold medal!

"We've always thought that we have a respon-sibility, living in the Adirondacks, to the envi-

And the gold medal goes to . . . YOU! Congratulations!

ronment," says James McKenna, president of the Lake Placid Visitors Bureau.

The tourism bureau bought hybrid cars for the office, but decided to take it a step further with visitors. "We wanted to identify these people as leaders," McKenna says of hybrid drivers.

Sportsmanship with a Blowtorch

In the 1980 Lake Placid Winter Olympics, the men's 15K cross-country skiing event was an intense, hair-splitting race between Thomas Wassberg of Sweden and Juha Mieto of Finland.

So close, in fact, that Wassberg edged out Mieto for the gold by one one-hundredth of a second! After the race, Wassberg, knowing how much Mieto wanted the gold medal, said to him: "We must split this medal in half as one one-hundredth of a second is nothing in a 15-kilometer race!"

Even the International Ski Federation agreed that it was a ridiculous margin, and from that point on, began rounding all of their times to the nearest one-tenth of a second.

It would've been easy enough to say, "Sure, give me half your gold medal!" But demonstrating what an honest, respectable athlete he was, Mieto replied: "A gold medal should not be split in half."

The story has become somewhat of an urban legend. (Can you have an "urban" legend in the Adirondacks, where there are no cities?) Some say Wassberg had his medal cut in half anyway and that the medals were re-welded as half gold, half silver. One man, on a visit to the Olympic Center, even claimed to have seen one of the half-and-half medals.

The truth is, the medals were never split. "At one point, Thomas Wassberg said he thought it should be split, but it never was," said Nat Brown, a former Olympic coach in cross-country skiing and a friend of Wassberg's. "I doubt if Mieto would have accepted it," Brown added. "He was—and is—far too proud a man."

Thomas, meanwhile, "was never very proud of that medal," Brown said. In fact, he had trouble finding it after the ceremony, according to Brown, because it was "scrunched up in his pocket!"

Still, it was a true exchange of sportsmanship—even if it didn't *actually* involve a blowtorch—and the Olympic spirit among two competitors who genuinely earned the title Olympian.

Richard Austermann, of Southwick, Massachusetts, drove his family to Lake Placid in a Prius and came home with the gold. "It's cool," Austermann says. "You go on your vacation, you come back with a little perk . . . a gold medal!" Ever a humble medalist, Austermann says, "It's still hanging on our rearview mirror. We figured the car earned it, not us!"

The tourism bureau will take a picture of you with your car and medal and upload it to their Web site, www.lakeplacid.com, to forever recognize that you are champion in the sport of fuel efficiency! (Click on "Gold for Green" when it flashes under the search box to see all of the past medal winners.)

Imagine how much fun it will be at the next gathering of family or friends to say, "Hey, did I ever tell you about that time I won a gold medal in Lake Placid?"

To claim your "Gold for Green" medal, drive your hybrid car to the visitors bureau in Lake Placid's Olympic Center at 2610 Main Street (800-447-5224). It's open Monday through Saturday 9:00 a.m. to 5:00 p.m. and Saturdays and Sundays 8:00 a.m. to 4:00 p.m.

Good luck!

BREWIN' WITH THE BIG DOG
Lake Placid

When Chris Ericson got into the beer-brewing business, he needed a name for his beer. As it turns out, the first beer he made was pretty big as beers go, clocking in at 7 percent alcohol. (Most beers average 4 to 5 percent alcohol, 3 percent for baseball games to keep the crowd from getting too rowdy.)

So, he named the beer after one of the pub's most loyal regulars: a dog named Ubu!

"Ubu was a 125-pound chocolate lab with a head the size of a basketball," says Ericson, brewmaster and owner of Lake Placid Pub & Brewery. "We named the big beer after the big dog!"

Photo courtesy of Lake Placid Pub & Brewery

Ubrew. Brew! brew! brew! brew! (That's Labrador for "We hope you enjoy our beer.")

Ubu was legendary in Lake Placid. His owner used to stop in for a drink every night after work. Ubu knew the routine, so he'd bum around town all day, doing his big-dog thing, then head to the pub to wait for his owner. "Everyone in town knew Ubu," Ericson says.

Ubu Ale is a smooth, malty, garnet-red colored English Strong Ale. And, at 7 percent alcohol, it packs a punch. Don't act surprised if it takes you down like a chew toy. (Hey, we said Ubu Ale, not Chihuahua ale!)

The beer is so popular that it has a cult-like following in the Adirondacks and has won several national awards. Former President Bill Clinton liked the beer so much after a 2000 visit to Lake Placid, he had some Ubu Ale shipped to 1600 Pennsylvania Avenue!

Good brew, Ubu, good brew!

For more information visit www.ubuale.com or call (518) 523-3813.

★ ★

I'VE GOT A HANDFUL OF CREAM CHEESE. CATCH!

Lowville

Welcome to Lowville, home of the world's largest cream cheese factory!

What do you do with all that cream cheese?

Well, let's see. You can make the world's largest cheesecake. You can have a bagel-and-cream-cheese eating contest. Heck, you can even get crazy and have a cream cheese–tossing contest!

These are just some of the fun events at the annual Cream Cheese Festival (www.cream cheesefestival.com) in Lowville (rhymes with "How-ville").

Welcome to cow country. My name is Lady LeWinDa Milkzalot!

There's also a cream cheese recipe contest, cream cheese bingo, and a feed-your-partner-cheesecake contest. Try your waitressing skills in the milk-tray relay, carrying a tray filled with glasses of milk. Put the pedal to the metal in the tractor race or leave it to lady luck in the tractor raffle.

If you're wondering why all this creamy, cheesy goodness is here in Lowville instead of Philadelphia, it's because this is where the world's largest cream cheese plant is. Also, remember that I told you New York is the third-largest dairy-producing state and here, in the western foothills of the Adirondacks, there are twice as many cows as people!

Trivia

Spreading the Truth

Where was cream cheese invented?

You said Philadelphia, right?

Wrong!

Hand me that butter knife. I've got some truth to spread!

Cream cheese was invented in 1872 by a dairyman in Chester, New York, which is about 250 miles south of Lowville and 150 miles north of Philadelphia.

So, how did Philadelphia wind up getting all the credit?

When A.L. Reynolds started distributing the cheese in tinfoil wrappers in 1880, Kraft says, he called it "Philadelphia Brand" cream cheese because, at that time, a lot of high-quality foods were being produced in Philadelphia. The city's name became synonymous with quality. You would say that something was "Philadelphia quality."

Because it was referring to a standard and not a city, in some cases, the packaging would have the word "Philadelphia" in quotes.

So, the next time you say, "We need to buy Philadelphia cream cheese," be sure to add some air quotes with your fingers on the word "Philadelphia" for added amusement and historical accuracy!

While you're in Lowville, be sure to try the cheese curd and Croghan Bologna, which is similar to kielbasa but sliced like pepperoni, according to Michelle Castor of nearby Copenhagen. It's such a popular combination, Castor says, "it's like peanut butter and jelly" here!

For the uninitiated on the divine gift that is cheese curd, here's a little tip: "You know it's fresh because it squeaks!" says Gert Horning (of Copenhagen bandwagon fame). "If you refrigerate it, it takes the squeak out!"

For that perfect I-went-to-dairy-country photo op, head to the Lowville Producers Cheese Store on Route 12 and get your picture taken with Lady LeWinDa Milkzalot, billed as "the largest dairy cow in New York State." (Don't forget to say "cheese!") Her measurements are 10'6" high, 15' long, and 5' wide. Her name, the product of a local contest, is a nod to the area's dairy farming and giant windmill farm.

During the off-season, practice your cream cheese tossing and shop online at www.gotgoodcheese.com.

ACROBATIC GREEN GIANTS
Lowville

Aside from the cream cheese tossing and giant cow, there's something magical about visiting Lowville.

As you drive through the rolling hills of cow and farmland, a 12-mile procession of about 200 windmills winds through the landscape. Each has three silver blades, tumbling through the wind, making it look like a troupe of giant acrobats!

This is the Maple Ridge Wind Farm, the second-largest wind farm in the U.S. (The largest is in Texas.) The windmills look skinny on the horizon, but it's an optical illusion. Each one is 320 feet tall, almost the length of a football field standing upright.

One blade, alone, is 130 feet long. And, while the windmills appear to be doing a slow ballet number, they're actually tumbling at 140 miles an hour!

If Don Quixote saw this—*Ay, dios mio!*—he'd think it was an invasion!

Combined, the windmills have a capacity of 320 megawatts, the same as a midsize power plant. But these are green giants: The

★ ★

Ready. And a one-two-three, one-two-three . . .
Pick up the pace, ladies!

American Wind Energy Association says that one megawatt of wind-generated power offsets so much carbon dioxide in the air that it's the equivalent of about one square mile of new forest.

Each windmill is capable of providing electricity for about 500 homes. Plus, the wind farm doesn't own any of the land. It leases it from farmers, the local school, and other residents and businesses, paying them thousands of dollars a year in rent! In an area where the main job opportunities are dairy farming and the Kraft cream cheese plant, this arrangement makes a huge impact on the local economy.

The reason why they chose this spot for a windmill farm is because it's 1,600 to 1,800 feet above sea level and catches strong lake-effect winds from Lake Ontario. (The rent money is a nice consolation for residents who've been grappling with those gale-force winds for years!)

They named it Maple Ridge because Lewis County (of twice as many cows as people fame) is the top maple-syrup-producing county in the state.

Canst thou not see these monstrous giants? Thou should! With three great arms whirling back behind the cows and corn!

For more information visit www.mapleridgewind.com or call (315) 376-8812.

DUDE, YOU'RE THE *MAN*!
Mayfield

For thirty years, the 24-foot tall Leather Guy stood outside Alvord's House of Leather on Route 30, greeting customers and welcoming visitors to the Adirondacks.

He wore a tan, fringed jacket, jeans, and matching knee-high boots. He had a brown comb-over haircut with sideburns, a moustache, and oddly shaped beard. He wore thick black glasses. He was known at times as The Leather Guy, The Hippie Dude, or The Big Man.

He was the kind of guy that whenever you arrived in the Adirondacks, you wanted to pat him on the back (well, the back of the ankle, anyway) and be like, "Dude, what's *up*?!"

So, when Steve Alvord took him down, it raised concern among the locals as well as longtime tourists.

Oh no. Did someone . . . uh . . . stick it to The Man?

Nope! He's just found a new job since Alvord's Leather closed. He's moved up the road, but still on Route 30. Now, he's the spokes-dude for Adirondack Traditions (www.adirondacktraditions.com), a company that builds Daniel Boone Log Homes.

He got a makeover to pull his look out of the 1970s. So, sorry, ladies, love 'em or leave 'em, the sideburns are gone, as are the goofy glasses.

"He's the perfect Daniel Boone guy," says Marty Greco, owner of Adirondack Traditions. "Steve had the statue made to look like him. It was actually called Big Steve. I want to call him Daniel Boone."

The Big Guy is a great calling card for a business, but beyond that, Greco says, he's a gateway to the Adirondacks. As a kid, you knew you were getting close to camp when you saw him. "He was a mile marker," Greco says. "You knew you were there."

"If I didn't have a business," Greco adds, "I would've bought him anyway and dedicated him to every father that ever took his kid to camp in the Adirondacks."

So, the next time you're headed to the Adirondacks via Route 30 and someone from the backseat yells, "Are we there yet?" you can say, "Not yet. We're waiting for The Big Guy!"

Photo by Annie Greco

The Big Guy gets a little help with his career transition.

FASTER THAN A LOCOMOTIVE!

North Creek

If you secretly believe you have Superman tendencies, now is your chance. Put yourself to the "Faster than a speeding bullet! More powerful than a locomotive! Able to leap tall buildings in a single bound!" test and actually race a train.

Race the Train is a scenic 8.4-mile race on the Upper Hudson Railroad (www.uhrr.com) from Riparius to North Creek station. The proceeds go to Dollars for Scholars, an organization that raises money for local college-bound students.

Spectators can buy a ticket to ride the train with the runners. The runners get dropped off in Riparius, where they literally race the train

★ ★

back to North Creek. The spectators get to stay and cheer on their superpeople from the train.

The race starts on a bridge, with whitewater rushing below. As they exit the bridge, the dirt road curves uphill, and one by one, they taper the cacophony and vanish around the corner to run alongside the train and the Hudson River.

So, does anyone ever beat the train?

Among the more than 200 runners that compete, "there are a certain number of racers each year who do beat the train," says Ann Arsenault, codirector of the race and president of the local Dollars for Scholars chapter.

This would probably be a good time to tell you that they don't actually run the trains at "full speed ahead." The trains are set to 8 miles an hour, or an 8-mile minute as they say in runner lingo. The trip takes one hour, seven minutes for the train. One of the past winners pulled it off in just over forty-five minutes, which put him at a 5.23-minute mile!

"I'll tell ya, he was the real locomotive!" Arsenault says.

After the race, there's a second race called a Family Fun Run. This is a simple 1-mile race, Arsenault says, designed to encourage kids who aren't ready for the big race but are still excited about it.

One fun historical tidbit for you: The North Creek train station was where, in 1901, then–Vice President Theodore Roosevelt found out that McKinley had died and that he would be the next president of the United States. It's preserved exactly as it was at that time period as a museum in addition to a train station.

The race is held the first Saturday of August. For more information call (518) 251-2602. To register visit www.adirondackrunners.com and click on "races," then scroll down to "Race the Train."

THE ADIRONDACK TIMBUCTOO

North Elba

How many times have you said something like, "Oh, that place? It's way out there in Timbuctoo!"?

Today, Timbuctoo has become some far-flung funny-named place, but once upon a time, it was a very real, very unfunny place right here in New York State.

In 1846, abolitionist Gerrit Smith decided to give forty acres of land in Essex, Franklin, and Hamilton counties to newly freed slaves. It wasn't the best land. Some farms were very hilly; others were under water. But as landowners, these former slaves could now vote.

Way out there in Timbuctoo, John Brown's farm.

The area, just south of Lake Placid in the northern Adirondacks, was unofficially dubbed Timbuctoo, after a city of the same name in central Africa that was desirable but hard to reach.

In May 1849, a white man named John Brown moved his family to the Adirondack Timbuctoo to help the community.

"Most of the newly freed slaves were city slickers—from Schenectady, Albany, and New York City—and didn't know much about farming," says Brendan Mills, historic site assistant at the John Brown Farm. Brown shared everything he knew about farming and frontier living with the community to help them make a go of it. They grew what they could on the land: mostly potatoes, but also hay, rye, corn, peas, and turnips.

Timbuctoo ultimately became more of a stepping-stone to a free life. Some of the former city dwellers never adjusted to farm life, while others found the land too tough to tend. Most of the families left within ten years.

Today, John Brown's farm is all that remains of Timbuctoo. You can visit the farm, restored to a typical 19th-century Adirondack farmhouse. There, next to a large rock Brown used to call his "thinking rock," the body of John Brown is interred.

So, the next time you hear someone say "out there in Timbuctoo," you'll know exactly where that is and what it means.

For more information visit http://nysparks.state.ny.us/sites/ or call (518) 523-3900.

CHRISTMAS IN JULY
North Pole

You might've thought that Santa was toiling away up there at the northern tip of the Earth's axis, but if you paid attention in geography class, you'd know that the North Pole is actually in the middle of the Arctic Ocean!

Don't worry, though, I found him! All this time, his workshop was right here in North Pole, New York!

Opened in 1949, this North Pole was the very first theme park—predating even Disney. (In fact, Walt Disney studied the North Pole before he built Disneyland in 1955.) The North Pole was created by Julian Reiss, a Lake Placid businessman, who wanted to make his daughter's dream of visiting Santa's workshop come true. Adirondack artist Art Monaco brought that dream to life.

The park, on the slopes of Whiteface Mountain near Lake Placid, features all sorts of specialty shops, amusement rides, Santa's house, a reindeer stable, and live musical shows. There's even a Talking Tannenbaum and a real, solid ice North Pole that stays frozen—even in July!

Walking through Santa's candyscape village is magical, even for adults, as elves show you how they make the toys and the candy, and fairy-tale characters such as Red Riding Hood and Little Bo Peep pass by. You can visit with Santa's live reindeer in the barn and watch them fly with Santa during the show!

That's cold, Santa.

It's a hot July day, and a bunch of giggling kids run up and press their hands on the frozen North Pole. "Feel my hand!" one boy yells.

"You see the magic every day and it's so real to the kids," says Matt Stanley, a park operation manager. "If they're on the verge of not believing, after visiting here, they do!"

In fact, when kids walk out of Santa's house, you'll hear them say, "I think that's really him!"

I didn't realize until around 4:00 p.m., when I heard a child crying, that I hadn't heard a single kid cry all afternoon until that moment. "That's because they have to leave!" Matt explains.

Aw, man! Is it time to leave already?

For more information visit www.northpoleny.com or call (800) 806-0215.

THE JUMPING FROGS OF HERKIMER COUNTY
Old Forge

If you're a bett'n man, I reckon you're gonna like this next story.

Every Father's Day in Old Forge, people run out and git themselves the most edercated frog they can find, then they bring 'em to town for a frog-jumpin' contest.

You're not allowed to touch the little fellers—that means no punchin' 'em, Smiley—but you can blow on 'em with a straw or cup your hands around 'em to see if that'll get 'em jumpin'.

The winn'n frog is measured by the total distance of one . . . two . . . three! . . . jumps. If you miscalcerlated and got yerself a walkin' frog instead of a jumpin' frog, well, that's gonna cost you. Every step counts as a jump.

There are awards for the fastest frog, fastest business frog (not an MBA-edercated frog, but rather, a frog sponsored by one a them local businesses), heaviest frog, lightest frog, longest jump, and furthest-traveled frog. They also give an award to the dad with the ugliest tie. You reckon yours is uglier'n all the other ties in Herkimer County?

A few tips: Catch 'em the night before. (The frogs, not the ties.) Change the water in the morning, cause it gets mighty cold at night and there's nothin' makes a frog more ornery than a cold bum. Don't hold 'em in yer hands too long, neither, because there ain't no award for best baked frog.

★ ★

You'd best keep 'em in a separate can from them other frogs. Once, there were these two brothers brought their frogs tergether, and when they opened the can, well, let's just say, there was only one frog ther!

Maybe you've had experience with frogs and maybe you're only an amateur. The only requirement is that you can't be a squeamish feller. Dealin' with frogs, now, you're gonna get wet and slimy.

I ain't got no frog, but iff'n I did, I'd bet you that's a dern good way to spend Father's Day!

For more information on the Father's Day Frog Jump, visit www .oldforgeny.com.

THE OLYMPIC PRISON

Ray Brook

If you've ever been to Lake Placid, looked around and said, "Gee, where did they put everyone during the Olympics?" here's your answer:

Prison.

That's right, they threw them in prison! Welcome to America! As a gesture of goodwill and peace, we've got your cell right here!

No, no. It wasn't like that. Here's what happened:

Hosting the Olympics is expensive. So much so, that the Lake Placid Club, which is the reason the Olympics ever came to Lake Placid in the first place, was forced to shut down under a mound of debt following the 1980 games.

So, that year, Lake Placid got a little help from the federal government. But, there was one teensy-tiny stipulation: As soon as the Olympics were over, the Olympic Village dormitories that housed the athletes were to be converted into a prison.

The Olympic Village was built 7 miles from Lake Placid in Ray Brook, halfway between the host city and Saranac Lake, as a security precaution after eleven Israeli athletes and coaches were killed at the 1972 Olympics in Munich. One small mountain road went in and out, there were 12-foot high chain-link fences, and the dormitories had narrow windows.

In other words, with apologies to the athletes who had to stay there, it was a perfect prison!

Today, the Adirondack Correctional Facility at Ray Brook is a medium-security facility that houses seven hundred inmates.

Aside from Olympic athletes, this place has had some other famous guests, including John Gotti Jr., who spent five years here for racketeering.

YOU NAME IT, HE'S GOT IT
Rensselaer Falls

Everything in Kyle "Fireball" Hartman's world is an opportunity. But it's not about finding one door that opens; it's about finding 1,000 of them!

Literally, Hartman has a collection of 1,000 doors and counting. He's also got 1,500 windows, 1,000 shutters, and 80 classic cars. (He got his nickname, "Fireball," for his love of restoring and racing old cars.)

Hartman has a collection of just about everything imaginable, from mannequins and manual washing machines to church pews and antique taxidermy—even a collection of coffins!

River House Wares and Restoration (www.riverhousewares.com) is the name of the architectural salvage business, but the Hartmans call it "Kyle's World."

Kyle's World is housed in three buildings: the main house they call River House; a former Purina Chow Mill–turned–art gallery (run by his wife, Sally); and a replica of an old railroad station that Hartman constructed in 1985 to house the thousands of salvaged items he has for sale.

The main house has a second-story open porch that displays some of Hartman's taxidermy, which he calls his "Dead Head" collection. Hartman strolls the porch like it's a museum you can walk through

Ding! Ding! Ding! Now entering Kyle's World station!

with a beer, then stops to tell the story of the 150-year-old taxidermic puma. "I took him drinking one night!" Hartman says mischievously. I'm still not exactly sure what happened, but all I know is, there was some sort of scuffle and the puma came home with only one eye!

Out front is the Volkswagen tree house (literally, a Volkswagen in a tree!) that Hartman built for his son.

"Growing up, I didn't have a swing set," David Hartman says. "I had a Volkswagen!"

They say if you're looking for an odd-shaped window or other hard-to-find item, Hartman probably has two. (Seriously—he buys one to sell and one to keep for himself.)

Kyle's World runs from 208 to 317 Front Street in downtown Rensselaer Falls, which Hartman calls "The Honeymoon Capital of

★ ★

the North Country." Stop by to purchase that hard-to-find restoration item, add to your own collections, or just browse through it as a museum. If you can't find Hartman right away, look for the big kid zipping down Front Street in a golf cart.

Kyle's World is "open by chance or appointment." Call (315) 344-8882 or 344-7247. You can also send him a postcard from anywhere in the world. Mail it to: Kyle 13860 USA.

They'll know *exactly* who you're talking about!

Trivia

Shall We Vacate?

The Adirondack region is a great vacation destination, but did you know that the word "vacation" originated in the Adirondacks?

By the early 1900s city people had begun to realize that the summer months were prime time for deadly diseases. So, they started "vacating" their homes in the city and heading for the fresh mountain air of the Adirondacks.

This time period was loaded with misconceptions and hoaxes (hello, Cardiff Giant), but if you've been paying attention, you know that there is definitely some truth to feeling better in mountain air. Remember the negative ions of Niagara Falls? Well, there is also a concentration of negative ions around mountains and forests. And guess what? The Adirondack region has both!

So, if you've ever wondered why Americans take a "vacation" instead of a "holiday," like the British, that's why—it came from the need to vacate cities and avoid disease!

Now, who's up for a vacation in New York City?

NO SPITTING, PLEASE
Saranac Lake

Not only did people vacation in the Adirondacks to avoid deadly diseases, they used to go there to be cured!

Saranac Lake became known as a cure community for tuberculosis after Edward L. Trudeau, infected with TB, went there in 1873, planning to spend his remaining days in a serene mountain setting, only to make a full recovery!

Not one to take his cure and run, Dr. Trudeau set up a facility for other TB patients called the Adirondack Cottage Sanitarium (later renamed the Trudeau Sanatorium), which helped many other patients recover as well. The sanitarium was so popular that it was overflowing, prompting locals to convert their homes into "cure cottages." (This was before they discovered that TB was contagious.) In old photographs, you'll often see the porches of these cure cottages lined with beds so patients could take in the "curative" mountain air.

Of course, the air wasn't some magic cure, but it did give a boost to the patients' immune systems. Antibiotics hadn't been invented yet, and the immune system was a patient's only defense against TB.

The patients were encouraged to rest but weren't bedridden. "There were no restricted activities," says Mary Hotaling, executive director of Historic Saranac Lake. "So, they went horseback riding—it was like a vacation!" Performers were brought in by the William Morris Agency to entertain patients and raise money; as a result, there are still weekly concerts and theater events in Saranac Lake today.

The Trudeau Institute, now a broader medical research facility, isn't open to the public, but if you're in Saranac Lake, you can see the statue of Dr. Trudeau out front, created by the same artist who designed Mount Rushmore! His former lab, the Saranac Laboratory on Church Street, is being converted into a museum. As you walk around this picturesque mountain town, try to pick out the "cure cottages" by their long porches. Saranac Lake also has a thriving art community and variety of wellness programs.

A Prisoner's Palace

Saranac Lake

What do you get when you mix kind-hearted royalty, prison labor, and a famous comic-strip artist?

The Saranac Lake Winter Carnival!

In order to break up the long Adirondack winter, every February, Saranac Lake hosts a 10-day winter carnival, featuring a coronation ceremony of the king, queen, and court, selected for their contributions to the community. There are theatrical performances, sporting events, woodsmen's events, an ice-sculpture contest, and funny competitions such as the Ladies Frying Pan Toss. There are also two parades and two sets of fireworks, set high above the carnival's famous Ice Palace.

Sure beats making license plates.

Photo by Mark Kurtz

It's like Disney World in the Adirondacks! (Only, it eventually melts.)

The Ice Palace is a 50-foot high castle built of hundreds of ice blocks chipped out of a nearby lake. Sounds like pretty hard labor, right? Well, you can volunteer if you want to, but, for more than twenty years, they've had a little help from inmates at the nearby Camp Gabriels state prison! (Don't worry, though, it's a minimum-security facility and the labor is securely monitored.)

Another fun bit of trivia about the festival is that the illustration for the carnival commemorative button is designed by Doonesbury creator Gary Trudeau. Trudeau, the great-grandson of TB-cure community founder Edward Trudeau, spent part of his childhood here and continues to give back to the community by doing the illustration every year for the winter festival.

For more information visit www.saranaclakewintercarnival.com. If you can't make it to the festival, you can pick up a button year-round at the Town Hall on the corner of River and Main Streets in Saranac Lake.

★ ★

So head on over to Saranac Lake and take a nice deep breath of that fresh mountain air. Oh! I should warn you: Whatever you do, don't spit! A holdover from the area's TB past, there's still a village "expectoration" law on the books that says you'll be fined up to $250 if you're caught, well, expectorating.

But, seriously. I shouldn't have had to tell you that. You should know better!

For more information visit www.saranaclake.com and www.trudeauinstitute.org.

GETTING A LEG UP
Saratoga Battlefield

The map says that stop number seven on the Saratoga Battlefield tour is Breymann Redoubt, commemorating a key win for the American side during the American Revolution.

What they don't play up too much is that there is a monument to Benedict Arnold's leg here!

I guess they *can't* play it up too much, given that whole traitor thing. The inscription on the back of the monument doesn't even mention him by name. Instead, it says, "In Memory of the most brilliant soldier of the Continental Army, who was desperately wounded on this spot . . . 7th October 1777 . . . winning for his countrymen the Decisive Battle of the American Revolution and for himself the rank of Major General."

You have to remember this was P.T. (pre-treachery) and Arnold *was* one of the best generals we had. He was crucial in winning the Battle of Saratoga, the turning point of the Revolution. He was severely wounded in the leg during this battle, the same leg that had been injured previously in Quebec.

Purportedly, the monument refers to the response Arnold got from an American soldier he'd taken captive while working for the British army A.T. (after his famous traitorous act). He'd asked the soldier what the Americans would do if they captured him. The soldier

Your leg, we shall honor. The rest of you? Not so much.

replied: "We would cut your leg off and bury it with full military honors for your work at Quebec and Saratoga. The rest of you we would hang."

For the record, it never came to that. After he got busted for trying to surrender West Point to the British and narrowly escaped via the Hudson River, Arnold commanded troops for the British army for a few years and then retired to London, where he died in 1801.

The real leg, incidentally, is buried at St. Mary's Church, Battersea in London, along with the rest of him.

To figure out how to get to that leg monument, visit www.nps.gov/sara or call (518) 664-9821, extension 224.

★ ★

ON YOUR MARK. WAKE UP. GO!

Schroon Lake

You know what they say: If you snooze, you lose.

In Schroon Lake, there's no sleeping on the job. That's because they not only sleep in their beds, they also race them!

Ken Hedden, owner of the Wayfarer Motel (www.wayfarermotel .com), had fond memories of attending a bed race every year in Lake George with his wife and some camping buddies. So, when they stopped holding the race, he decided to start one up in Schroon (pro-nounced "skroon") Lake.

It's exactly what it sounds like: You run with a bed. There are four runners who guide the bed, which is on wheels, across the finish line. People use all different kinds of wheels, Hedden says, everything from wheelbarrow wheels to bicycle wheels and handcart wheels. One person sits on top of the bed.

Photo by Geri Hedden

Do NOT hit the snooze button. You got it, buddy?

★ ★

You can leave the box springs at home, but beds still get pretty heavy, especially when the rules say "no handles." So, the race itself is only about 35 yards.

"It's not a long race, but it's a fast, furious race!" Hedden says.

There are $100 prizes for the fastest bed and for the most creative bed. Even if you're not too fast, you get points—and cash—for style! Past beds have been patriotic- and hospital-themed, shaped like a fire truck, and made from an Adirondack log. Once, there was even a bed made to look like a boat, complete with a "water-skier" on a skateboard in the back!

Um, was it a *water* bed?

The race is held every year on the Saturday of Memorial Day weekend. For more information visit www.schroonlake.org and click on "Calendar/Events," or call Rosemarie at the Schroon Lake Chamber of Commerce at (888) 724-7666.

THIS HERE'S A ROBBERY!
Thendara

Shortly after the train chugged out of Thendara station, a woman came through the aisle in a mighty purdy yellow dress.

"My name is Miss Lill," she said. "I'm handin' out government money just in case somethin' happens. . . . It won't. Naw, we won't need it. But iff'n we do . . . "

We were chattin' it up real nice with Miss Lill when all of a sudden . . . four men appear outside the train window, some on horseback, some firin' guns!

"Dougy, we're going to get robbed!" shouted Sandy, a fellow passenger across the aisle. Chrissy, in a raspberry derby, giggled excitedly as she looked out the window.

Next thing we know, a few a them bandits boarded the train, bickering. Annie Oakley was hot on their heels, attempting to fight them off, along with the help of some growls and cheers from the kids on the train. But it was no use: We had to hand over that "government money" Miss Lill gave us.

★ ★

"It's been a pleasure robbin' you today!" one a them bandits shouted, just before we entered Carter station.

On the way back to Thendara, we met some other characters, including a mail-order bride, Miss Prudence, and a man who introduced himself as Sam Wayne. They call him One-Shot Wayne, Quick-Draw Wayne, or Frilly-Knickers Wayne, but don't ask about that!

Outside, the scene unfolds again, and, while the bandits were ultimately defeated in a dramatic shoot-out, we never did get that government money back.

Oh well.

Wait just a dern minute. I thought we wuz the ones doin' the robbin'?

Being from New York City, it seemed odd to pay money to get "robbed" on a train, but here in the Adirondacks, where a friend once said it's so safe you could leave a bag of money in your unlocked car and no one would take it, that's just a fun way to spend the afternoon!

The "Loomis Gang Train Robberies," based on a famous 19th-century family of thieves, are held every Wednesday in July and August on the Adirondack Scenic Railroad. Most of the actors come from the Mystery Company theater troop from Rochester.

The plots and characters are always changing, so you never know who's gonna rob you. Just take my advice and have your government money ready!

For more information visit www.adirondackrail.com or www.mysterycompany.net.

A TALE OF TWO CASTLES
Thousand Islands

There are not one but two castles in the Thousand Islands. They were both built at the turn of the 20th century, but their stories are quite different. One is a romantic fairy-tale castle, the other is a peculiar mystery-novel castle!

Boldt Castle (www.boldtcastle.com) is better known because it has been open to the public longer. It's called a "Monument to Love" because it was built by George C. Boldt, millionaire proprietor of the Waldorf-Astoria Hotel in New York City, as a Valentine's Day present for his wife, Louise. It's located on Heart Island, and the heart-shaped motif infiltrates every last nook and cranny, from the stained-glass ceiling to the garden—even the island's seawall is in the shape of a heart! Alas, this love story has a tragic ending: Louise died suddenly before the castle was completed. Heartbroken, Boldt immediately ordered all 300 workers to cease construction. He walked away and never returned.

Boldt Castle remained abandoned and unfinished for an astounding seventy-three years, exposed to wind, rain, snow, and vandals. The Thousand Islands Bridge Authority assumed ownership of the castle in 1977 and began the long process of restoration. It remains unfinished today, but you can still take a fascinating self-guided tour.

If Boldt Castle is the princess of castles, then Singer Castle is her black-nail-polish-wearing Goth sister!

Singer Castle (www.singercastle.com), located on the appropriately named "Dark Island," was a private residence for about one hundred years before being opened for public tours in 2003. It was built as a summer home for Frederic Bourne, director of the Singer Sewing Machine Company.

Welcome to Singer Castle. Don't lean against any bookcases. You never know!

★ ★

The architect modeled Singer Castle after a castle he read about in Sir Walter Scott's novel, *Woodstock*. There are hidden passageways, accessed through trick bookcases and other clever disguises, and secret lookout spots through ventilation grates and even—how cool, how cliché—through a painting! It was really a child's (i.e., my) fantasy come to life, but the practical application was that the servants would always be able to monitor when someone needed a refill of their drink without ever having to pass through and disrupt the conversation. (Well, excuse me!) There's also a fully equipped dungeon (though never used as one), an underground labyrinth, and lots of odd gadgets, high-tech for their time, including an "electric light-bath cabinet." (There's a reason you've never heard of it!)

Oh, and in case you're wondering, the two millionaire castle owners did indeed know each other. They used to race their speedboats between the two castles.

That is *totally* what I would do if I owned a castle on an island!

You can take a boat to both castles with Uncle Sam Boat Tours in Alexandria Bay (www.unclesamboattours.com).

ARE THERE REALLY A THOUSAND?

Thousand Islands

Why do they call them the Thousand Islands? Are there really 1,000 islands in the St. Lawrence River?

In fact, there are actually *more* than 1,000. I guess "One Thousand, Eight Hundred and Sixty-Four Islands" was too much of a tongue twister for the French explorers who named the area! The number is technically closer to 2,000, but you can't say Two Thousand Islands because 1) that's just weird, and 2) it's not true!

So, we'll leave it at a cool 1,000 then. Isn't that grand? (Har har.)

(Look, I know this whole thing was decided in French, but my jokes are in English, okay?)

In order to qualify as one of the Thousand Islands, an island has to be at least 1 foot in diameter, host one tree or shrub, and be above water 365 days a year.

Trash Talking on Your Own Island

Thousand Islands

Do you think that you or I could just buy one of the Thousand (1,684) Islands? I mean, if there are so many of them, why not?

The quick answer is: Yes! Anyone can buy an island, since most of them are private property. But it's not as easy as you think, being your own island.

First, winters are cold, so most of the private islands are vacation properties. (Yeah, my second home is an island.) Second, you're going to pay at least half a million for your own island, probably more like a *couple* million. (OK, I fold. But I'll continue telling the rest of the story in case you're still interested.)

Then, there's the little matter of electricity. Most islands have electricity through underwater cables, as with telephones, says Gary DeYoung, director of the 1000 Islands Tourism Council. Some islands still don't have electricity; they use generators or gas-powered appliances. If you want to have underwater cables installed, here's a reality check: It costs about $150 per foot!

"Internet is a challenge, outside of dial-up," DeYoung says, adding that some islands now use wireless Internet. (Yeah, my island has Wi-Fi.)

Now, it's time to do a little trash talking. There is no curbside pickup on an island and you can't just throw it overboard—I mean, over porch! Taking out the trash means putting it in your boat and hauling it to the nearest mainland landfill. Each town has a transfer station, DeYoung says.

"It's like when you go grocery shopping," explains Melanie Curley of Thousand Islands Realty. "You put it in your boat and drive it to your island."

You may not even need a car once you get to shore. "The super-market in Alexandria Bay has a dock in its parking lot," DeYoung says, adding that "municipal parking" often includes boat docks.

The key to private-island living, Curley says, is planning ahead. You have to check the weather, so you're not boating to your island in a massive thunderstorm. Plus, she adds: "When you run out of toilet paper, you have to get back in your boat and go back to the mainland!"

Oh, and there are no street numbers on a river. So, in case of an emergency, DeYoung says, have your GPS coordinates handy!

Why is everyone pretending they don't see the big, white lighthouse in the middle of the room?!

The smallest island is Tom Thumb, a 3-square-foot hunk of rock with a tree sticking out. Another island is called Just Room Enough because it has just enough room for one house. (How cute is that?) The largest is Wolfe Island, part of Canada, at 49 square miles. (The U.S.-Canada border zigzags between the islands.)

Sisters Island is famous because there's a lighthouse going straight through the middle of the island's only house, but the residents carry on about their business like no one notices the big elephant—er, lighthouse—in the middle of the room. Deer Island is owned by a member of the clandestine Skull and Bones society, and the local chapter has held retreats there.

Another fun bit of Thousand Islands trivia is the fact that there are more than one hundred shipwrecks in this channel. (Hey, it's not easy navigating 1,864 islands, cut them some slack!)

And, to answer your other burning question, yes, Thousand Islands salad dressing was invented here!

As the story goes, around the turn of the 20th century, Sophie LaLonde of Clayton created it and served it to dinner guests. Its public debut was at the Thousand Islands Inn, but it really caught on after George Boldt, hotel magnate and lover extraordinaire, found out about it and started serving it at the Waldorf.

The rest is, as they say, dressing on the salad!

For more information, visit www.visit1000islands.com. For a tour check out www.unclesamboattours.com.

GRAB THE AX, CHAINSAW, AND THIS HERE GREASED POLE!
Tupper Lake

Is your closest lumberjack connection using Brawny paper towels? Wearing a flannel shirt in winter?

Well, put down the paper towels, Nancy, cuz we're headed to the Adirondacks for some good, ol' fashioned lumberjackin' and we're gonna get dirty! (Cue the banjo: Dug, dugga dig a dug dug, doog doo doo . . . digga digga dooga dug doo . . .)

If you want to really experience the mountain life in the Adirondacks, head to Tupper Lake in July for the annual Woodsmen's Days (www.woodsmendays.com). The festival features Lumberjack and Lumberjill contests, where men and women compete in log rolling (it's much harder than you think!), ax throwing, tree-felling, and other events. There's also a chainsaw-carving contest; a horse-pull competition; and the pièce de résistance, the Saturday night main event—the greased-pole climb! (It's a team sport, so it's sort of like a mountain-man totem pole with Crisco added.)

Ladies and Gentlemen. Start your chainsaws!

It's great entertainment and an excellent opportunity to buy the little missus a chainsaw-carved bear for the porch!

There are at least three other lumberjack festivals in New York State. They're held throughout the summer, so you can find the one that fits best with your schedule, or spend the whole summer hoppin' from one log roll to the next, like the lumberjack groupie that you are!

Also in July is the Lumberjack Festival in Deposit (between Binghamton and the Catskills). There's a sidewalk sale, carnival rides, a beautiful baby contest, a log truck "cherry picker" contest, horseshoe tournament, tractor pull, and more.

In August, Boonville (in the foothills of the Adirondacks) holds its Woodsmen's Field Days (www.starwebhosting.net/woodsmen), featuring log rolling, ax throwing, a truck pull, a Miss Forest pageant,

★ ★

and a truck rodeo. Macedon (near Rochester) gets its chainsaws revved and poles greased in September.

You never knew there was so much elbow grease in New York State, did you?

DIRECTIONS TO THE FUNNY FARM

Warrensburg

When people used to drive by the late Forrest Lanfair's house on East Schroon River Road in Warrensburg, they slowed down. Some got out of the car. Others walked right up on the lawn to see what the heck was going on there!

Lanfair, a former postmaster and self-taught artist, had created dozens of life-size comical sculptures on his lawn: a farmer and his horse, the farmer's wife chasing a goat with a broom, a cave family,

Looking for the funny farm? You found it, buddy!

a tree family, a couple of town drunks, an elf, even an Adirondack skeeter!

He called it "Fun & Farm," which he told the *Glens Falls Post Star* was a play on "funny farm."

When Lanfair passed away in 2003, his daughter inherited the house and lawn museum, but she died a few years later after a brief illness. Lanfair was a private man, and his wish was that, when he died, someone would dig a hole and bury the sculptures. But his daughter's family was left with big medical bills, and they decided to sell or auction most of the collection, much to the delight of longtime fans such as Bill Dow and Susie West.

Dow, who owns the Boardwalk Restaurant and Lake George Steamboat Company in Old Forge, bought a dozen of the sculptures, including the town drunks (er, let's call them lamppost people) and an elf, which is perched on the restaurant's wooden railing, as well as the skeeter. He plans to display the rest at his businesses in Old Forge after some much-needed repairs. A few others were sold to Magic Forest, a small theme park in Lake George, according to an article in *Adirondack Life* magazine.

Perhaps the most popular, the farmer, with his belly poking out of his worn-out shirt, and his tired old horse, with its tongue lolling out, were bought at auction by West, Lanfair's first cousin once removed (Lanfair's mother and West's grandfather were siblings).

The farmer and horse were, like many of the concrete and mesh sculptures, in pretty bad shape. The horse had two broken legs and needed a lot of repairs. West recalls, "My husband said, 'Can you believe my wife bought a dead horse?!'"

How does that expression go—if you can't beat a dead horse, join him?!

The Wests repaired the sculptures, added cement bases, and today proudly display them on their front lawn on Route 418, across from Schroon River.

So, if you think you're about ready for the funny farm, drive around Old Forge and Warrensburg and you'll find it!

4

Southeast, the Catskills, and Hudson Valley
Fender Rockets and Sleeping Beer

The southeastern part of New York has long been a getaway for weary city folk, with plenty of restful spots nestled in the Catskill Mountains and in the picturesque Hudson Valley.

As you're driving to your little chalet—well, here they call them motels—you'll soon realize the area's got a knack for kitsch—everything from an oversized fork at, appropriately, a fork in the road, to the world's largest garden gnome.

It was on the way to the world's largest kaleidoscope (of course) that a friend and I discovered one of the best curiosities—rockets made from 1950s car parts shooting out of the ground at Steve Heller's Fabulous Furniture on Route 28. And, if you've ever said, "Oh, I'd love to have my own castle—if only I were rich," then you need to go to Millbrook to meet Peter Wing, a man who built his own castle out of found objects.

Speaking of castles, little known fact: They're great for storage of explosives or other items you might have lying around, as you'll learn at Bannerman Castle on Pollepel Island in the Hudson River.

A few words of advice before you go: If you're touring Howe Caverns, shhhhhhhhhh! Be quiet or you'll wake the beer. And, if you're in Canajoharie, always stay to the right of the Dummy Light.

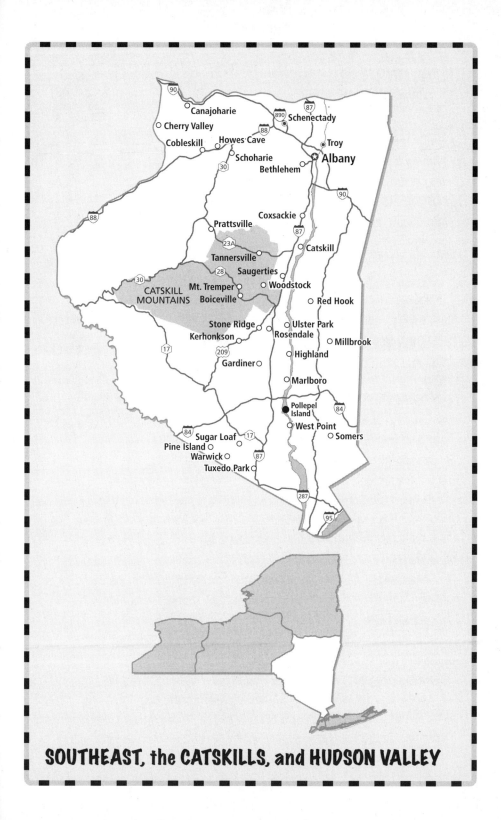

SOUTHEAST, the CATSKILLS, and HUDSON VALLEY

★ ★

A LITTLE NIPPY UP THERE

Albany

On the outskirts of Albany, a four-ton dog sits on top of the Arnoff building, with his head cocked like maybe he just heard the word "treats."

If he looks familiar, that's because this building used to house an RCA distributor, and he's Nipper, the famous dog from the RCA ads. This fiberglass-and-steel-mesh Nipper was erected in 1954. Many RCA buildings used to have Nippers like this one; only this one and another in Baltimore remain.

One ear tuned to the "treat" channel, the other monitoring traffic!

He's an old dog, that's for sure: The real Nipper, whom the statue was based on, was a bull terrier/fox terrier mix born in 1884 in Bristol, England. He got his name because he liked to nip at the back of people's ankles.

After Nipper died in 1895, his owner, a struggling artist named Francis Barraud, painted a famous picture of Nipper looking into the bell of a phonograph. Nipper was, apparently, puzzled by where the voices were coming from when the phonograph was on. The title, *His Master's Voice,* suggests that maybe he was listening to the voice of his former owner, Francis's deceased brother Mark. (Or maybe it suggests the painter was having a hard time selling the painting.)

The painting was ultimately bought by the Gramophone Company in 1899. Nipper became a trademark for HMV Records and RCA.

"His Master's Voice" also became the name of a record label. RCA updated the Nipper ads in 1991 with a little Nipper-snapper named Chipper; actor dogs continue to play both dogs today.

The Nipper-topped building in Albany is now home to Arnoff Moving and Storage Company, but these guys just can't bear to let an old dog down.

The real Nipper is buried under some magnolia trees in a London park. The original painting resides at EMI Music's Gloucester Place headquarters, also in London. And the big dog, well, he sits on the Arnoff building at Broadway and Tivoli streets, listening to the sound of the cars whizzing by.

PANDA, THE SEEING-EYE HORSE
Bethlehem

Some blind people use a cane to navigate. Others use a guide dog.

Ann Edie uses a guide horse!

Edie has been guided by Panda, a 2½-foot-tall black-and-white miniature pony, since 2003. Panda is one of three or four seeing eye horses in the U.S.

"I go a lot of different places with my job," says Edie, a special-education teacher. The main reason to have a guide animal is that it "allows me to travel more smoothly and faster than with a cane."

But isn't it hard getting around with a horse?

Nope. Edie says she takes Panda everywhere—grocery stores, hotels, train stations—even bookstores.

What about restaurants? Surely they turn away a woman with a horse.

Nope! "We always get the best service when I take Panda," Edie says. "All the waiters fight over who gets to wait on the table with the horse!"

"The only place I've had a problem is with airlines," Edie says. "The FAA has some concerns about her size. Unlike a dog, she doesn't fit under the seat!"

★ ★

That's true. So, why a horse instead of a dog?

It costs less to feed a horse than a dog, Edie says. Plus, dogs are more easily distracted by small animals. Horses are more deliberate in their footing and can identify overhead obstacles like tree branches that dogs can't reach. Perhaps most importantly, horses live up to thirty years longer than dogs.

Panda taps her foot to let Edie know when to step up, and puts her nose up to doorknobs to guide Edie's hand. If Panda needs to go out to her shed to see a man about a—nevermind—she rings a jingle bell on a doorknob with her nose. She might even nibble on some grass while she's out there.

Inside—yes, she's allowed inside—Panda enjoys playing Frisbee and other retrieval games. And, when Edie's chopping vegetables in the kitchen, you'll find her glued to Edie's side, hoping for a handout.

What's a girl have to do to get a carrot around here?

You truly haven't lived until you've heard the clip-clip of a horse's hoofs on the kitchen linoleum!

For more information about horses as guide animals, visit www.theclicker center.com.

FABULOUS FENDER ROCKETS

Boiceville

Steve Heller makes beautiful—sorry, *fabulous*—organic-shaped wooden furniture out of odd or misshapen trees that he and his team retrieve themselves.

But the first thing you notice when you drive by Steve Heller's Fabulous Furniture on Route 28 in the Catskills is that there are rockets shooting out of the front lawn!

Wait a minute, is that a fender?!

Heller's been looking for old trees to carve since his paper-route days, and he started tinkering with recycled metal from his father's scrap collection. But Heller says his real passion is cars.

He takes the fins off of 1950s cars—his favorite make is Cadillac—and seamlessly welds them together to create these amazing rockets and spaceships.

"I'm just putting them back together the way they should've been!" Heller says.

He also turns vintage car parts into furniture; those big Caddy trunks, if you stand them upright, make a great bookshelf. And the tail lights? Of course, a floor lamp!

"My father took me to the Museum of Modern Art when I was a kid," Heller says. "I saw Picasso's *Baboon and Young.* The head of the baboon was two toy cars put together. It freaked me out! I knew from then that this is what I needed to do."

An old cement mixer becomes a spaceship. An unwanted box of wrenches becomes a flame-shooting, soapbox-derby-winning wrenchosaurus!

His masterpiece is a brand-new Mercury Marquis that he stripped and restored with 1950s car parts from ten different cars. So, it's vintage on the outside, brand-new on the inside! It seems implausible but Heller pops open the trunk and you can see where the old trunk ends and the new one begins. Or, wait, is it the other way around?

★ ★

On this sleepy stretch of Route 28, Steve Heller's Fabulous Furniture is a magical glitch in the matrix, where things go in broken down and come out transformed into something amazing.

The only thing that's bugging me is the "fabulous" part. Heller is a cool, laid-back biker-type dude, the kind of guy you want to grab a beer with after you buy something from him. He just doesn't strike me as the kind of guy who would use the word "fabulous."

Well, unless it was #*@%-ing fabulous.

Which it is.

NASA's got nothing on Steve Heller!

Check him out at www .fabulousfurnitureon28.com or call (845) 657-6317.

Wait. You know what? Don't do that. Just go. Trust me.

THE DUMMY LIGHT

Canajoharie

Five roads converge on the small town of Canajoharie, making it necessary in the days before cars to have a policeman directing traffic.

There was also a monument, with built-in bowls for the horses to drink water, right in the middle of the five-way intersection!

When the automobile came along, it became a lot more dangerous. In 1926 they moved the monument to a nearby park and installed one of those newfangled pedestals, or "dummy" lights, to direct traffic with lights that turned red, yellow, and green.

★ ★

It was all very confusing. No one knew what any of those lights meant. So, the *Canajoharie Courier* printed lengthy instructions, including: "Go ahead on GREEN and stop on RED." It advised caution when making a left turn and set the conditions for turning right on red. "Cut out this summary and paste in your hat," it said.

You can imagine the scene that followed: When approaching the intersection, people were taking their hats off, left and right, to consult the directions!

When the new wave of technology brought hanging traffic lights, the state wanted to replace the dummy light, but the people of Canajoharie protested and the state backed down. Today, there are two traffic lights in Canajoharie, and, you guessed it, the dummy light is one of them! It's one of only a few dummy lights left in the United States.

There's a sign on the pedestal that says KEEP RIGHT SO, even if you're making a left turn, you stay to the right of the light to avoid an accident. Not everyone gets that, and, let's just say, people notice.

"People just abuse it," says Barbara Spraker, the unofficial town historian, wearing an "I Have Seen the Light!" dummy light T-shirt. "They disrespect it."

They may not know how to use it, but they've all seen the light.

Please, get it right.

★ ★

"Anyone who's been here knows that light," says Phyllis Lapi, owner of the Picture Perfect Art Gallery in downtown Canajoharie. "My husband was stationed in Guam. We met people and they asked where in the U.S. we were from. When we told them Canajoharie, they said, 'Oh, that town with the light!'"

Now, if only everyone who drives past it would learn how to use it!

SOMEONE HAD TO DO IT
Canajoharie

H-h-hey, are you throwing out that paper bag? Before you do, let me tell you something about that bag.

It was during the Civil War, and cotton was scarce. Canajoharie businessman James Arkell started tinkering with some paper and what do you know? He invented the paper bag!

It was a much bigger deal than creating a vehicle for your five-patty burger and supersize jumbolicious fries. It freed up cotton supplies, making more available for bandages for the Union troops.

"Imagine the ingenuity to take paper, lay it out, put folds in it and put it through a machine to glue it together," remarks Barbara Spraker, the unofficial town historian of Canajoharie. "You don't just put the paper in there and it comes out a paper bag!"

Arkell and Smith, as the company was known, had struck gold—well, paper—and the business expanded rapidly. They made paper bags for just about anything you can think of—sugar, salt, dog food, fertilizer, cement, you name it.

Everyone in Canajoharie has either worked at the Arkell factory or knows someone who did. "When you were a new employee," recalls local resident Sue Beaver, "they'd send you out to look for the bag stretcher!" (There wasn't one.)

Arkell's son, Bartlett, inherited his father's nose for business and went on to found the Beech-Nut Packing Company with a few other business partners. It's Arkell money, says Spraker, that has kept the town going. So, if you're driving through and think to

★ ★

yourself, "Wow! That's a really nice museum for a small town," you know it was made possible by ham, ketchup, peanut butter, gum, baby food—and paper bags!

There's a mural of James Arkell and his great invention, with nurses applying bandages to Union troops in the background, at the Canajoharie Post Office on Main Street.

For more on Arkell and Beech-Nut, visit www.arkellmuseum.org.

SENG IT FROM THE MOUNTAINTOPS

Catskill

Mark Twain's dad was into it. So was Daniel Boone. Ditto for John Jacob Astor, one of the richest men in U.S. history. Heck, Bob Beyfuss has a shoulder-to-elbow tattoo of it!

I am, of course, referring to ginseng, a root known for its energy-enhancing and youth-preserving abilities. Some say it can alleviate fatigue in cancer patients and that it has other . . . um . . . uplifting effects.

The United States has been exporting the coveted herb for nearly 300 years, and New York, particularly the Catskill region, is known to have some of the best soil in the world for growing ginseng. "One guy—he was from Ohio or Virginia—called New York ginseng, 'ginseng on steroids'!" recalls Dr. Beyfuss, a specialist with the Cornell Cooperative

Gnarly, dude! That's a twenty-two-year-old ginseng root.

195

Extension who has studied ginseng for more than twenty-five years and organizes the Catskill Ginseng/Medicinal Herb Festival.

The most potent is wild ginseng, grown in the woods. The older and more gnarly the root, the better. The theory is that, when a plant lives a long time, it accumulates a strong chi (pronounced "chee"), or life force, that is transferred to you when you consume it raw, in tea, or as an elixir. You can tell how old a root is because it has scars for each year, like rings on a tree stump.

If you're wondering what rock you've been under that you've never heard of New York ginseng, that's because it's a pretty secretive business. (Think *The Orchid Thief* meets fountain of youth.) Growers won't even tell you where their ginseng farms are for fear of poachers. They protect their crops with cameras, motion detectors, dogs—even guns.

Sure, you can buy a bottle of ginseng tablets at a health-food store for $16 but it's not the same. At the quaint Catskill ginseng festival, Ziploc bags of wild ginseng root were marked $500 and $1,000 per pound! A really old root can run into the thousands—*plural*.

Beyfuss says he's had people offer to pay him $1,000 just to show them where the ginseng is!

Now, don't go getting all starry-eyed that you're going to get rich quick on ginseng; it takes a minimum of eight to ten years to mature. And no Meryl Streep/Chris Cooper–type adventures looking for the secret ginseng farms, OK? Next thing you know, you get shot, someone gets arrested, and I'm hauled in for questioning.

But maybe, the next time you're driving through the sleepy Catskills, you'll look at those forest-covered mountains just a little bit differently.

SIGN HERE FOR THE CHILI
Cherry Valley

Few things say Americana like a four-story (55-foot) tepee.

As you drive by it, you can't help but wonder why someone would

We come in peace, prepared to sign the Great Chili Treaty of Cherry Valley.

go to all the trouble . . . Your inner monologue brakes only after a hair-raising shout of "CAN WE STOP?!" from the backseat.

You know it's inevitable. Oh yeah. You're stopping at the tepee.

The TePee (that's literally what it's called), on Route 20 in Cherry Valley, was built in 1950 and has all the makings of a typical tourist trap, but the current owners, sisters Donna and Dale Latella, have a great eye. It's a really well-done gift shop.

Native Americans in this area never actually lived in tepees (they lived in longhouses), but the Native gifts at the TePee—such as deerskin moccasins and dream catchers—are authentically Native-made. The shop also has a beautiful selection of jewelry, pottery, pewter, wood carvings, and more. The TePee-branded items are

also surprisingly tasteful, like the tiny tepee in a snow globe and the TePee Taffy!

Next door is TePee Pete's Chow Wagon, operated by Donna and Dale's brother, Pete. Sure, he serves your average roadside fare of hamburgers and hots, but he's also got a few items you didn't see coming, including hot apple salsa, red tart cherry salsa, buffalo burgers, and Pete's special Seven-Pepper Chili, the only chili for which you'll ever have to sign a release form! (Seriously, you can't eat it if you don't sign it!)

Picnic tables between the TePee and Chow Wagon make for one of the most pleasant roadside stops in the entire state. Just try to be discreet if you order a buffalo burger; don't brandish it in front of Buffy the Buffalo, the fiberglass beauty who's been keeping watch on Route 20 for the past twenty-five years!

This is one time it's worth giving in to the backseat contingency.

The TePee is located at 7632 U.S. Highway 20. For more information visit www.thetepee.biz or call (607) 264-3987.

GET YOUR KNICKERS STRAIGHT
Cherry Valley

When moviemakers need an army of tweed knickers, where do they go?

Do they scour vintage stores until they find the fifty pairs of pants they need? Do they buy imitation tweed and ask the costume designers to just fake it?

No, they call Rabbit Goody, who runs Thistle Hill Weavers, a textiles manufacturer that reproduces 17th-, 18th-, and 19th-century fabrics for vintage clothing as well as historic homes (curtains, bedspreads, rugs) and vintage automobiles.

As we're sitting in her office, in walks the FedEx guy with a letter and swatch of fabric from a movie producer. Goody inspects the gray herringbone wool with her magnifying glass. "What's neat about this is that it has a colored yarn in it. You see? It has a purple thread in it!"

Her clients usually send a swatch of fabric, but sometimes they include a whole article of clothing. "We'll have a brief overnight visit from the pants if necessary," Goody says matter-of-factly, as if the pants were in-laws.

Thistle Hill made the fabric for the children's World War II–era clothing in *The Chronicles of Narnia: The Lion, the Witch and the Wardrobe,* the striped prison fabric in *O, Brother Where Art Thou?,* and the fabric for Tom Hanks's suit in *Road to Perdition,* among other films.

What makes the shop unique, Goody says, is that it can make smaller-quantity orders than big commercial mills. Thistle Hill has a 20-yard minimum; most mills won't run a fabric order for less than 5,000 yards.

"Companies in China can't do custom," Goody says. "That's our niche."

Most of the equipment was purchased secondhand from mills going out of business. Only one loom is computerized; the rest are old hand-run looms, guided by a pattern punched in paper.

Doing things by hand has been a lifelong philosophy for Goody, who has a degree in anthropology and lived without electricity for fifteen years. "I didn't need a generator," Goody says. "I wanted to use systems that were in place 200 years ago."

So, the next time you need a pair of 200-year-old pants, you know whom to call.

For more information visit www.thistlehillweavers.com or call (518) 284-2729.

THE ODD CAVE COUPLE
Cobleskill

Much like the Thousand Islands has its tale of two castles, so Cobleskill has a dark tale of two very different caves. (Literally, it's dark down there!)

Howe Caverns is like the Disney World of caves, with its preppy-jacketed guides and brick path. Secret Caverns, by contrast, is like the

The Cradle of the Cave

Howes Cave

Howe Caverns may be the Disney World of caves but there's something unexpected lurking under that tarp around the corner. No, it's not Gollum hiding out until the *Lord of the Rings* reunion special. It's beer and cheese!

Fly Creek Cidermill has a couple hundred pounds of McCadam's (what else) New York cheddar aging in the cave and Cooperstown's Ommegang Brewery has a couple hundred cases of Belgian-style beer down there.

Look out for cavern monsters and beer when you're spelunking in Cobleskill!

The cave provides perfect conditions: At 156 feet below ground, the temperature remains at fifty-two degrees Fahrenheit year-round.

Cave aging isn't a new concept; it's how they used to age beer and wine before refrigeration, and it's still used in the Champagne region of France today.

"We set out to replicate as closely as possible the conditions that produce extraordinary champagnes," says Ommegang Brewmaster Randy Thiel. "There is no doubt that these dark, silent, subterranean 'cathedrals' are the ideal surroundings for secondary fermentation and maturation of wines (and beers)."

For beer, keeping it between fifty and fifty-five degrees slows the maturation and leads to greater complexity, Thiel says.

As for the cheese, the cool temperature and humidity of the cave allows the cheese "to age and mellow far better than other methods," according to Fly Creek. "The result: a sharper yet smoother New York cheddar." You can buy some of the cave-aged cheddar at Howe's gift shop and decide for yourself.

In the fall, the cave hosts a "Waking the Beer" party, with hors d'oeuvres and beer tasting to properly welcome the beer into the drinking world.

Until then, shhhhhhhhhhhhhh! Keep your voice down or you'll wake the beer!

Grateful Dead's underground den, with goateed guides and uneven stairs.

You know something is different about Secret Caverns by the psychedelic billboards you encounter on your way to the cave. There are graphics of cavemen, dinosaurs, and bats, with cheeky slogans such as "Like a Limestone Cowboy: Secret Caverns" and "Four out of Five Dentists Prefer Our Cavity." One billboard was upside down and said something like, "You'll Flip for Secret Caverns!" (I nearly wrecked the rental car on that one!)

Howe's slogans, meanwhile, would be what they call tongue-in-cheek. (Try to suck your cheeks in a little when you say that.) "It's the 'Coolest' Place Around!" Howe's marketing department jests, adding, "Let Us Show You Howe!"

You descend to Howe Caverns via an elevator with two buttons: "L" for Lodge and "C" for Cave. (I actually did laugh at that one!) At Secret Caverns, you take the stairs, buddy.

At Howe Caverns, they'll tell you what a "cave kiss" is: drips of water from calcite. At Secret Caverns, you'll learn what "cow snot" is: flow stone.

Howe Caverns has "Titan's Temple," a 65-foot-high room with great acoustics, and a "Bridal Altar," with a 6-inch piece of semi-transparent heart-shaped calcite set in the brick floor and lit from below. Secret Caverns has cave formations it calls "The Cavern Monster" and "Alligator."

Howe Caverns will encourage you to come caroling in the cave at Christmas, or to have your wedding at the bridal altar. Steve, our guide at Secret Caverns, stresses: "Being cold, wet, and miserable is crucial to the cave experience!" (It wasn't, but it's the thought that counts!)

The pièce de résistance at Howe is an underground boat ride on the Lake of Venus, while the big guitar-slammin' finish at Secret Caverns is a 100-foot waterfall.

I would take my mom to Howe Caverns and my teenage son (if I had one) to Secret Caverns, but personally, I think everyone should go to both!

For more information visit www.secretcaverns.com and www .howecaverns.com.

HAY! IT'S SCIENCE, BUDDY.
Coxsackie

Before the Bronx, there were the Broncks, and they were just a little bit country.

Jonas Bronck of Holland settled the area of New York City we now call the Bronx. His son, Pieter, went farther up the Hudson River to Coxsackie.

Pieter's home is now a museum and thought to be the oldest home remaining in the Hudson Valley. How old is it? So old that he bought the land it's built on from Mohican Indians in 1662!

The property was used as a working farm by eight generations of Broncks. There are 11 buildings in the Bronck complex, including 3 very different barns, which tell a Bronck's tale of 276 years of agricultural evolution.

The first barn was a Victorian horse barn, which is now a local history museum. The family's primary crop was wheat, so the next barn was a New World Dutch–style barn, with a large area for grain storage and a "threshing floor."

Perhaps the most fascinating is a thirteen-sided barn, built in the 1830s when farmers were taking a more scientific approach and the Broncks switched to dairy farming. The weight of the roof rests on the thirteen walls, like a lid on a cookie jar. Well, it was used to store hay, so that would make it a hay jar. The only interior structural element is a large pole to support the middle of the roof. The structure now houses a collection of horse-drawn vehicles.

Why go to such creative lengths for . . . hay? Quite simple: You can drive a wagon inside, around the perimeter, and dump the hay in the middle!

OK. That makes sense. But a cupola . . . for hay? If you look at the sides of the barn, there are no windows! Light had to get in there somehow.

Hay! Let there be light. Now that's using your head for something more than a hay rack.

The farm-turned-museum is owned by the Green County Historical Society and tours run from Memorial Day to mid-October. For more information visit www.gchistory.org or call (518) 731-6490.

Try not to drop a needle in this haystack. It will be like looking for, you know . . .

NO, I DECLARED BEFORE YOU DECLARED
Coxsackie

When in the course of human events it becomes necessary to hit the panic button, let us hold these truths to be self-evident, maintain our God-given right to live . . . oh, and I call shotgun!

Concerned by the violence they were seeing as the American Revolution began, more than 200 Coxsackie residents got together in 1775, a year before the U.S. Declaration of Independence, and whipped up their own declaration!

Known as the Coxsackie Declaration of Independence, the document was signed at the Bronck House, now a museum, and later found in an Albany attic by the former president of the Albany Institute of History & Art, where it remains today.

The signers were "convinced of the necessity of preventing the anarchy and confusion" that come with a revolution. They declared that they were "never to become slaves" and agreed to associate based on religion, honor, and love of their country. (Mm hmm. Mm hmm. I'm with you . . .)

They opposed the execution of "several arbitrary and oppressive acts of the British Parliament." (Yeah! Darn, right!) But here's where it gets weird. The rest of that sentence reads: "until a reconciliation between Great Britain and America or constitutional principles . . . can be obtained."

"If you read it, it wasn't a declaration of independence at all!" says Greene County Historian Ray Beecher. "What it did was reaffirm allegiance to the king of Great Britain!"

Oops. Maybe that's why someone buried it in the attic. Thank goodness for that *other* declaration!

MAY I BORROW THOSE TOMATOES?
Gardiner

At the town library in Gardiner, not only can you check out books, you can check out seeds!

The "seed library" has more than sixty varieties of vegetables, flowers, and herbs, including peas, Brussels sprouts, beans, eight kinds of heirloom tomatoes, sunflowers, hollyhocks, and lettuce.

Wait, how do you "return" seeds?

At the end of the season, you collect seeds from your own crop and return them to the library to replace the ones you borrowed. If you don't know how, the library offers classes on how to do it. In one workshop, they'll show you how to dry out tomato seeds, which are covered in that jelly-like coating to protect them from seeding too

★ ★

soon. Another class is called "Seeds and Salsa," where you learn how to save seeds from tomatoes, cilantro, and peppers, and then use the deseeded ingredients to make salsa!

The seed library also has an extensive collection of gardening books to really get you growing.

Basically, checking out tomatoes is exactly like checking out books, except you get to eat the tomatoes before you bring them back!

The concept sounds like a ready-made *Seinfeld* episode, but it was designed with a loftier goal in mind: "to build a publicly-owned and maintained seed source for the community," says Ken Greene, co-founder of the seed library. He adds that the group hopes to intro-duce the concept to other libraries to "help communities across the country build their own food sources."

For more information contact info@seedlibrary.org or call (845) 255-1255.

YOU'RE HIRED! (TO MAKE ME A KILT)
Highland

So, you're getting married and you want to wear a kilt to honor your Scottish heritage.

N-n-no, wait. I know. You and your buddies are going to a *Brave-heart* reenactment and you're gonna need a kiltload of that special Mel Gibson tartan.

Have I got the place for you!

And guess what? It doesn't involve a trip to Scotland!

Across the Hudson River from Poughkeepsie, in a town appropri-ately named Highland, is the Kiltmaker's Apprentice, a shop devoted entirely to handmade kilts. They order all of their tartan fabrics from Scotland and will even special order your family tartan.

If you're not up for the commitment of owning your own kilt, you can rent one from them—even if you live in California! In fact, the owners, Doreen and Robert Browning, say they do most of their busi-ness over the Internet.

It's not just kilts: You can buy the whole Celt-lovin' getup, from the Prince Charlie jacket to a belt, hose, and shoes. Of course, you're gonna need a sporran, which is a man-purse-type thing, because kilts don't have pockets. "That was probably the original fanny pack!" Bob says.

They've really thought of everything, from a tartan bridal gown to a camouflage kilt for the soldiers in Iraq—even a bride and kilt-wearing groom cake topper!

Doreen says the most common question they get is: What's worn beneath a kilt? Bob jumps in with the *correct* answer: "Nothing is worn beneath the kilt; it's all in working order!"

I SAID it's a sporran, not a purse!

Visit the Kiltmaker's Apprentice at 54 Vineyard Avenue in Highland (800-859-KILT) or order online at www.highlandkiltshop.com.

HELLO, MY GNOME IS CHOMSKY
Kerhonkson

Gnomes have been gknown to nap in the garden. Guard treasures. Get you good deals on hotel rooms.

This one welcomes you to what may be the world's only edible mini-golf course and—oh, how sweet, you shouldn't have—he's picked you a bouquet of wildflowers!

His name is Chomsky (Get it? Gnome Chomsky!) and at 13 feet, 6 inches tall, he is officially the world's largest garden gnome.

He stands on Route 209 in front of Kelder's Farm and Homegrown

Mini-Golf, a ten-hole course landscaped with real fruits, vegetables, herbs, and the occasional chicken!

In the summer Chomsky often holds a bouquet of wild-flowers, since the farm features pick-your-own flowers as well as vegetables and fruits. After a flood in the area, they gave him a life jacket (I always say, make your gnome a prepared gnome) and the local 4-H made him a scarf to keep him warm in the winter.

Sha-gnome! And welcome to Kelder's Farm.

Stealing garden gnomes has been a favorite American pastime, but I wouldn't mess with Chomsky. Have you read any of his work? You don't want to get on that guy's bad side. Plus, he may look like an innocent country bumpkgnome, but this guy grew up in New York City!

Well, that, and he's more than 13 feet tall.

For more information visit www.gnomeonthegrange.com or call (845) 626-7137.

MORE FUN THAN A BARREL OF GRAPES

Marlboro

So, you have a hankering to get closer to your food chain? Missing old-world Europe?

Well, take off your shoes and head up to the Benmarl Winery in the Hudson Valley because we are going to do some grape stomping!

Every fall, after the grape harvest, the winery holds a Harvest Grape Stomping Festival, featuring music and wine tasting, tours of the winery, and, yes, grape stomping.

There are two big tubs with spigots so you can compete with your friends to see who makes the most juice!

Before you get grossed out, you should know that it's just for novelty; they don't actually make wine from the grapes stomped by all those stinky feet! In fact, they use Concord grapes, which aren't used in wine.

To make it more interesting, they often toss the winemaker in one of the barrels, so you can ask him any questions about the winemaking process while you're pretending to be Italian. (You know, spin around and hum—Dit da dada. Dit da dada. Dit da dadada da. Hey!)

You'll learn the secret to one of the winery's signature wines, Baco Noir, an extraordinary cherry-vanilla flavored wine with a peppery finish. "I like a lot of fruit," says winemaker Kristop Brown, with his pants rolled up to the knees and his feet dyed wine red up to the calves. "I taste the juice and think that's delicious. I don't want to lose it."

The name Benmarl comes from the Scottish Gaelic *ben,* meaning small hill, and *marl,* meaning slate, which is a major component of the soil where the grapes are grown. "I believe it's the oily slate in the ground that makes our Baco so good," explains Benmarl owner Victor Spaccarelli Jr.

Making Feet-o Noir at the Benmarl Winery.

★ ★

After you've finished your rousing rendition of *Stomp!* and had your feet hosed down, grab some wine and cheese and head to the round white tables behind the winery, to take advantage of the spectacular hilltop view of the Hudson River and valley.

For more information visit www.benmarl.com or call (845) 236-4265.

They also do grape stomping at nearby Brotherhood Winery, the Cobblestone Farm Winery in the Finger Lakes Region, and at Casa Larga Vineyards near Rochester.

I mean, you have to put your foot down sometime.

EXCUSE ME, ARE YOU USING THAT BRIDGE?

Millbrook

Here's proof that your last name doesn't have to be Hearst to live in a castle.

Peter Wing didn't have a lot of money when he returned from Vietnam in 1969 and got married. So, he scrounged around and spent the next thirty years building his own castle out of found objects!

He salvaged a large quantity of stone from an old railroad bridge that had been blown up. You'll also see remnants of old barns, churches, or buildings, as well as household objects. The spires, for example, are made from toilet-bowl balls and upside-down wrought-iron plant stands! He even borrowed the books to study architecture!

The castle is a melting pot of styles—Spanish, German, Greek, Tibetan, and Japanese—with a healthy dose of organic liberty. You'll find unexpected stained-glass windows in the passageways, as well as human forms protruding from the stone. "I found a rock that looked like a torso," Wing says, as if he had no choice. There's even a Gaudí-inspired mosaic staircase of two dragons. "Walking between dragons is good luck," Wing explains.

The living room has a balcony that looks like the bow of a ship protruding from the second-floor landing. Surprisingly, in this land of

A man's home is his castle.

recycled make believe, it was never a ship, but created from an old wooden porch arch and barn beams. A floor-to-ceiling fireplace on the opposite wall looks like a cathedral.

Wing and his castle give off an esoteric, macabre vibe, like you just walked onto the set of a Fellini film. Where most people put wreaths and eucalyptus sprays on the mantle face, Wing has a fan of knives. Overhead, a vintage velvet military coat looms, with the head from a suit of armor. Suspended from the ceiling are carousel horses that Wing says he "bought from a carny for $2 each."

The bathroom is a clover-shaped, palatial oasis, complete with an antique bird feeder for a sink and a Victorian–era golden garden planter for a tub!

★ ★

Of course, no castle would be complete without a moat: This one doubles as a swimming pool, with a hot tub on one end!

With all that weaponry, I wouldn't dare launch an assault on the castle. I might linger in the moat, though!

If you call (845) 677-9085, Wing or his wife Toni will give you a tour. In the summer they host "Shakespeare at the Castle," part of a children's summer camp put on by the Annandale Shakespeare Troupe.

THE WORLD'S LARGEST KALEIDOSCOPE

Mount Tremper

Remember kaleidoscopes? As kids, we used to peep through them until our squint muscles hurt, dazzled by the twists and turns of the colorful objects trapped in an obscure space at the end.

Well, Mount Tremper, in the heart of the Catskills, is home to the Guinness-stamped World's Largest Kaleidoscope!

It's housed in an old animal-feed silo, 60 feet tall, with a giant pyramid of mirrors at the top.

A video of brightly colored patterns and pop-culture images is aimed through the opening at the top and reflected through the mirror-mid.

The kaleidoscope opened in the late 1990s, but it has that retro 1960s feel. In one of the ten-minute shows, the faces of Native Americans, Lincoln, Nixon, Elvis, Marilyn Monroe, and others

It used to store animal feed, now it houses Lincoln, Nixon, and Elvis!

flash through the scope, punctuated by images of American flags, trains, and marijuana leaves.

The giant scope seats—er, stands—twenty people, though the best seat in the house is actually on the floor.

Lying there, I felt like I should be wearing a headband and tie-dye and saying things like "Far out."

The silo-scope is attached to a barn-turned–upscale mall called Emerson Place. The groovy vibe of the kaleidoscope is totally mismatched with the posh self-importance of Emerson Place, making it feel a little like the hippy gardener at a Hamptons estate.

This place is so money, it should come as no surprise that you exit the world's largest kaleidoscope into a huge kaleidoshop, which has everything from $3 scopes to fine-art scopes priced in the thousands.

Sitting in the corner like Tom Thumb is the World's Smallest Kaleidoscope, a little 1-inch wonder displayed in a ring box. Another cool item is a groovy coffee table with a kaleidoscope on each corner for group scoping.

The shop was cool, but I couldn't help but be disappointed with the World's Largest Kaleidoscope. I guess what I really wanted was giant beads and gallons of colored oils in an esoteric tumbler overhead instead of Lincoln and weed.

You'll leave with some pain in your neck and squinting muscles, perhaps also your pocketbook, but hey, check another "world's largest" off the list!

The World's Largest Kaleidoscope is on Route 28 in Mount Tremper.

PSSSST. I'VE GOT SOME DIRT.
Pine Island

Before I tell you this next story, I should warn you that it's a little bit dirty. Oh, and please don't cry.

The hamlet of Pine Island, in the town of Warwick, was once known as the "Onion Capital of the World."

★ ★

That's because 12,000 years ago, the valleys were filled with a gla-cial lake that melted into a swamp. When Polish immigrants arrived one hundred years ago, they settled in Pine Island because the val-leys and fertile soil reminded them of home. They drained the land, revealing "black dirt," rich soil that was perfect for growing onions. The dirt is literally so black, you can see the "Black Dirt Region" from space!

Another curious fact is that there isn't any oxygen in the muck, as the farmers call it, which slows decomposition. As a result, this area has one of the highest concentrations of mastodon remains!

"We find Indian arrowheads, cow bones," says onion grower Chris Pawelski of Pawelski Farms. "Mastodons are dime a dozen," he adds. During my visit, the Pawelskis popped open a big, blue Tupperware tub, revealing what they believe are the remains of a 12,000-year-old moose elk!

It's like going to a natural history museum and farmers' market all at once! Taste the difference of the region's fresh, robust onions and other produce at the Warwick Farmers' Market (www.warwickinfo .net/farmersmarket), on Sundays in the summer and fall.

Some farms, such as the Rogowski Farm (www.rogowskifarm .com), which grows 250 different types of produce, hold their own daily markets. Farmer Cheryl Rogowski, who writes "The Black Dirt Blog" and hosts weekly a radio show on WTBQ, sometimes holds culinary classes in the farm's kitchen. She's also been nationally rec-ognized for innovative programs such as English-language classes for the farm's migrant workers.

Perhaps you want to leave the preparation to the pros. Area res-taurants that use local produce include the Crystal Inn, Landmark Inn, and Old Forge Inn. If you're not hungry just yet, try a hot-air balloon ride to get a bird's-eye view of the black-dirt region and work up your appetite!

For more information contact Orange County Tourism at www .orangetourism.org or call (845) 291-2136.

A LITTLE JOY IN YOUR HIKE

Pine Island

Andrea Colman and her daughter Elizabeth were on vacation in Utah when Elizabeth accidentally left her newest prize possessions, two little doggy dolls, in one of the stores. She was about six years old then, so this was devastating. She went to the car sobbing.

Andrea told Elizabeth that she must've lost them for a reason. They weren't really hers to begin with. She was just holding on to them until some kid who really needed them—maybe a kid whose parents had just divorced—found them. She always taught her daughter that you should give to the universe and it will come back to you.

Later that day, they were hiking off-trail in Zion National Park. They stopped to take a picture when Andrea noticed something dangling into the frame that was ruining the shot.

She said, "Lizzy, what is that? A dish rag?"

Elizabeth replied, "Oh my gosh, it's a doll!"

The doll was lovingly hand-stitched with the words "walking joy" embroidered on it. They were touched by this gesture of a stranger. That day, they knew it was meant for Elizabeth.

Since then, they've made a couple dozen "walking-joy dolls" and left them in the woods to bring joy to someone else.

The dolls are made without sewing, using fabric remnants, twine, raffia, twigs—whatever materials they can find. Sometimes they sit down at the dining room table, other times they just tuck a few pieces of fabric and twine in their backpack and make them right there in the woods.

The only requirements are that there is no sewing involved and that the doll is made with love. "It has to be so beautiful, you don't want to give it away!" Andrea says.

Andrea says her favorites are the ones that they don't draw faces on. That way, "the person who finds it can imagine the emotion," Andrea says. "If they're having a good day, they can have a happy,

★ ★

Photo by Andrea Colman

laughing doll. If they're having a bad day, it could be a commiserating doll."

So, the next time you find a little surprise in the woods, maybe it's a friendly greeting from Andrea and Elizabeth. And maybe—just maybe—you'll leave something nice for the next person.

Andrea runs the Glenwood House Bed & Breakfast (www.glen woodbb.com) with her husband, Kevin, in Pine Island.

A CASTLE AS THE ULTIMATE STORAGE SOLUTION
Poltepel Island

For years, train passengers have been elbowing their travel companions in amazement as they spot what appears to be a castle on an island in the Hudson River just north of Cold Spring.

★ ★

No one knew too much about it, so the curiosity generally ended there. Well, let me tell you the story of that castle.

It was built by Francis Bannerman VI in 1901. Bannerman ran what may have been the first army-navy surplus store. He sold helmets and military gear, rifles, revolvers, cannons—you name it. He ran the business from Brooklyn, and later expanded into Manhattan.

After the Spanish-American War in 1898, Bannerman bought his biggest supply of military surplus, including a large stock of black powder. His neighbors in Brooklyn weren't happy. They said, "Fugheddaboudit! You're not storing that stuff here! One false move and we all go sky high!" (OK, that was a loose, dramatic reenactment of what they said.)

So, Bannerman did what any of us would do: He bought an island and built a castle on it to house his munitions!

He modeled it after European castles, reflecting his Scottish heritage. He also made some interesting architectural choices: The towers of the castle are smaller at the bottom and wider at the top, giving the illusion that the castle is bigger than it really is. No one knows why he did it, perhaps to make the building more imposing to passersby.

After Bannerman's death in 1918, his wife and sons took over the business. Two years later, the "powder house," used to house that gunpowder supply,

A castle fit for a queen . . . or a keg of gunpowder!

exploded. No one was killed, but the castle suffered some structural damage. According to accounts of the incident, the blast was felt from Poughkeepsie to Peeksill. (And by my account, you could hear the big, fat "I told you so!" all the way from Brooklyn!)

A massive fire in 1969 destroyed most of the buildings on the island. Firefighters had rushed to the scene, but when they realized no one was in danger, they let the fire burn itself out. Some spectacular ruins remain.

The island is now owned by New York State, but a group known as the Bannerman Castle Trust began operating public tours there in 2003.

Boat tours to Bannerman Castle depart from Newburgh and Beacon. For more information visit www.bannermancastle.org or call (845) 220-2120.

CARVING HIS PLACE IN HISTORY
Prattsville

There's an odd set of small, white objects set into the rock high above Route 23, just outside of Prattsville.

It's been called "New York's Mount Rushmore," but quite honestly, it looks like someone got tired of all the knickknacks in his living room and, for kicks, decided to bolt them to the side of the striated rock!

There are a couple of busts, a horse, a tree, a wreath, a scroll, and, like a broken toy found behind the sofa, an arm wielding a hammer.

This is Pratt's Rock, a three-dimensional biography of not a living room, but Zadock Pratt, a wealthy entrepreneur and congressman. The story goes that, one day in 1843, he was approached by a beggar. Pratt, a firm believer in hard work not handouts, asked the man what his trade was. When the man replied that he was a stonecutter, Pratt put the man to work, carving his life story into the cliff.

When we said you should write your life story, we thought you knew that we meant *on paper!*

Pratt owned the largest shoe-leather tannery in the world (well, until he cut down all the hemlock trees in the Catskills). So, the tree is a hemlock and the horse represents the animals that carried the bark to the tannery. There's the Pratt coat of arms and a wreath containing the names of his children. One bust is, of course, Pratt; the other, his son George, who was killed in the Civil War. Who knows what that arm and hammer represent. Perhaps it was the manual labor involved in tanning leather, or maybe it was just an early example of product placement (Keep your life story fresh with Arm & Hammer!)

Pratt had intended to be buried in the cliffside, but the tomb, which you enter through a doorway carved in the rock, leaked. So, that's now just a nice little stopping point; Pratt is buried in the town cemetery. However, he did bury six of his favorite horses and dogs at the site, down near the picnic tables.

★ ★

Pratt's Rock Park is open to the public. It's a gorgeous little hike: Switchbacks take you up the 500 feet to the monument and the top offers spectacular views of the Schoharie River across the street. There's also a Zadock Pratt Museum on Main Street in Prattsville.

For more information visit www.prattmuseum.com or call (518) 299-3395.

SOMEONE MUST BE HUNGARY!
Rock City

Wow. That's one big fork in the road.

Literally, at 31 feet tall, it's the world's largest fork!

The fork, located at the intersection of Routes 308 and 199 in Rock City, is jammed straight into the ground, as if the Jolly Green Giant was eating a salad of trees and grass and stabbed his fork down for a second while he ran to the bathroom.

OK, when you get to the fork in the road . . .

The back of the fork officially says the "punny sculpture" was made by Stephen B. Schreiber, president of the Rock City Arts Council.

But Schreiber, a local real-estate entrepreneur with his tongue planted firmly in cheek, told the *Poughkeepsie Journal* in a 2003 interview that he did it as a joke.

"I didn't think they would let me leave it there," Schreiber is quoted as saying. "Nobody has said anything."

★ ★

So, there it stands. The world's largest fork at a fork in the road. A joke that just keeps on . . . ahem . . . sticking it to you!

When you're taking your companion's picture, try to play along and be a punny guy. Say something like: "Hey, your nose is running and your feet smell!" Or, maybe stick with the food theme and try this one, compliments of www.punoftheday.com:

"I like European food so I decided to Russia over there because I was Hungary. After Czech'ing the menu I ordered Turkey. When I was Finnished I told the waiter 'Spain good but there is Norway I could eat another bite!'"

Once you're all punned out, you can make the big decision everyone faces when they come to a giant fork in the road: Are you going to Rhinebeck or Red Hook?!

IT'S A PICKLE PARTY!
Rosendale

When Eri Yamaguchi came to visit her friends in America, she told them she wanted to have a "pickle party."

"We didn't have a clue," said Bill and Cathy Brooks, "but we could always throw a pretty good party!"

A dozen years later, the Brooks are still throwing annual pickle parties, now known as the Rosendale International Pickle Festival. The festival aims to expand people's culinary and cultural horizons "through the simple, but alluring, PICKLE!"

Here, you'll learn they can pickle just about anything—carrots, onions, mushrooms, beets, garlic, olives—even lemons! They can also make anything out of actual pickles, from pickle soup to pickle chili, pickle pizza, and—wait for it—deep-fried pickles!

The festival is truly international, with a Japanese tea ceremony, traditional German dancing, and an African drumming performance mixed in with the bluegrass. "From sushi to sauerbraten" and "kimonos and lederhosen," the festival boasts, there's something for everyone.

★ ★

If you're going to a Picklefest, you might as well ride in style!

Amid all this cultural-horizon expanding, the festival truly is a family affair and events such as the pickle-eating, pickle-juice-drinking, and pickle-tossing contests, have a "Sure, I'll try that!" feel to them. A lot of kids compete in all the events, and I can tell you that I didn't find a single professional-circuit pickle eater in the bunch!

These pickle people have a pretty good sense of humor, too. There were, of course, the T-shirts, such as "Pickles—get hooked! They're the real dill." And, let's not forget *the accessories*. Tracy Krawitt, owner of Spacey Tracy's Pickles and maker of a mean fried pickle, sported dangly pickle-chip earrings she bought through Pickle Packers International.

Mike Mongeon, the "chief brine brewer" of Mike's Grenades, named his pickles after ammunition because of their "shape and burst of flavor." He also brings his Picklemobile for a prop at the festival. He uses it in Adirondack sled racing, so he can—you had to see this coming—"slide down the hill in a garlic dill."

All pickle puns aside, the food is extraordinary. Don't forget to check out winners from the pickling contest. Awards are given for best pickles, best relish, best green beans, and best chutney, as well as for specialty items such as watermelon-rind pickles, pickled heart-shaped beets, and pickled carrots with cinnamon and cloves.

Suddenly, I look around, and the whole world looks like one, great, big pickling opportunity!

For more information visit www.picklefest.com or call (845) 658-9649.

MR. FITE'S OPUS
Saugerties

From the rubble of an abandoned bluestone quarry near Woodstock rises a six-and-one-half-acre stone sculpture that *Architectural Digest* once described as "one of the largest and most beguiling works of art on the entire continent."

It is a series of swirling rock formations that form steps, paths, tunnels, and platforms, topped by a nine-ton monolith. The massive formation is comprised of a series of flat rocks, tightly stacked, one on top of the other, by one man.

That man was Harvey Fite, a self-taught artist and former professor at Bard College. He initially created it as a place to display his bulbous, Picasso-esque sculptures of people. But the pedestal formation became so stunning in and of itself, it began to overpower Fite's sculptures, and he was mature enough at that point to realize you listen to your art when it grabs you by the scruff of the neck and says, "This is not right!"

I say he was "mature enough" because it took him thirty-seven years to lay down all of those rocks! He'd bought the quarry in 1938 for a measly $250 after it became worthless when concrete came along and replaced bluestone as the primary material used to make sidewalks.

223

He called it *Opus 40* because, he joked, composers had an easier time of naming—well, numbering—their work! And, by the time he named the piece in 1972, he'd been at it for several decades (so, you add these two . . . hum hum hmm . . . carry the one . . .) and estimated that it would take a total of forty years to complete.

Sadly, or poetically, however you want to look at it, Fite never made it to forty years. He died three years short of that goal when his lawnmower jammed and tossed him over the edge of the quarry.

He was seventy-two years old and died at the hand of his beloved masterpiece, which, as an artist, isn't too shabby.

Today, you can take a self-guided tour of *Opus 40* in all of its massive glory, including the unfinished wall and pile of bluestone where Fite's work abruptly ended. There's also a

The pedestal becomes the art.

Quarryman's Museum that Fite built to display traditional quarryman's tools.

For more information visit www.opus40.org or call (845) 246-3400.

★ ★

GO AHEAD, WIG OUT!

Schenectady

I'll bet you have always wanted to know where Gene Simmons buys his makeup.

Well, it's out of the frying pan and into . . . Schenectady!

I have no idea where the lizard tongue came from but I can tell you that those star-framed eyes were all Schenectady. The makeup came from a shop called The Costumer, which typically specializes in renting costumes for high-school musicals.

The owner, Kathe Sheehan, is a former teacher who directed high school, college, and community theater. She and her husband Jack, who passed away in 2006, saw a void and decided someone needed to make quality costumes, makeup, and props available for the kids. "This led us to 'change hats' and become costumers," Kathe says.

Now, after providing makeup and costumes for the famous rock band, The Costumer not only outfits high school students but also "every Kiss tribute band that comes down the pike!" says Deborah Trowbridge, store supervisor at The Costumer.

You know? I think that's one retail line I wouldn't mind waiting in!

They also rent or sell costumes to commercial production companies, reality TV shows, MTV, *Saturday Night Live,* and everyday people looking to up the Halloween ante or dress their groomsmen as Beefeaters.

"We do a huge Internet business," Trowbridge says. "We ship Santa Clauses, Easter Bunnies, high school mascots—you name it."

It's a gigantic warehouse, with thousands of characters mingling on the racks. There's the gang from *West Side Story* stepping and snapping next to the fringe-shaking fabrics of *Thoroughly Modern Millie.* Hey wait, was that a ketchup costume trying to get close to Miss Millie? I think she's got bigger aspirations than you, buddy!

There are knights and hippies. Showgirls and princesses. Kings and Fruits of the Loom. Oh, and Elvis is definitely *in* the building.

225

★ ★

We're just trying to get a-head!

Awesome! You can't see me right now, but I'm totally sticking my tongue out as far as it will go—like the rock star I know they can dress me to be!

For more information visit www.thecostumer.com or call (877) 218-1289. Tours are available.

THAT'S SCHENECITALIA!

Schenectady

So, you've been to Italy and it's ruined you for the food they pass off as Italian here in the U.S.

Great news! We've got your Italia right here. No, not in Little Italy, silly. In Schenectady!

At the Villa Italia bakery in downtown Schenectady, the pastry recipes were handed down to owner Bobby Mallozzi from his grandparents, who owned a bakery in Italy. "Every recipe is from Italy—what my grandmother made," Mallozzi says.

What really sets this bakery apart and makes you think you've died and gone to Italian heaven is that most of the ingredients in the pastries actually come from Italy, like the chocolate-covered cannoli shells and the flavoring for the gelato. "You can tell the intensity is different," Mallozzi says.

Just about everything, right down to the $300,000 refrigerated display cases Mallozzi had custom-made, came from Italy. I'm sorry, no. I meant right down to the three cabinetmakers he imported from Italy to put that display case together!

Even the paper napkins on the table . . . yep, from Italy!

"We're just trying to bring something unique to the table," Mallozzi says. "The flavors, tastes, and smells you get from products [in Italy] are different than the ones you get domestically," he explains. "The majority of the bakeries in this country are all buying from the same place."

You might be sitting in your cubicle, asking no one in particular, "Schenectady? Really?" Look, if you're not up for the trip, don't worry about it. That just means more for Chuck Mangione, Dom DeLuise, Ray Romano—all fans of the Schenectady bakery—and the rest of us!

Villa Italia is so popular that they actually advise you to try *not* to come on Fridays and Saturdays, and at Christmastime, they have a police officer directing traffic in front of the bakery!

Mmmmmm. Can you smell that? That, my friend, is a Sicilian cannoli shell.

For more information visit www.villaitaliabakery.com or call (518) 355-1144.

AQUATIC DAYS ARE HERE AGAIN

Schenectady

The sign on top of Jumpin' Jack's Drive-In says SKI SHOW EVERY TUESDAY 7 PM.

Wait, what year is it? Is Fonzie going to be in this show?

You might think that it has to be either 1950 or a theme park in Florida for a human pyramid on water skis, but in July and August, you can see one every Tuesday night in Schenectady—for free!

Schenectady is home to the U.S. Water Ski Show Team, a dedicated group of about thirty-five skiers who compete in team water-skiing and, between practices, put on shows for the locals, complete with spangled costumes and set to music.

"It's the closest thing you can get to a Broadway show on water!" says Kara Pangburn, president of the ski team.

Then Tuesday comes . . . we'll have some fun . . .
Ready to entertain you!

Photo by Wendy Benjamin

If you've ever tried dancing, you know how difficult it is *on land* to hold your leg out in front of you. (If you haven't, take a moment to try it now.)

During a show, you'll see a "ballet line" of synchronized skiers, each on a single ski. They start with one leg pointed out front and one arm curved gracefully in the air. Then—don't blink—they flip away from the rope, using a swivel ski, so their foot is pointed behind them, holding the rope. It's like the aquatic Rockettes!

A team of barefoot skiers creates a stunning wall of water to dazzle the crowd. The jumpers do spectacular acrobatic spins and flips—as if gravity hasn't already been defied!

The strap-double acts offer up lifts straight out of a ballroom-dancing championship, only on water and being pulled by a boat! The ropes are connected to a strap around the men's waists as they hoist their partners overhead, sometimes even inverted! In some acts, there may be ten or more couples on the water at the same time.

The big finale is the human pyramid, the ultimate display of strength, grace, and teamwork, which can be anywhere from three to four tiers tall, involving up to twenty people.

Well, the boat picks up two, three, and four . . . When the clock strikes five, six, and seven . . . we're gonna rock . . . gonna rock . . . gonna rock it all aquatic tonight!

Shows are held on the Mohawk River, behind Jumpin' Jack's Drive-In snack shack on the Scotia side of the river. For more information visit www.uswaterskishowteam.com or call (518) 346-7405.

TALKIN' AT THE DRIVE-IN
Schoharie

If it weren't for Ed Scribner, Danny and Sandy would've been singing a very different tune at the drive-in.

Something like: *"Silence" is the word is the word* . . .

Scribner designed and built the sound system for the first outdoor movie with sound, shown on Main Street, Schoharie, on June 11, 1931.

Scribner didn't have a lot of money growing up, but "I had a lot of make believe," he said in a September 2006 interview. And, unlike some of us daydreamers, he had the technical skills to back it up.

"Everyone said it will never work outdoors," Scribner said, but "I knew I could do it."

For people who knew him, it was no surprise that Scribner, who was always building something, was the guy who made it happen.

In 2002, when Schoharie was featured on "The Late Show with David Letterman," 500 of the town's 1,000 population were bussed in for the taping. Letterman joked that it was part of an audience-exchange program and that the same number of New Yorkers were, at that moment, in Schoharie "watching Ed Scribner wire up a toaster!"

THE ELEPHANT HOTEL
Somers

At the intersection of routes 100 and 202 in Somers is a three-story building that has "Elephant Hotel" in big letters on the front and a monument of an elephant in the front yard.

What is this, some kind of elephants-only hotel? Where pachyderms pack it in for the night?

Nope. This building has been a meeting place for menagerie/circus owners, a stagecoach stop, a dance hall, a bank, the town clerk's office, and a museum, but never an actual elephant hotel!

Its name is a nod to Somers's circus past. It was built between 1820 and 1825 by Hachaliah Bailey, who is not the "& Bailey" in the Ringling Bros. circus, but was one of the first Americans to tour a menagerie of exotic animals. (In fact, he predates the Ringling Bros. and was said to be a role model for the famous carnival barker P.T. Barnum.)

This Bailey, a farmer-turned-circus showman, started his menagerie in 1827 with an elephant known as Old Bet. He'd transported his share of cattle, so moving a menagerie was no sweat. Soon, other

Maybe they need a monument to remember, but I'll never forget!

menageries began sprouting up around the Somers area, earning it the nickname, "Cradle of the American Circus." In fact, a lot of homes in the area have some oddly large rooms—something that was necessary when you were boarding a menagerie!

Bailey built the Elephant Hotel as a memorial to his beloved elephants. Old pictures show a few elephants did visit the hotel as promotional stunts, but to my knowledge, none ever spent the night!

Today, the Elephant Hotel houses the town clerk's office, the Somers Historical Society, and the Museum of the Early American Circus, which is a small but worthwhile stop.

But please, leave your luggage in the car.

The Elephant Hotel hasn't been an actual hotel since the town bought it in 1927. Nonetheless, "we still sometimes get folks arriving in the town clerk's office, or at a town board meeting, with suitcases, wanting to book a room in the hotel!" says Terry Ariano, curator of the circus museum.

For more information visit www.somershistoricalsoc.org/elephant hotel.html or call (914) 277-4977.

ALL TOGETHER NOW
Stone Ridge

Being a teacher in a one-room schoolhouse was a lot like being one of those entertainers who spins plates.

You had to juggle twenty to thirty kids, spanning at least six different grades, making sure everyone stayed in line. That would be enough to drive anyone to dri—no, no, no! According to the "Rules for Teachers" posted at the Kripplebush Schoolhouse when it opened in 1857, you weren't allowed to drink, smoke, or get "shaved in a barbershop." (Scandalous!)

Teachers were allowed some recess time, though. The rules stated that male teachers were allowed one night per week for "courting purposes," two if they went to church regularly! Female teachers, however, were dismissed for getting married or engaging in "unseemly conduct." (Well, I never . . .)

The Kripplebush Schoolhouse, which held classes until 1951, is now a museum, offering all kinds of insight—and entertainment—about what it was like to work and study in a one-room schoolhouse. Today, thanks to a dedicated corps of volunteers, the museum is set up exactly as it would've been if school were in session, with chalkboards, iron-legged desks, a watercooler—even an outhouse key. The rules are posted on the back wall.

Arlita Perry, who attended school here in the 1940s, says having all the grades together was tricky, but it worked. Older kids helped

★ ★

younger kids. Students did their homework while other lessons were going on. That way, homework never had to come *home* with you!

She recalls the moral lessons from penmanship class, with classic one-liners such as "Always do your best" and "Beauty is as beauty does!" And, with just one room, the reward for being good was obvious: time outside this educational sardine can. "If you were good, you could clap erasers outside!" Perry says.

The Kripplebush one-room schoolhouse museum is a wonderful walk back in time, when you *could* put all those kids in a room without mayhem ensuing and one man or woman could keep all the plates spinning, as long as he didn't do any drinking or barbering and she didn't engage in marriage or unseemly conduct!

Class! School is in session!

★ ★

The museum is located at 204 Kripplebush Road, off of Route 209. It's run by volunteers, so the hours are limited to Sundays from 2:00 to 4:00 p.m. June through September, or by appointment. For more information visit www.ulster-web.com/schoolhouse or call (845) 687-9229.

JUST LIKE OLD TIMES

Sugar Loaf

The proliferation of superstores like Wal-Mart has driven small mom-and-pop shops out of business, but one little craft hamlet has stood the test of time.

Sugar Loaf is an artisan community of more than fifty shops and restaurants, offering handmade goods such as soap, candles, folk-art pillows, and wood-carved and leather items. The hamlet is

A walk in time, and Into Leather.

surrounded by apple orchards and horse farms, and the shops are located in barns and buildings from the 18th and 19th centuries. The Barnsider Restaurant, for example, is housed in what used to be the general store.

In the mid-1700s, when the village was formed, this was where farmers came to buy supplies and trade horses. By the 1800s, there was a wagon maker, a carpenter, a blacksmith, a tannery, a cheese factory, and other businesses.

Its preservation is credited to two men, Walter Kannon, who owned a barn-siding business, and Jarvis Boone, a wood carver. When the craft-revival movement swept America in the late 1960s, these two decided to establish Sugar Loaf as a craft community, and soon attracted other artisans. By 1971, the hamlet's population had doubled in size.

What makes it truly unique is that, like their predecessors, these artists and craftsmen not only work but also live in the hamlet.

A lot of wood-carved signs are done with machines now, but Jarvis Boone's son, Clay, still does all his carving the old-fashioned way, by hand. "There's character in a hand-carved sign that you don't get with a machine," Boone says, as he shows us a huge, wooden dining table he's working on for a firehouse in New York City.

Character, I understand. But when you're doing it by hand, wouldn't you be worried you'd mess up and cut off part of the design?

"We never make mistakes," Boone says, "but occasionally we have to redesign."

Israeli-born Yaron Rosner was working as a photographer in France when he met his wife Kiki. He decided to turn his soap-making hobby into a business, but decided to set up shop in Sugar Loaf because there was more room here for a family than in Paris.

Well, soap, surely *that* would be easier to do with a machine?

"No machines," Rosner says firmly. "Part of the quality of soap is in small quantity. Salad for six tastes better than 600!"

For a complete list of shops and directions, visit www.sugarloafny chamber.com or www.sugarloafartsvillage.com or call (845) 469-9181.

JUST FOLLOW THE BUBBLES
Tannersville

As you drive down Main Street in Tannersville, it looks like the whole town is playing one big game of Pictionary.

There are cartoon soap suds painted on the Laundromat and liquor bottles on the shutters of the village liquor store. Wine and cheese icons offer a taste of what's to come at the Last Chance Restaurant, and a picture-book laundry line of clothes dangles from the front of the Clothes Line boutique.

The buildings are painted in eye-popping shades of squeeze-mustard yellow, aqua, lime green, and cherry.

What's going on here? Did the village get an extreme makeover from Nickelodeon?

The village did get a makeover, but it was inspired by Elena Agostinis Patterson, an artist who moved here in the mid-1980s with her investment banker husband. Patterson got a little tired of the hum-drum look of her house, so, she painted it orange,

Bubbles are a universal language.

yellow, periwinkle, and green. Then she decided to paint pictures on the shutters depicting what was going on in that room. So, there are dentures on the bedroom shutters (har har) and a toothpaste tube on the bathroom shutters!

Well, before long, people started veering off of Main Street to check out the house like the bright lights of suburbia at Christmas-time.

Meanwhile, the sleepy little village of Tannersville was trying to figure out how to jump-start its tourism industry—and the local econ-omy—which had languished since the automobile and airplane came along and whisked the once-thriving tourism industry off to more exotic, faraway places.

Patterson had a bright idea: What if they could recreate her for-mula across the whole village and drive that gawking traffic onto Main Street?

So, she pitched her idea to the mayor, who thought it was a great plan. Today, there are about a dozen businesses that have gotten a Patterson-inspired makeover and Tannersville is billed as "The Painted Village in the Sky."

Tannersville is on Route 23A in the Catskills. I'd be more specific, but honestly, you'll know it when you see it!

My only question is: If you lived in Tannersville, what would be painted on *your* shutters?!

HAM FROM UNCLE SAM

Troy

We all know the iconic image of Uncle Sam: that tall hat, white goa-tee, and finger pointed straight at you to let you know that he wants YOU for the U.S. Army.

What a lot of people don't know is that Uncle Sam was a real guy!

His name was Sam Wilson. He was a meat packer from Troy who shipped rations to U.S. troops during the War of 1812. The soldiers

★ ★

would receive these packages stamped "U.S." When someone asked who it was from, they would jokingly reply, "It's from Uncle Sam!"

The "U.S." stamp became an indicator of top-quality meat inspected by Sam Wilson. Soon, the Army stopped accepting any meat that wasn't passed through Uncle Sam.

The face of the famous finger-pointing Uncle Sam, used on recruiting posters during both world wars, was actually modeled after the artist, J.M. Flagg, not Sam Wilson. The gesture came from a similar British Army recruiting poster featuring not a white-goateed guy but a guy with a handlebar moustache that looked like it belonged on one of the Village People.

The real Uncle Sam, Sam Wilson, is buried in Oakwood Cemetery in Troy. A statue of him stands in downtown Troy. Everything from the bowling alley to the parking garage is named after him, and, for the past thirty years, the city has held an annual parade in his honor.

I'm not saying you have to go to Troy or anything; it's just something I want YOU to know.

BEWARE OF "COLLECTORS" AT HALLOWEEN!

Ulster Park

If you've got no use for your socks, then head over to the Headless Horseman Hayride and Haunted Houses in Ulster Park and prepare to have them knocked off. Or (cue the creepy organ music) taken by a "collector" along with your feet!

This Halloween horror fest is unlike anything you've ever seen. It starts with a haunted hayride. As you chug along the 1 mile of open farmland in the dark of night, you'll come upon a town with some strange occurrences. Two men stand over a woman, who levitates and then poof! She vanishes into thin air. A bartender serves up a severed head. A murderous mortician opens a box to display his preserved bride-to-be, who never made it to the altar but will remain with him forever.

In the pitch black interludes between these houses of horror, with your legs dangling off the side of the hayride, "collectors" will chase after you with chainsaws looking to add your body parts to their collection. And suddenly, the moment everyone's been waiting for: The Headless Horseman emerges from the darkness for one final spine-tingling ride.

With your heart still pounding, you'll get dumped into a labyrinth corn maze. Good luck finding your way out! Ah ha ha ha!

The maze ends in a series of haunted houses. Creepy characters pop out of walls, a vampire swoops overhead and someone is following you . . . "Your eyeballs look tasty!" he whispers.

More than one hundred actors are recruited to scare the crap out of you during this Hollywood-style fright fest, which was named the number one haunted attraction in America by *Hauntworld* magazine two years in a row. It's all the brainchild of Mike Jubie, a former Kingston detective with a penchant for the macabre.

Allow a few hours for the whole thing, as there are also three food-court shacks, six gift shops, and a not-to-be-missed sideshow act, where John Shaw does everything from putting a nail in his nose to hanging paint cans from his eyelids with hooks.

It's not for children under eight years old or the faint of heart, so consider yourself warned!

The Headless Horseman Hayrides and Haunted Houses are held weekends in September and October in Ulster Park on Route 9W. For more information visit www.headlesshorseman.com or call (845) 339-BOOO (2666).

SOMETHING IS UP
Warwick

Ask anyone in Warwick and they know about "the doors." No, I'm not referring to Jim Morrison's rock band, I'm talking about a curious decorating choice at the Landmark Inn restaurant.

"People know," says owner Michael DiMartino. They'll be in the bar, then drag their friends into the dining room saying, "'You have to see the doors!'" he says.

Um, the doors?

★ ★

Let me start at the beginning. The inn was built in 1778, with a dining room added on by then-owner Gordon Richardson in 1954. Richardson's wife Cynthia got a little ahead of herself and booked the dining room for a wedding before it was completed. The bride-to-be was horrified when she came by for a walk-through, declaring: "There's no way I'm getting married in this place with the paper ceiling!"

Knock knock. What's up?

Richardson was a pretty eccentric guy, so he came up with a creative solution. The Red Swan Inn, where he'd tended bar, was being torn down. So, he salvaged dozens of doors from the old inn, and nailed them to the ceiling of his dining room!

The bride, incidentally, did wind up getting married there, in the place—not with the paper ceiling, but—with all the doors on the ceiling!

Richardson had a pretty odd sense of humor, DiMartino says. If you came into his restaurant wearing a tie, he'd cut it off and tack it to the wall! And, there *is* a dinghy on top of the awning over the bar. Still, no one knows exactly why he chose to put the doors up instead of Sheetrock. Alcohol may or may not have been involved. "There are a lot of hammer marks where they missed," DiMartino says. "Some have four nails in them, some have fourteen!"

In the psychedelic 1960s, Richardson painted the doors every shade of the rainbow, including gold, and some had murals painted by his daughter. One of the subsequent owners painted the doors a nice, tasteful shade of brown, which remains today.

"Parents like to scare their kids," DiMartino says. "It's the same joke all the time: 'Hey, you never know who's gonna come through that door!'"

The Landmark Inn (845-986-5444) is at 126 Route 94, near the intersection of 17A, in Warwick.

A DIVINE PIPE DREAM
West Point

Military accommodations tend to be pretty sparse, but not at the West Point Cadet Chapel.

This Gothic chapel, on par with some of most spectacular cathedrals, is home to the world's largest working organ in a religious structure.

The West Point organ, built in 1911 and subsequently enlarged, is the size of about fifteen good-size church organs put together, says Grant Chapman, curator of organs at West Point.

There are at least 23,500 pipes, which run the length of the massive chapel—on either side of the altar, wrapping around both side bays, even over the door at the far back entrance. Those are called *trumpet en chamade* (meaning "pointing at you") pipes, Chapman says, and, by my layman's estimate, they're what you might expect to greet you at the gates of Heaven!

"A big organ like this has no speakers," Chapman explains. "Everything runs on air!" Though, "the intention is not to be louder, but richer."

There are four keyboards on the organ, with 874 "stop controls" (each one controls a different set of pipes), 244 notes to be played by hand, and thirty-two notes for the feet!

Craig Williams, who is only the fourth organist the academy has hired, says that periodically an aunt will ask to play the organ for her niece or nephew's wedding. "They sit down and say, 'That's not my

★ ★

church organ!'" Williams says. "They take one look at it and say, 'What am I doing here?!'"

"Most organs don't have a gong crash," Williams says, referring to the buttons below the keyboards, which are mostly percussion and special effects.

Williams says the organ can be overwhelming even for him at times, but mostly, it's inspiring. "There are almost an infinite number of possibilities," he says. "If there's a sound in my head, I know I can make it happen on this organ."

The sound that comes from the West Point organ, echoing through the halls of this divine medieval-like fortress, is unlike anything you've ever heard. I don't care how deep or shallow a person you are, it will find your soul and touch it, before sending a ripple up your spine.

These are just a handful of the more than 23,500 pipes in the West Point organ.

Sunday church services are open to the public, as are special concerts held in the chapel. For a schedule visit www.usma.edu/chaplain and click on "Events."

THE FORTY-YEAR DRIP
Woodstock

When most people get a drip, they call someone to fix it right away. Not Barbara and Dennis Moss—they've had a drip going for the past forty years and counting!

It's a drip candle that was started by the Mosses' friend Kenny in his Manhattan apartment in the 1960s. You know how it goes. One candle melts down and you just jam another one in there, thinking, "I'll clean it later."

Four inches of wax on the table later and Kenny still hadn't gotten around to it. By that point, in 1969, Dennis was opening a candle shop down the street. Kenny, seeing his window of opportunity, asked Dennis if he wanted this mound of a drip candle. Dennis said, "Sure, why not."

So, they cut off the legs and put the wax-covered tabletop in the window.

When they moved the shop up to Woodstock a few years later, they took Kenny's drip-candle table with them. "It's like a mascot or something," Barbara says.

They haven't moved the candle since 1971 and have continued to add candles to it. Today, that tabletop has an 8-foot mountain of wax on top of it!

The Mosses call it "The Mountain."

In a fitting tribute to its '60s roots and home in Woodstock, this is a rainbow-colored mountain, with knobby drips of red, white, yellow, aqua, purple, pink, and neon green wax, with peaks at the top like a castle.

The candle mountain is magical for kids, who like to look into all the little nooks and crannies for hidden figurines, like the white-bearded

You know what, Kenny? At this point, don't even worry about it.

dude playing guitar, the boy on the unicycle, and the bear on a blue surfboard.

It's all about peace, love, and wax, man.

Visit "The Mountain" at the Candlestock candle shop at 16 Mill Hill Road in Woodstock. For more information go to www.candle stock.com or call (845) 679-8711.

5

New York City and Long Island

Wild Parrots in Brooklyn and a Naked Cowboy in Times Square

First, let's clear up one thing: You can look at a map on a New York street without getting mugged. Just don't do it in a Hawaiian shirt and fanny pack. Do it with style and, most importantly, conviction.

New York is an orchestral cacophony of cultures that can transport you to faraway lands, from the lively Russian supper clubs in Brighton Beach, Brooklyn—Tonight, is dancing girls!—to the hookah cafes on the block known as "Little Egypt" in Astoria, Queens.

Of course, we've got plenty of Americana, too, from the competitive Christmas-light extravaganza in Brooklyn's Dyker Heights to the man whose pants precede him, the Naked Cowboy in Times Square.

There's more wildlife here than you'd expect, from Pale Male and Lola, the famous red-tailed hawks of Fifth Avenue, to the cluster of green monk parrots that mingle with the pigeons in Brooklyn and Long Island's Big Duck.

We pride ourselves on education here in New York. For all you would-be Wallendas, there's the New York Trapeze School. If you're more the nail-up-the-nose type, well step right up to Coney Island's Sideshow School and get your freak on!

There are plenty of ways to unwind, too. You can have someone beat you with an oak-leaf broom and then douse you in ice-cold water at the Russian and Turkish Baths. Or, rent a YeloCab for a 15-minute power nap before your next curiosity.

Are you ready to see the real New York?

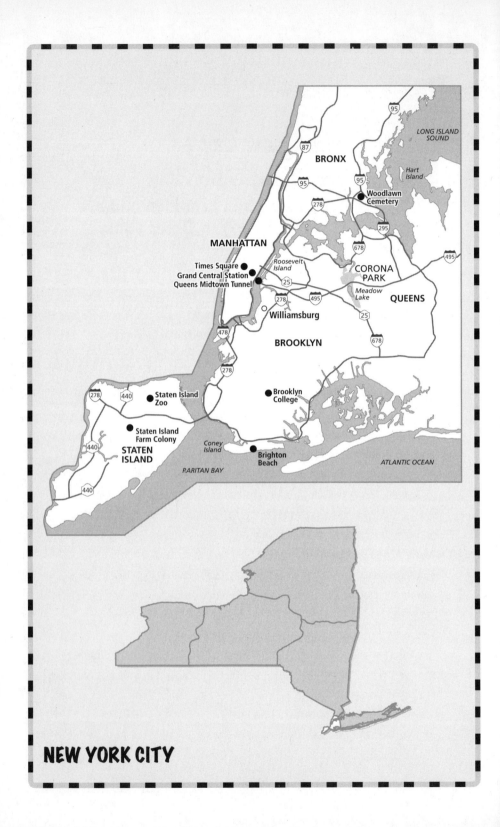

NEW YORK CITY

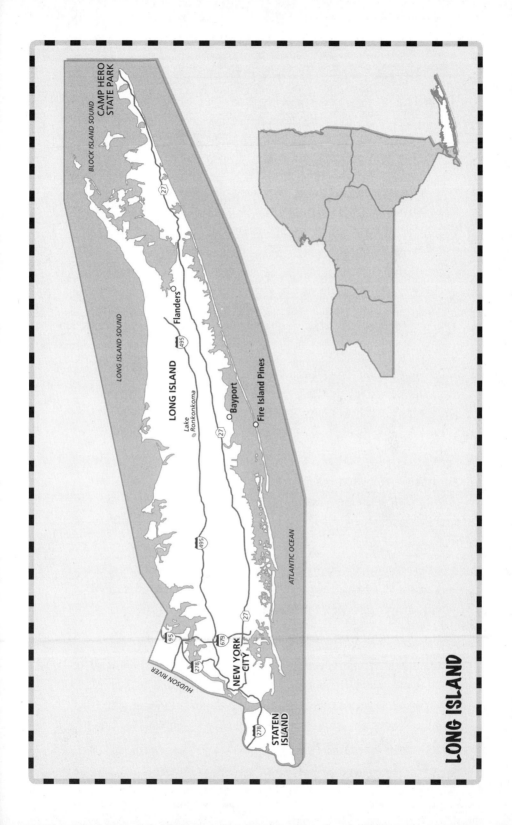

LONG ISLAND

King of New York

Pop quiz: What county is New York City in?

Even if you're a New Yorker, that's probably a tough question. You may only have learned the county you live in when you registered to vote. Here, people identify themselves more by borough than by county.

Your first guess might be that New York is in New York County. Well, that's partially right. Each of the five boroughs that comprise New York City is in a different county, and Manhattan is the only one in New York County.

Two of the boroughs—the Bronx and Queens—share the same name as their county, residing in Bronx County and Queens County, respectively.

So, ninety-nine bottles of borough on the wall, that leaves us with two more to go, right?

Brooklyn, contrary to what you might expect, isn't in Brooklyn County. (I wonder how many people write *that* on their voter registration forms!) It's actually in Kings County. And Staten Island, the third tenor of the boroughs as it's often forgotten, is in Richmond County.

Here's how it went down. The Dutch, in 1646, were the first to settle the area we know today as Brooklyn, and they named it Breuckelen, after a town in the Netherlands. But about twenty years later the English arrived and got all up in their business. They told the Dutch to fugheddaboudit.

Brooklyn, true to its tough reputation, kept its name. But when New York was divided into counties, the English daddios named it Kings County, after their king at that time, King Charles II of England.

Queens was named for Charles's wife, Queen Catherine of Braganza.

Staten Island (seriously, you forgot about it, didn't you?) kept it all in the family, and Richmond County was named for one of Charles's numerous illegitimate sons, the Duke of Richmond. Who, incidentally, is said to be the ancestor of both Princess Diana and Camilla Parker Bowles, the now Mrs. Prince Charles.

Think you can remember it now?!

★ ★

DID YOU SEE SAW LADY?

New York City

In the bustling Times Square subway station, there's a strange sound. It's angelic. It's otherworldly.

Woo woo woo woo eee ahh oh oooh . . .

You can't quite put your finger on it. A violin? No, wait. An opera singer. Hold on a sec. Is it even . . . *gulp* . . . human?

Jaded New Yorkers might stop you right there and caution that it's probably some subway huckster with a tape recorder and dancing puppets, so either get your buck out and tip him, bub, or keep it moving.

Finally, 257 eyebrow-raised New Yorkers and a flash mob of Japanese tourists later, the source is revealed: A slim woman with long, brown hair. But she's not singing. She's got a bow—but wait—that's not a violin. It looks like a saw! A real-life, build-you-a-house, chop-you-some-firewood household saw!

Photo by Ricardo Oyarzo

Natalia Paruz is armed, but not dangerous.

Her name is Natalia Paruz. Born in Israel, Paruz came to New York, where her professional dance career was cut short by an accident. Her parents took her on a vacation to Austria to cheer her up. It was there that she heard a saw played for the first time. Moved by the experience, when she returned to New

We're Not Going to Take It, But Yes, We're Lying Down

On the Woodlawn Cemetery plot of artist Patricia Cronin and her partner, Deborah Kass, is a larger-than-life (literally) marble sculpture of the couple lying in bed, in what has been described as a postcoital embrace. It is as striking as Michelangelo's *David* but with a tenderness that is a sharp contrast to David's sideways can't-be-bothered look.

As you take in the sculpture, titled *Memorial to a Marriage*, you can become consumed by its sweetness and love. Before you go embarrassing yourself by asking, "Oh, how did she die?," try, if you will, to think outside the . . . casket. The couple is very much alive, thank you very much.

So, why a sculpture for the living in a resting place for the dead? Cronin explains that, as a gay couple, she and Kass share as many legal documents as the law will allow—wills, health-care proxies, powers of attorney—but those papers are "all about the end of our lives." She wanted to create "the most elegant official object" she could think of to address the issue. And, since the government seemed so fixated on the death part, why not a cemetery? (Cronin also explains, for the historically challenged, that before museums, art was found in cemeteries.)

Instead of being one of those artists eternally griping about The Man and The System, Cronin worked the system. Oh yeah, government? I'll see your death and raise you two lives. And so, while Cronin is off in Rome on her next project or picking out a new sofa with Kass, the sculpture is out there diligently, day after day, on the front lines of the gay rights movement, touching visitors with the ordinariness and beauty of their relationship.

Shhhhh. Can you hear what they're saying?

There are also several smaller versions of the sculpture that tour the country, traveling soldiers who lie down in museums from coast to coast, quietly making their statement, without ever having to get out of bed. The version at Woodlawn is on all of the cemetery's walking tours. Or, see it online at www.patriciacronin.net.

York, she picked up her landlady's rusty old saw and well, the rest, is, as they say, hist-saw-ry.

She's played with orchestras and been featured on commercials. She's played big concert halls, including Lincoln Center in New York and Verizon Hall in Philadelphia—known for its top-notch acoustics—but she credits the New York City subway as having the *best* acoustics in the world. "I don't know," Paruz says. "Maybe it has something to do with all the concrete!"

Playing in the subway, Paruz says she's met all kinds of people—rich, poor, homeless, and thieves. "You just can't get that in a concert hall!"

Paruz goes underground about three days a week. Catch her at one of her favorite stops, including Times Square (42nd Street), Union Square (14th Street), and Lexington Avenue (59th Street). Check her out online at www.sawlady.com, where she has CDs for sale and a performance schedule.

Oh, and in case you're wondering, you post-9/11 skeptic you, Natalia's saw is toothless and not considered a deadly weapon. (And yes, she once had to explain this to the police.)

THE DA VINCI CODE OF TOOTHPASTE

The Bronx

Woodlawn Cemetery in the Bronx has some of the most famous graves in the world.

There are jazz greats like Miles Davis and Duke Ellington, and the father of the blues, W.C. Handy. There are more monuments to *Titanic* victims here than anywhere else in the U.S. There are also many household names, including R.H. Macy, J.C. Penney, and F.W. Woolworth. There are six former New York mayors, as well as master developer Robert Moses, who was famous for wrapping New York parks in highways. (He is, appropriately, buried next to an on-ramp to the Major Deegan Expressway.)

The sprawling 400-acre city cemetery has all the charms of its rural counterparts, with rolling green hills, dappled sunlight through the treetops, and even a waterfall.

But the real reason to visit the cemetery isn't its famous residents or idyllic setting. The secret to its charm lies in the people that you've never heard of and the stories their tombstones tell.

The "Inventor of the Artists' Color Tube" is here, according to one headstone shaped like an artist's palette and paint tube. This invention had an even greater cultural impact when they started putting toothpaste in those tubes.

You can also read the sad yet charming story of George Spencer Millet, who died at age fifteen. His tombstone reads: "Lost life by stab in falling on ink eraser, evading six young women trying to give him birthday kisses in office of Metropolitan Life Building."

You can get lost in all the stories. "It's your own little Da Vinci Code," says Susan Olsen, executive director of Friends of the Woodlawn Cemetery, "trying to figure out what they [the family] meant" when they designed each tombstone and mausoleum.

There are guided tours, though a little-known secret is that the security guards tell the best stories, albeit less accurate. There's a life-size statue of a bride, Clara Sulzer, who guards will tell you slipped on her gown and died on her wedding day. In fact, the cause was appendicitis before the wedding.

Woodlawn's famous bride, Clara Sulzer.

The Bronx Cheer

Like Archie Bunker, we've all been known to blow a few raspberries from time to time. You just stick your tongue out and make a flatulence noise.

There are, for whatever reason, certain occasions, where the only obvious response is that of a six-year-old. It's fun to make a raspberry on a baby's belly and very gratifying to deliver one to your spouse when he or she does something you don't like.

You just give 'em a big pfffffllllllllt.

That highly evolved act of disapproval is actually known as a "Bronx Cheer," probably because Yankee Stadium is located in the Bronx and when fans didn't like an umpire's call, they delivered raspberries by the truckload.

Now, raspberries are pretty sweet and unassuming, so how did they land such an unsavory association? Wordsmith.org notes that British Cockney rhyming slang of the early 20th century turned "raspberry tart" into code for "fart." I mean, would any of us still be doing this if it were called a mouth fart? Probably not. That's pretty gross. But say "blow a raspberry," and I'll give you one right now.

Call it a "Bronx cheer" and it sounds downright patriotic.

And so, while our friends in the Bronx didn't invent it, they certainly made it all-American.

Before you leave, be sure to do an air toast to Jerry Thomas, father of the cocktail, who's also here. And next time you're squeezing the last drop out of the Crest, shout out to the paint-tube guy.

For more information go to www.thewoodlawncemetery.org or call (877) 496-6352.

STICKBALL BOULEVARD
South Bronx

City kids don't have the luxury of running around in the yard like their suburban counterparts, but they have no less energy zipping around inside of them. So, they take their games to the streets.

Many games have held court in the city's streets over the years, from handball and stoop ball to hit the penny and skelly, which involves flicking bottle caps. But none have endured like stickball, which is often called "poor man's baseball."

There are many variations of stickball, but the equipment is basically the same: a broom handle and a rubber ball. Manhole covers are bases; cars and buildings, the foul lines. (Um, you have auto insurance, right?)

Steve Mercado, a former New York City firefighter and a legend in the Bronx stickball world, used to say it's not a game, it's a tradition—one that started with Irish and Italian immigrants in the 1930s and one he helped pass down to the next generation in the Bronx as president of the New York Emperors Stickball League.

There are many leagues all over the city and in the United States, and it's even spawned several Web sites including www.streetplay. com, which hosts the Stickball Hall of Fame. And every year over Memorial Day weekend, the Bronx is host to a tournament on, what else, Stickball Boulevard.

Yes, the game is so popular, there was even a street named after it. Formerly Newman Avenue, Stickball Boulevard is between Seward and Lacombe Avenues in the southeastern part of the Bronx.

255

★ ★

If you've already got a barbeque planned for Memorial Day, don't hang up your broom handle just yet: Games are held on Stickball Boulevard every Sunday morning April through September. For more information check out www.stickball.com.

LITTLE GREEN INVADERS IN BROOKLYN
Brooklyn

Little green creatures have invaded Brooklyn. They gather in groups of fifty or sixty, building elaborate colonies, with landing strips and lookout posts. They have a sophisticated communications system that seems almost human. They laugh. They argue. They dispatch warnings. And sometimes, they appear to be conspiring.

But don't go opening an X-File or calling the paranormal experts. These invaders aren't here to take over.

They are monk parrots, also known as Quaker parrots. They have a green robe of feathers, which makes them monk-like, and a ruffled gray chest, for that dash of Quaker style. They are native to Argentina. The story varies as to how they found their way to Brooklyn, but the long-standing theory is that they were being shipped to JFK Airport around 1968 when the crate broke apart. A man named Vinny may or may not have been involved, but if you like your kneecaps, you'll leave it at that.

You may think of parrots as delicate, tropical birds that couldn't survive the winter in New York, but these tough guys came from the mountains of Argentina, so they're used to the cold and actually thrive here year-round.

You'll find them on the athletic field of Brooklyn College—they've built condo-style nests up in the stadium lights—or in nearby trees and fire escapes. They huddle in groups of two or three to stay warm in the winter. Another major colony has set up shop in the huge Gothic-style entrance gate to Green-Wood Cemetery. You might even find them mixing it up with the local pigeons at dinnertime.

Photo by Steve Baldwin, BrooklynParrots.com

A rumble in Brooklyn.

Make no mistake, though, these Brooklyn birds take crap from no one. At the first sign of a predator, their charming banter turns to an "Eeeee! Ack! Ack! Ack!" sound that the *Washington Post* once described as like "metal scraping metal." They're super-smart and extremely strong, so they'll go after that predator, a little winged army zigzagging through the sky. You don't mess with a bird from Brooklyn.

"They're gutsy little creatures," says Steve Baldwin, who runs a Web site devoted to the parrots, called www.BrooklynParrots.com. To watch them go up against a predator, it's "like a game of chicken between a motorcycle and a tractor trailer," Baldwin says.

To learn more about the parrots, check out Steve's Web site, which includes photos, videos, and even a song he wrote for them, "Ballad of the Brooklyn Parrots." Or, join him on a "Wild Brooklyn Parrot Safari," held on the first Saturday of each month.

★ ★

A BROOKLYN-STYLE WELCOME

Brooklyn

If you've ever been to Brooklyn, you know what it is to have Brooklyn style and Brooklyn attitude.

If you've ever driven to Brooklyn, they set you straight from the get-go.

At key entry points on the expressways, overhead signs say things like WELCOME TO BROOKLYN: BELIEVE THE HYPE and WELCOME TO BROOKLYN: HOW SWEET IT IS!

There are about a dozen of these signs, part of a campaign by Brooklyn Borough President Marty Markowitz.

Nobody loves Brooklyn like this guy, who calls himself "Mr. Brooklyn." Oh, and he's earned it. Markowitz was the guy with the megaphone on the Brooklyn Bridge during the Blackout of 2003, greeting melting Brooklynites with a resounding, "Welcome home to Brooklyn!" In the freezing cold of the December 2005 transit strike, he was back on the bridge with that megaphone, cheering, "We'll get through this!"

Markowitz even launched a tourism campaign for Brooklyn—yes, *that* Brooklyn—to show off the borough's assets, such as the Coney Island amusement park and beach and the borough's cultural cornu-copia of restaurants. Check it out at www.brooklyntourism.org.

Only a true Brooklynite would know how to spell "Fugheddaboudit!"

In Markowitz's opinion, "You shouldn't be leaving Brooklyn for almost anything." So, if you even *think* about it, he's got a street sign for that, too: LEAVING BROOKLYN—FUGHEDDABOUDIT!

For a listing of the locations of the Brooklyn signs, visit www.brooklyn-usa.org/Press/2003/july21.htm.

DAILY COMMUTE: BROOKLYN TO CRETE

Bay Ridge, Brooklyn

George Kortsolakis grew up on the Greek island of Crete (pronounced "kreet-y") and came to New York in 1955. He spent years working as a tailor to the stars, everyone from Frank Sinatra and Mrs. Frank Sinatra, as Kortsolakis refers to them, to Paul Newman and prizefighter Mike Tyson. (For the record, Kortsolakis has both ears intact. I checked.)

When Kortsolakis retired in 1990, he turned to his garden, a small swatch of roughly 7x20 feet, between his house and the sidewalk. He dreamed of returning to Crete, so one day, he built a 7-foot-long replica of Crete right there in his garden! He added moss for grass and pieces of slate down the middle for the main road. Chunks of concrete stand in for Crete's mountains. Turquoise aquarium rocks represent the sea. There are dozens of houses, churches, cars, boats, tiny people, and farm animals—even a representation of Kortsolakis's childhood home.

"This is one of a kind!" Kortsolakis proudly declares in his thick Greek accent, happy to explain his masterpiece—and the history of Crete—to passersby, pointing out the clock in the back under the shell-spelled banner CRETE TIME.

"Up in the mountains, you see here?" he says pointing. "These are the kri-kri, jumping goats that you find only in Crete."

Also represented are mythical figures such as Icarus ("eek-a-russ"), who glued feathers together with wax to fly, and Alexander the Great's sister, who drank forbidden water, leaped into the ocean, and became an immortal half-fish half-human.

★ ★

Welcome to George's Crete. Please watch your step and enjoy your stay.

Kortsolakis is out there every day, before dawn, and well after dusk, always thinking about what he can add next. "The island was too dark," Kortsolakis explains. "It needed lights." So, he recruited an electrician to help him make streetlights, tiny white lights covered with clear pen caps.

Kortsolakis built a temple-like structure of Plexiglas trimmed with gold-painted molding to protect his island from the elements, then added rope lights on the ceiling for stars. He rigged systems for simulated weather patterns. "I put rain inside. Snow inside. I make stars inside. It's a beautiful thing . . . looks exactly like Crete," he says.

"He's always dreaming up things that don't exist with household objects," says Magda Capurso, one of his daughters, while Kortsolakis stands nearby, planning his next Cretian wonder.

"We're very proud of him," his wife Flora adds.

"I still have a lot of work. I never finish. Next, I have to put in the sun and the moon," says Kortsolakis, now eighty years old. "I'm going to work until I die. When I die, then I stop."

TONIGHT, IS DANCING GIRLS!
Brighton Beach, Brooklyn

When you think of Russia, a few things probably come to mind: Vodka. The KGB. Furry hats. An accent that's fun to impersonate.

Well, here are a few more visuals: Men in tight pants and cabana wear. Women in nude unitards with strategically placed sequins. Bongos. Plumage.

Everybody, tequila! I mean, vodka.

★ ★

Where might you find this star-spangled Russia?

In Brighton Beach, Brooklyn, a seaside community that's sometimes referred to as Little Odessa because of all the Russian and Ukrainian immigrants. The restaurants, fruit stands, and Russian-language signs seem to instantly transport you to the land of furry hats and funny accents.

You are still wondering about sequins, yes?

One of Brighton Beach's most transporting experiences is its lively Russian supper clubs. In Russia and other eastern European countries, such clubs are a posh experience. In Brighton Beach, these fancy clubs under the elevated subway tracks make the experience more like a campy low-budget Vegas act.

Most are banquet style, which means you'll eat like a king in a grand ballroom while a steady stream of entertainment—and vodka—flows. The elaborate spreads often involve a couple dozen dishes—everything from beef tongue to blintzes—for about $50+ per person.

At the National (273 Brighton Beach Avenue), the music and costumes change quicker than you can say, "More vodka, please!" At one performance, strategically placed sequins starred in a "Tequila!" number, which was equal parts lady jumping out of a cake, Julie Andrews twirling an umbrella, and Robert Palmer video. The showgirl numbers were punctuated by soloists, including a stocky Russian crooner in a brown velvet jacket and amber-tinted J-Lo shades and a well-endowed, bustier-clad blonde in silver eye shadow.

"We have gypsy show!" said a manager at Odessa (1113 Brighton Beach Avenue), who added that the show's music is in a variety of languages. A dishwasher at Rasputin (2670 Coney Island Avenue), described the show there as "a human zoo," with performers in animal costumes and pop music. "There is toro [bull]. There are dogs," he said. "Las Vegas–type thing." And at Primorski (282 Brighton Beach Avenue), an employee summed up the show this way: "Very good music. Believe me."

To get to Brighton Beach, take the B or Q train to the Brighton Beach stop. Or, get a preview of the dancing girls and appetizers at their Web sites: the National (www.come2national.com), Odessa (www.restaurantodessa.com), Primorski (www.primorski.net), and Rasputin (www.rasputincabaret.com).

You have very good time. Believe me.

THE MAN WHO FIXES BROKEN ANGELS
Clinton Hill, Brooklyn

Arthur Wood's view of the world doesn't involve boundaries. His creativity spills from the canvas onto the floor, the wall, the ceilings, and beyond. In 1979, he bought the former headquarters of the Brooklyn Trolley, an ordinary building by any measure, and bent, built, and twisted it into a masterpiece.

The building, which he named Broken Angel, has been described as "a Rubik's Cube of a spaceship" by Brooklyn President Marty Markowitz, and "Alice in Wonderland on acid," by Chris Wood, Arthur's son, who grew up in the house. It's a gravity-defying structure straight out of a Dr. Seuss book, lopsided boxes piled up on top of each other, dotted with random acts of colorful mosaic. To look at it, you half expect Things One and Two to pop out of the oddly shaped windows.

Parts of the structure are fully enclosed, while others are wide open. The stairs are steep planks with cleats. Wood says he wanted to transcend the standard "walking on the bottom of a cube" structure of a room and instead "make it possible so you can exist in any place in that cube—even float in air!" The mosaic windows are made of everything from car-accident glass to colored bottles, ashtrays, saltshakers, and candy dishes. I think I even saw Mrs. Butterworth in there.

The name "Broken Angel" came during a stroll in Staten Island. Wood found a broken statue—first a hand holding a torch. Then an arm. A torso. A head. "I reassembled the parts into a position I thought would be graceful," Wood says. "And then I told my wife,

★ ★

'Someday, I'll build you a house like that.'"

Wood built Broken Angel over twenty-three years on a budget of $300 a month—including food for his family. It helps that he's as charming as he is creative, and he knows how to get dinner and a movie for free.

Alas, there was a fire and a court battle, and the original Broken Angel is being torn down. Wood, now in his seventies, brokered a deal to spare some small part of his life's work by converting it into condos. It's not Wood's ideal outcome; he calls the venture "Gaudí," the great Spanish architect, "meets IKEA."

Overlapping triangles over the doorway are Wood's own superhero logo, A.W.

One thing is for sure: Nothing will stop Wood's wild creative exploration. He'll tell you about the time he spent six months building an artificial woman, and he'll show you his blueprints for the crown jewel of the building: a retired helicopter from Arizona's aviation "boneyard" that will become a futuristic whale-shaped building, with a hydraulic chair that ascends through a hatch in the roof.

"Imagine," Wood said, "sparks fly, the hatch opens, and up you go!"

Check out photos of the original Broken Angel at www.flickr.com/photos/onebadapple. Or, see it in Dave Chappelle's *Block Party*, which was filmed right in front of the house.

★ ★

IS IT HOT IN HERE, OR IS IT JUST ME "SWEATING GRAVY"?
Coney Island, Brooklyn

By now, you've probably heard of the great American Fourth of July tradition, the Nathan's Hot Dog Eating Contest in Coney Island, Brooklyn.

Now, don't go rolling your eyes. Competitive eating is a wildly entertaining sport—oh yes, I said "sport"—complete with star players and a national federation that signs them to contracts. There are announcers who call the shots and offer stats, and the sport has its own vocabulary. It's like the NFL, only with a much greater chance of a player puking.

Photo courtesy of IFOCE

. It's a man-eat-dog world out there.

Sorry, my bad. The first rule of eating club is you don't say "puke." Or "vomit" or "hurl," for that matter. You say "reversal." As in: "For Joey Chestnut, reversal is not an option at this point!" And, so you know, reversals *do* happen, but not as often as you'd think, according to George Shea, the P.T. Barnum of the sport and chairman of the International Federation of Competitive Eating.

The IFOCE, based in Manhattan, puts on about one hundred eating contests per year worldwide. You can pretty much eat your way to fame with any number of foods, though only the top few competitors eat their way to fortune. Takeru Kobayashi, who won the Nathan's contest for several years running, is one of the sport's top earners. He's also held titles in hamburgers, bratwurst, and cow brains. American Joey Chestnut finally became top dog on July 4, 2007, eating sixty-six hot dogs in twelve minutes. He also holds titles in asparagus, grilled cheese, and pulled pork.

There's Sonya "The Black Widow" Thomas, weighing in at just over 100 pounds, with nearly 30 titles behind her size small belt, including chicken wings, baked beans, and oysters. Eric "Badlands" Booker, who subsidizes his eating earnings by selling CDs of himself rapping about eating, holds the corned-beef hash record and, according to Shea, "sweats gravy." (Meat events, apparently, are the most sweat-inducing.)

As for training (what, you thought it was just show up and eat?), the most common technique is to drink large quantities of water to stretch the stomach's capacity. Or the buffet-water combo. Thomas estimates her stomach can hold eighteen pounds of food, Kobayashi, more than twenty pounds.

To learn more and brush up on your eaters, check out www.ifoce .com. There's also an indie league, www.competitiveeaters.com, which declares itself "Home of Picnic Style Rules."

May you have many happy returns, but never a reversal.

WHERE THE MERMAIDS MAMBO
Coney Island, Brooklyn

Everyone it seems, has their day. There's Mother's Day. Father's Day. St. Patrick's Day. Presidents' Day. Even the fools have their day.

But what about the merpeople? They get no love from Hallmark. None.

Well—and this isn't the first time you'll find yourself saying this—thank goodness for Coney Island! They understand that it ain't easy being half-lady, half-fish!

Coney Island holds a Mermaid Parade every year in late June. The ladies get all decked out in their best tails. Some walk, some ride floats. Some ride bikes. Some even walk on stilts.

Even the guys get into it. A father dressed as a fisherman pulls his merdaughter. There are Mambo mermaids and Egyptian mermaids. French (mer)maids. There's a mer-bride, and a mer-momma-to-be-maid. There are pirate mermaids, belly-dancing mermaids, and even hula-hooping mermaids. They're joined by crabs, lobster, and other glittering sea life. Marching bands, tambourine bands, and even a kazoo band.

The parade, led by the "Permanently Unelected Mayor of Coney Island," Dick Zigun, and a celebrity King Neptune and Queen Mermaid, kicks off

Aw, look at the mer-baby!

★ ★

on the Coney Island boardwalk and winds through the streets, where awards are given out for best costume. In the final leg—or fin—the Queen leads the masses of merfolk down the beach, where she cuts four ribbons—one for each season. The parade ends in the ocean, where all the costume parade-goers jump in and toss fruit out to sea as an offering to the gods. Mayor Zigun holds up a giant key, and the ocean is unlocked for the summer swimming season.

That night is a Mermaid Parade Ball complete with live music, burlesque, and sideshow acts.

For more information walk or swim to www.coneyisland.com/mermaid.shtml.

STEP RIGHT UP, FREAK
Coney Island, Brooklyn

Sure, we all say we're freaks from time to time, but how many of us have a certificate to prove it?

If you aren't quite ready for the face tattoo but would like to make your freak status official, you're in luck. Professor Todd Robbins, a longtime sideshow entertainer and chairman of Coney Island USA, will teach you how to perform sideshow stunts at the Coney Island Sideshow School, right there on the stage of the actual Coney Island Sideshow!

He'll teach you how to walk barefoot on cut glass, eat fire, swallow a sword without perforating your esophagus and drive a nail into your nose, which, in the biz, is called the Human Blockhead.

OK, OK. C'mon, professor. Come clean with us. That stuff sounds great, but it's all fake, isn't it?

"The fun thing about sideshow is that half of it is fake and half of it is real," Robbins says. "The irony of it is that which you think is fake is probably real and what thought was real is probably fake."

The old lady-in-the-box-punctured-by-swords trick, for example, "looks impossible until you get up there and look in. There's a way to twist yourself around the blades," Robbins explains.

It's all "based on principles of physics and anatomy," he says, and mastering the risk factors. Of course there are exceptions like glass eating, which is—literally—a crapshoot. You wait a couple days and hope that everything comes out all right.

To be sure, Robbins won't teach you anything that risky. His number-one priority in class is safety. Outside of class, however, he has been known to attend a party, drink his martini, and then eat the glass.

That, my friends, is how they roll in Coney Island.

Sideshow School isn't cheap: It costs $600 for a five-week course (or weeklong intensive), but you will leave there with some great party tricks—and unemployment insurance. Should you ever lose your job, just stand on the street corner and hammer a nail into your nose for money.

Move over, bearded lady. There's a new freak in town.

For more information, check out www.coneyisland.com/sideshow_school.shtml.

MY JESUS HAS HAIR
Dyker Heights, Brooklyn

When my friend asked me if I wanted to go on a pilgrimage to Brooklyn to see the Christmas lights, I quickly agreed, visions of fun light-gazing trips with my mom dancing in my head.

And then, I spotted the life-size Mary and Joseph wearing wigs.

And all I can tell you is: These aren't your mother's Christmas lights. Frankly, these aren't even the lights of that crazy guy who lives on the way to your grandmother's house.

Oh no.

These are the lights of Dyker Heights.

In the Dyker Heights section of Brooklyn, McMansions fill the blocks, with sweeping staircases, topiaries, and decorative gates. And at Christmas, there's only one way to describe what goes on here: It's "keeping up with the Joneses" on cra—Christmas.

★ ★

Stepping out of the car, we were greeted by the wig-clad, Nativity-going mannequins, flanked by signs advertising Christmas-decorating services—one for the lights, the other for the Nativity scene. Here, residents pay professional contractors up to $20,000 to deck out their homes for the holidays.

At that price, it goes without saying that there are lights on pretty much everything. Keep your children and pets in sight at all times during the ODS (Official Decorating Season).

There are armies of plastic angels. Rows of lawndy canes. Carolers and Clauses. Sleighs and snowflakes. Wreaths the size of a Manhattan apartment.

Bring it on! It's Christmas in Brooklyn, baby!

One house features dancing dolls spinning on pedestals. Another has cherubic ice-skaters in snowsuits—bearing an eerie resemblance to Oompa Loompas—frolicking with furry polar bears. Another has a full-scale diorama of *A Christmas Carol,* complete with soundtrack.

It's not hard to figure out which house belongs to the "Joneses" that everyone's trying to keep up with. That's 1145 84th Street, between 11th and 12th Avenues. The centerpiece of that display is a giant, casually posed Santa, flanked by two toy soldiers more than 20 feet tall, rearing horse statues, and giant carousels that spin. You can climb the stairs, but a rope will keep you from actually walking up and sitting on Santa's lap. Not that you'd want to.

Standing beneath casual Claus, both dazzled and terrified, it felt more like the Hollywood set of a horror movie than Christmas in Brooklyn. I half-expected Jack Nicholson to jump out with an ax. At one point, I swear I saw the shrubbery take an aggressive stance. Up on the balconies, dancing reindeer seemed to mock my fear of the festivity.

The "light district" stretches from 83rd to 86th Streets and 11th to 13th Avenues in the Dyker Heights section of Brooklyn.

LIFE, LIBERTY, AND THE PURSUIT OF HELLO
Greenwood Heights, Brooklyn

Millions of people visit the Statue of Liberty each year. She is one of the most recognized icons in the world. There she is in the New York Harbor, torch to the sky, saluting America in all of its liberated glory. What most people don't know is that, across the harbor, on Brooklyn's southwestern shore, someone is waving back. And she's been doing it for more than eighty years.

She is Minerva, the Roman Goddess of Wisdom. She is made of bronze, roughly 7 feet tall, and she resides in Green-Wood Cemetery on Battle Hill, Brooklyn's highest natural point, and the site of the first and largest battle of the Revolutionary War. She's loaded up with all her Roman warrior-goddess gear, including a helmet, but her left arm is raised in a friendly wave to her old pal, Lady Liberty.

Despite its historical significance, we all would've forgotten about the battle that took place here. The truth is, we lost that battle—and nearly lost the war at that point—and who wants to dwell on defeat? (It would be pretty hard to sell stars-and-stripes paper plates and ballpark franks in July had we not actually won our independence.) But Charles Higgins, who made his fortune selling Higgins India Ink, thought the battle was pretty important and wanted to make sure that we didn't forget. So he had Minerva built, and he donated her to the people of Brooklyn.

There is no disputing that Minerva, built more than thirty years later, was intended to face the Statue of Liberty. But the Statue of Liberty is another story. Some say she faces France, who gave her to us. The official Statue Web site says she faces the harbor to greet incoming ships.

But Green-Wood Cemetery has always maintained that she's facing Brooklyn, and Battle Hill, as a way of recognizing the starting point of our liberation.

Hey, Lib! How's the weather over there?

"If she's facing France, I guess that's possible," says Green-Wood Cemetery Historian Jeff Richman. "You'll have to stand behind her and see if you can see the Eiffel Tower in the distance!"

The amazing thing is that, in New York City, with all of its revised zoning laws to clear the path for ever-skyward buildings, the view between the two ladies of liberty remains unobstructed. One building between the old gals had threatened to block their greeting, but the builders agreed to cut out a corner so as not to interrupt.

And so, Minerva, and the Statue of Liberty, now 122 years old, will forever exchange greetings, like a couple of old ladies on the way to the market.

The next time you're visiting the Statue of Liberty, mugging for the camera in your green foam crown, gaze across the harbor and give a shout-out to Minerva. Better yet, visit Green-Wood at 500 25th Street in Brooklyn (www.green-wood.com).

THE DANCING OF THE GIGLIO
Williamsburg, Brooklyn

Every summer, just as June is melting into July, there's a street festival in the Italian part of Williamsburg, Brooklyn, near Our Lady of Mount Carmel Church. It has all of the usual street-fair fare—refreshments, cotton candy, and carnival games—and, of course, Italian specialties. But twice during this festival, something extraordinary happens. Out from between the carts of Italian sausage and deep-fried zeppole emerges a towering spire, five stories tall—and it appears to be dancing.

The spire, which has a priest and twelve-piece brass band at the base, weighs about five tons and is carried by 125 men down the street. It is the Giglio. (And no, it has nothing to do with J-Lo.) As the band plays an eccentric medley of Italian classics, "The Star-Spangled Banner," and even "The Rainbow Connection," the burly men, with cutoff sleeves, headbands, and backward baseball caps, carry the immense monument with lightly padded steel beams resting on their shoulders. Lieutenants on each side call out orders to *la paranza*, the lifters, and the entire regiment is overseen by one man, the *capo*. Bobbing, swaying, and turning it as they go, they pause every few minutes to wipe the sweat from their brows and take a swig of beer from the sidelines, the Giglio version of the Gatorade shot at a marathon. The crowd stands in awe.

The Dancing of the Giglio, as the feat is known, is a tradition that was brought to Brooklyn more than one hundred years ago by immigrants from the southern Italian town of Nola near Naples. The Giglio, which means "lily" in Italian, is topped with a statue of San Paolino, or Saint Paulinus, the patron saint of Nola. As the story goes, the Huns invaded Italy nearly 1,600 years ago and Paolino, a lawyer-turned-priest, escaped with the children of the town to protect

Dancing in the streets.

them. Upon his return, he soon realized that he'd missed one boy, who was captured. Paolino offered to trade himself into a life of slavery in exchange for the boy's freedom. When Paolino himself was finally freed, the people of Nola greeted him with bouquets of lilies. The town made this an annual tradition, carrying the lilies into the town square on big poles.

Brooklyn's Giglio is part of a two-week festival that celebrates both Our Lady of Mount Carmel and San Paolino. It begins with *La Questa,* when volunteers hand out bread in the neighborhood to remember San Paolino's sacrifice of all his worldly possessions. There are also Giglio dances in Harlem and Long Island.

For more information visit www.giglio-usa.org and www.olmcfeast.com.

THE HUMAN CAR WASH

East Village, Manhattan

New York is home to some of the best spas in the world. But why would you go for a froufrou spa treatment when you could simply get a beating with an oak-leaf broom, have a couple of ice-cold buckets of water dumped over your head, and then jump in a forty-five-degree pool?

Europeans and Russians have long used extreme temperatures—hot steam and cold pools—as a way to detoxify their bodies. In Russia, there's even a group called *morzhy,* or walruses, that jump into frozen rivers and lakes in the middle of winter.

Would you like wax or just the wash?

You can sample it for yourself at the Russian and Turkish Baths, the oldest bathhouse left in New York and a year-round gathering spot for the Polar Bear set. The idea is to toggle between hot and cold, starting with heat.

There are four rooms for heat, but the most popular is the Russian Room, where a huge oven heats 200 giant boulders to make dry, intense heat. With temperatures over 200 degrees, you'll actually grab one of those ice-cold buckets of water and dump it on yourself—multiple times. You take breaks by sitting in the hallway, jumping in the cold pool, or hitting the Swedish shower, which blasts you with cold water from all sides.

"You know, *shvitz*," the Yiddish word for sweat, "then cold pool, shvitz, then cold pool," explains Aron, an antiques dealer from Brooklyn who brings his own oak-leaf broom, known as a *Platza*. He and his friends—like Frank, who's been coming to the baths for forty years—take turns in the Russian Room, whacking each other with the brooms.

"The only way I can describe it, it's the closest you can get to God—spiritually, mentally, and physically," Frank says.

You can make up your own routine at the baths, with input from old pros like Frank and Aron, but there are two things not to be missed: the cold pool and the Platza. As you lay on the top shelf of the Russian steam room with a wet washcloth over your head, a Platza specialist will literally beat you with a broom made of oak leaves. Then, you sit up and they "whack you a couple times in the head," says Dmitry Shapiro, who runs the place with his brother, Jack. To be clear, it doesn't hurt. It's meant to intensify the heat. "You take detox to a new level," Dmitry says.

Platza, which comes from the Yiddish word for shoulders, "opens the pores, penetrates more heat," Aron explains.

"It's like a human car wash," Frank adds, which is an apt description, particularly when you're holding your breath and hot, wet leaves are coming down on both sides of your head.

It's certainly not the pampering you get at a spa. But when you walk out, your skin will feel like that of a newborn baby. "You're not necessarily going to look prettier when you come out" with bright, pink skin, Dmitry explains, "but you're going to feel better."

And when you're done, one of the charms of the baths is sitting around in the lounge/cafe, chatting in your standard-issue robe and rubber slippers while downing a fruit juice or Russian beer.

The Russian and Turkish Baths are at 268 East 10th Street (212-473-8806; www.russianturkishbaths.com). Most days are coed, but Wednesday mornings are ladies only and Sunday mornings are men only.

LIONS AND DRESSERS AND CHAIRS . . . OH MY!
East Village, Manhattan

On the corner of Houston and Elizabeth Streets, is a man with a long, blond ponytail wearing tinted glasses, a Chesterfield suit jacket, and jeans. He presides over a giant military-style tent with a steer skull over the doorway. The tent door is rolled up, beckoning like a mysterious carnival curiosity.

Inside, a skeleton in a vintage coat and embroidered scarf greets customers with a menacing smile. Behind him is a chandelier comprised of long tubes that looks like something straight out of Superman's lair. Overhead is literally a head—several of them, in fact—a few dancing skeletons, an ominous fortune-teller machine, and a vintage baby crib. A lion prowls on a ledge. Below is a china cabinet lined with skulls.

Elvis dances next to Jesus. A fox lurks on top of a vintage dresser, peeking out from behind a Victorian doll lamp. Up on the wall, Aunt Jemima entices you with her ready-made pancake mix.

This is Billy's Antiques & Props, where you can find every antique imaginable—from kitschy vintage signs to old leather chairs—as well as everything you'll need to make your own horror movie. It's the ultimate in one-stop shopping.

The shop is owned by William Leroy, a biker-turned-antiques dealer. Leroy considers it primarily a vintage-furniture store—that's his money maker—but he also likes to stock oddities, such as a 3,000-year-old mummy head he found at a flea market in Paris, just to keep customers on edge.

I'm going to ask you one more time. Would you like to buy this lamp?

"I don't want people to feel too comfortable," Leroy says with a sly grin, taking a drag on his thin cigar. Then, he pulls out a wall calendar by artist and former cannibal Nico Claux. "Now *that* is dark art," Leroy says, "not that Goth crap from some suburban kid in Jersey."

You can't argue with him there. That *is* dark art. And this, over here, is the edge of my seat.

Billy's Antiques, formerly known as Lot 76 and Manhattan Castles and Props, is at 76 E. Houston Street (917-576-6980).

THE CITY THAT NEVER SLEEPS, BUT NAPS OCCASIONALLY
Hell's Kitchen, Manhattan

New York may be known as the city that never sleeps, but the truth is, most New Yorkers are exhausted. Ditto for the tourists. There are so many stimuli, that they can suck the life force right out of you.

Finally, someone has heeded the call of the sleep-deprived and offered a spot for a quick power nap that doesn't involve drooling on the person sitting next to you on the subway. At Yelo, billed as an urban sanctuary, not a spa (that's so 1980), you can rent out a futuristic chamber called a YeloCab for anywhere from twenty to forty minutes. YeloCabs, not to be confused with their cacophonous counterparts, yellow taxi cabs, are set up for maximum relaxation and rejuvenation with 500-thread-count linens, purified air, and high-tech customized light. So, the next time it's pouring rain and one of those "other" cabs dispatches a wave of New York City gutter water all over your new suit, head over to 57th Street and hop in a YeloCab. To book your next nap, go to www.yelonyc.com or call (212) 245-8235.

CLICKETY-CLACK, THE WALLS WHISPER BACK
Midtown Manhattan

In Grand Central Station, thousands of commuters whiz by every day, filling the marble corridors with a cacophony of clacking heels and cell phone chatter as they make a mad dash for the next train.

But down below the main concourse, on the subterranean food-court level, people are whispering. A young girl runs into a corner and says softly, "Can you hear me?" On the opposite side of the corridor, diagonally, her friend quietly exclaims into the wall: "Yes, I can hear you!" and both run off giggling.

The girls are replaced by a father with his son on his shoulders. "I love you, Mommy!" the boy whispers into the wall, before meeting up with his beaming mother. A young man leans into the same wall, egged on by his friend. On the other side of the corridor, an attractive woman is startled when the wall whistles at her unexpectedly.

This is the Whispering Gallery, one of the charming secrets of Grand Central Terminal. It is located right outside the Oyster Bar. There are no signs pointing out the gallery's exact location, but a steady stream of people darting in and out of the whisper spots lets you know you've found it.

★ ★

Here's how it works: When you talk directly into the corner, the sound travels up and over the domed ceiling, covered in impervious Guastavino tile, and down the other side. To your friend on the other side, it sounds as if your voice is coming from a speaker tucked behind the tile about arms-length overhead. Or, depending on how you're standing, the sound may seem to come from elsewhere around you. I nearly jumped out of my skin thinking my friend, who was a good 30 feet away from me, was right behind me whispering in my ear.

I'd like two cheeseburgers, an order of fries . . .

Since the tile isn't absorbent, and there are no vents, rugs, or other sound-escaping or sound-absorbing items, there's no place for the sound to go but up and over, a spokesman for Metro-North Railroad explained. And even though you're on opposite sides of the corridor, the people buzzing through the corridor can't hear you. No one knows why the secret-communication ceiling was created, but it's been that way since Grand Central was built in 1913.

According to employees at the Oyster Bar, it's not just for idle chatter. The Whispering Gallery is a popular spot for marriage proposals. They're smart guys—that's one transmission you wouldn't want to get lost in a subway vent! All you have to do is make sure you have the right woman on the other side.

NIGHT OF A THOUSAND GOWNS
Midtown Manhattan

The hair is big. The gowns are big. The dance numbers are big. And most of all, their hearts are big.

This is the Night of a Thousand Gowns, an annual charity drag ball at the Marriott Marquis hotel in Times Square and one of the biggest events of the year on the gay society calendar.

It's put on by the Imperial Court of New York, a chapter of the International Court, and features dinner, dancing, Broadway-style entertainment, and an auction of fabulous things. (We're talking MAC Cosmetics, Swarovski-crystal bling, and yes, a portrait of Liza Minnelli.)

Photo by Joe Saporito for newyorkqnews.com

The emperor and empress, surrounded by their gorgeous man court.

★ ★

The guests wear lavish gowns, many of which they've made themselves (if you're 6'5", you may not fit into Miss USA's hand-me-downs), sequined cocktail dresses, leather numbers, or tasteful tuxedos.

The purpose of the event, aside from showing off your rhinestones and shaking your tail feathers, is to raise money for charity. At $200 a head, the ball raises thousands for a variety of charities including Broadway Cares/Equity Fights AIDS and PFLAG (Parents and Friends of Lesbians and Gays).

The ball includes awards for outstanding achievement in the gay community and offers a chance to brush satin-gloved elbows with celebrities—everyone from Boy George and Cyndi Lauper to cabaret star Dirty Martini and PBS personality Clover Honey.

The crown jewel of the event is the crowning of a new emperor and empress, chosen for his and his extraordinary fund-raising efforts. The royal couple reigns for one year as ambassadors of the court.

"It's like Broadway," says CJ Mingolelli, a Manhattan and Fire Island real-estate agent. "There's the passing of the crown. Each emperor and empress has an entourage. . . . It's kind of outlandish."

In case you're wondering—which, I know you are—CJ and his partner favor tuxedos. But they love the spectacle of it all, as well as the chance to see friends and raise money for a worthy cause.

The event is held in late March or early April, but tickets sell out fast. For more information visit www.imperialcourtny.org or www.gaycitynews.com.

THE ELEPHANTS RIDE AT MIDNIGHT
Midtown Manhattan

Speaking of large, what do you do if you're an elephant and you need to get to work in midtown Manhattan?

You take the train to the nearest stop, get off, and walk the last few blocks like everyone else.

★ ★

Ringling Bros. and Barnum & Bailey Circus travels from city to city by train. The performers—even the animals—live on the train. Now, that's a pretty big train, so there really isn't anyplace to park it in Manhattan; they leave it in Queens. Their human counterparts can hop on a subway to Madison Square Garden, but the elephants and horses walk to the arena, where they live for the duration of the performance. (The human performers go back to their "apartments" on the train in Queens every night.)

Excuse me, sir, which way to 34th Street?

Trying to avoid rush-hour traffic, the elephants do their commute at midnight a few days before the circus starts. They walk through the Queens Midtown Tunnel, turn on Third Avenue, and walk the length of 34th Street—past the Empire State Building, Macy's, and all the other bright lights—before heading into MSG through the shipping dock.

There are ten elephants in the circus—all girls—but one is a diva and refuses to walk. (I guess it's like humans, there's one in every bunch!) So, she gets the elephant equivalent of a limo: a special truck to drive her directly to work. Sometimes, she sneaks one of her friends into the elipha-limo.

As the rest march down 34th Street, each holding the tail in front of her with her trunk, the crowd goes wild. Hundreds of spectators, jammed up against the police barricades, snap pictures, while another

Retrospective: My Sock Collection

Have you ever been standing in the middle of your living room, looked around, and wondered what it would be like if someone in the year 2158 were giving a guided tour of this now-historic spot?

"Over here on the left, is Jim's sofa. You can see the indentation in the cushion where he sat most nights watching television. On the right, a pile of newspapers that he kept meaning to get around to reading . . . "

Amazingly, someone had the foresight to do just that: preserve homes from 150 years ago on Manhattan's Lower East Side.

It's called the Lower East Side Tenement Museum, and what you'll find on the tour is far more than a 19th-century butt print. You'll learn—and feel—what it was like for immigrants struggling to make it in America in the late 1800s and early 1900s.

Today's New Yorkers love to complain about *that time they lived in an apartment so small they could shower and stir a pot of spaghetti at the same time*, but the New Yorkers you'll encounter at the Tenement Museum would've considered such living a luxury. For them, coin-operated gas lighting and heat, indoor plumbing, and shared toilets were a treat. Before that, they used candles and went to the bathroom in the backyard.

On the tour, you'll get to know a few of the tenants of 97 Orchard Street, including Nathalie Gumpertz, a single mother from Prussia who ran a dressmaking business out of her tenement to support four kids after her husband went to work one day and never came home.

Unfortunately, Julius Gumpertz wasn't the only husband who vanished in the wake of the Panic of 1873 as severe economic depression gripped the nation. There were so many that the local newspaper had a "Missing Husbands" section. No one knows for

Thanks to the heavy iron, this is the kitchen, laundry room, and gym.

sure if men like Julius died or simply buckled under the pressure and ran away. But as one woman pointed out on the tour, "If they ever did come home, their wives would've killed them!"

You can take a virtual tour of several tenement apartments at www.tenement.org. Or, you can stop complaining about your desk job for five minutes, turn off your computer, make a pit stop at your indoor bathroom (don't forget to wash your hands under the running water), and head over to 108 Orchard Street (212-431-0233)—across the street from the preserved tenement building—where tours begin. Tours cost $15 and start about every half hour between 11:30 a.m. and 4:30 p.m.

hundred or so actually run/walk down the sidewalk to keep up with the elephants. (An elephant's stride is pretty long, so yes, you have to run.)

In fact, the elephants do this walk to the arena in every city in which they perform, but there's nothing like seeing elephants walk down 34th Street.

Well, unless you're *this* guy: While all the other spectators were yelling "Woooo!" and trying to get the attention of Bello, the performer with the spiky hair on the lead elephant, this guy was obsessed with the fact that there was no zebra.

"Where's the zebra? There was a zebra last year! I don't see the zebra!" the man repeatedly exclaimed to his friends.

There are elephants walking down 34th Street, and this guy wants to know where the zebra is. As the *New York Post*'s Cindy Adams says, "Only in New York, kids. Only in New York."

THE NAKED COWBOY
Times Square, Manhattan

If you've been to New York's Times Square, chances are you've seen the Naked Cowboy, pointed, and giggled. Any attempts to look away are generally futile.

For the uninitiated, the Naked Cowboy (aka Robert J. Burcke II of Secaucus, New Jersey) is the guy singing in the traffic divide at 45th and Broadway, wearing only a cowboy hat, boots, a guitar—and tighty whities with "Naked Cowboy" emblazoned on the butt.

He can't sing all that well, but then again, few people pretend that's why they stopped. Nonetheless, the Naked Cowboy's briefs are overflowing with . . .

Confidence.

The Cowboy will tell you he's the third top attraction in New York (after the Empire State Building and Statue of Liberty) and likens himself to Christ, Buddha, and Copernicus. "I, myself, am God Almighty!" he declares.

When he's not in Times Square or at the gym, you'll find this urban cowboy reading the work of great philosophers such as Nietzsche and Emerson, self-help guru Tony Robbins, and his own Web site. This is what fuels his confidence, which gets translated for the Times Square set into lyrics such as: "If you really wanna live / feel the way I feel / you've got to whip out! / your balls . . . of . . . steel," and "The homophobes say I'm a queer / but I like chicks and beer . . . "

The cowboy rides the wind on a brisk 30-degree day in January.

You can find him in Times Square most days—even cold winter days—though the Cowboy does occasionally "tour" other cities. In the early days, that meant him showing up someplace and playing in his underpants until he was either thrown out or arrested, which, for the record, was forty-nine times. Today, he's gotten a bit more recognition for his craft. He's been in a dozen commercials, including one for the Super Bowl, and may soon have his own underwear line at a chain store near you.

Once, a tourist asked the Cowboy: "Why do you do this?" He replied: "Because if I don't do it, It won't get done. You're not going to do it, are you?"

No, Cowboy, probably not. Thanks for taking one for the team.

On his Web site (www.nakedcowboy.com) you can find inspiration in *The Naked Cowboy's Prayer Book* and buy your own "Cowboy"

★ ★

gear, including the signature briefs—just in case, y'know, you feel like air guitar-ing naked cowboy-style in your living room.

SERIOUSLY, YOU WOULD LOOK GREAT IN A UNITARD
Tribeca, Manhattan

So, you've passed the point in your life where running off and joining the circus is a viable option. No problem. Step right up!

Tucked between the Hudson River and the West Side Highway is the New York Trapeze School. In the summer, the trapeze rig is all out in the open, so you can feel like you're really flying over Manhattan. In the winter, they put the rig in a tent.

Imagine yourself climbing up the ladder in your shiny sequined unitard, like the new kid on the Flying Wallenda block. OK, OK. You don't have to wear a unitard. (But it's fun to picture yourself in one, right?)

Standing on top of the platform, in your modern athletic wear, that top-of-the-roller-coaster giddiness will come rushing back. Your adult sensibility may interrupt with a gut-level alert of "Retreat! Retreat!" But your inner cheapskate will remind you that you've already paid sixty bucks for this experience, so just jump already.

As you fling yourself off the platform—23 feet in the air—you might scream. You

Turn this city upside down at the New York Trapeze School.

Photo by Jason Klein

might laugh. You might cry. But you're gonna freakin' love every minute of it.

Dangling upside down, trying to muster the courage to try a flip, you'll realize that this is *much* harder than it looks. In an inverted moment of epiphany, you'll completely understand why the pros make such dramatic "Ta da!" poses when they're done. You'll also make a note to self to clap much louder for these guys the next time you're at the circus.

Throughout your high-flying act, you'll have breathtaking views of the Statue of Liberty, World Financial Center, and the Hudson River. And you'll always have the bragging rights that you once performed in New York City!

Visit www.trapezeschool.com or call (917) 797-1872. Prices range from $47 to $65 per class. During the busy summer months, sign up in advance because classes book up quickly.

CELEBRITIES WHO EAT RATS

Upper East Side, Manhattan

In New York City, it's hard to stand out. But two high-flying Manhattan residents have managed to do just that. In a town full of celebrities, they *are* the celebrities. They've been in the tabloids. They've inspired a documentary. They even have their own Web site.

Their names are Pale Male and Lola. They are a pair of red-tailed hawks. Their story might not have drawn more than a passing mention if they lived in a treetop in eastern Pennsylvania. What rocketed this carnivorous duo to fame was the fact that they built their nest on the twelfth-floor ledge of a Manhattan apartment building. And not just any building: This one was on Fifth Avenue, which is dotted with names like Tiffany and Trump, and boasts other famous residents such as Mary Tyler Moore and Paula Zahn. Usually, in this town, it takes more than a few twigs to land such a prestigious address!

When Pale Male and Lola get hungry, they head to Central Park, which has a lot of wide-open spaces for hunting but is also home to

Photo by Donegal Browne, palemaleirregulars.blogspot.com

Great dinner, honey. The pigeon is delicious!

one of the city's most expensive restaurants, Tavern on the Green. So, while their human counterparts are inside dining on the likes of braised lamb and filet mignon, Pale Male and Lola are outside rounding up squirrels and pigeons to bring back to—you guessed it—Mary Tyler Moore's house.

The pair has drawn bird lovers from all over the world, but, like all celebrities, not everyone is a fan. (It may have something to do with the fact that their dinners are soaked in blood, not béarnaise sauce.) In 2004 they were temporarily evicted after outspoken residents (such as Zahn and her then-husband) had had enough of the unwanted attention and leftover carcasses from dinner that spilled onto the sidewalk below. But the bird lovers united—staging rallies and even circulating a 10,000-signature petition—and before too long, the birds were back in town.

You can visit Pale Male and Lola in person, or check them out online at sites including www.PaleMale.com, run by one of the pair's paparazzi, and http://palemaleirregulars.blogspot.com. The pictures are stunning, and the commentary is wildly entertaining. A December 1, 2005, entry on PaleMale.com reads: "Lola took off for parts unknown but PM was the master of his domain. Flying from his favorite tree . . . he was most likely looking for a late rat snack before turning in for the evening."

Mary Tyler Moore, following Elvis's lead, has left the building, but Pale Male and Lola still live at 927 Fifth Avenue.

WHAT TO DO WITH A SPARE ISLAND

Roosevelt Island

New York City is really a collection of dozens of islands. And, back before modern medicine, how did New Yorkers deal with contagious, sometimes deadly diseases? They shipped them out to another island! Imagine that: OK, this here is Plague Island. And this over here is Crazy Island. Got it? Good. Now go.

Roosevelt Island, which the Indians used to call Minnahononck ("It's nice to be here") Island and the Dutch called Hogs' Island, is a thin swatch of land in the middle of the East River between Manhattan and Queens. Because it was close to Manhattan but still isolated from the wider population, it became a favorite parking spot in the 19th century for the sick, crazy, and incarcerated.

Today, the island is popular with a loyal following of yuppies and diplomats, many of whom work for the United Nations, which is located a short tram or subway ride across the river in Manhattan. They love their condos and that small-town feel in the middle of the big city. But at the southern tip of the island lies a macabre reminder of the island's sordid past.

It is the ruins of the former smallpox hospital, built in 1856 by James Renwick, who is famous for his less-contagious work, St. Patrick's Cathedral. It's an imposing Gothic structure, with vines creeping through the pointed windows like ghosts of plagues past. At night, it's lit from below with an eerie greenish light, as if the building were doing some sort of Blair Witch impression, compliments of the lighting designer for the Statue of Liberty.

Roosevelt Island's former smallpox hospital is an eerie green beacon in the night.

You might think that living on an island steeped in years of disease, madness, and crime would be a bit of a bargain. Not true. Residents pay New York prices to live here, and over on Manhattan's eastern shore, residents pay a premium for a "view" of, well, a creepy hospital.

Ahhhh, New York. We're all a little bit crazy, aren't we?

RENT-A-HOOKAH
Astoria, Queens

Admit it: You dream of Arabian nights, though you're not exactly sure what that means. It just sounds exotic.

If you don't have the 1,500 bucks for a flight to Cairo and the global bazaar at Target isn't quite doing it for you, here's a way you can get a taste of the Middle East—literally.

★ ★

Head to Steinway Street in Astoria, Queens, between 28th Avenue and Astoria Boulevard, often referred to as Little Egypt because of all the Middle Eastern cafés, restaurants, and shops.

Wearing your jeans and sneakers, *you* may feel like the foreigner when you see some of the local women in their *hijab*, or head scarves. Just act like you left yours at home and press on to one of the block's many cafés, such as the Egyptian Coffee Shop, Egyptian Cafe, or Layali Beirut.

Take a stroll on Steinway, stop in for a hookah.

For about $5, you can rent a hookah for a few hours, with your choice of flavored tobacco. A hookah is a water pipe, usually made of brass and glass, which stands on the floor. Charcoal lights the tobacco and the smoke is filtered through water, which makes it light and airy—nothing like cigarette smoke. Attached to the pipe is a hose with a disposable plastic mouthpiece, through which you inhale the smoke. The tobacco often comes in fruit flavors such as apple, strawberry, cherry, and mango.

Now, a hookah may *look* like a bong, but to be clear, what you'll get in a hookah is tobacco and not an illegal drug. If some of you are disappointed by this, I offer no apologies. Remember, we're trying to have fun here, not get arrested.

While we're going over protocol, you should know that most authentic hookah cafes don't serve alcohol, as it's against Muslim custom. So don't get all frat boy on me and order a beer. Instead, try the Turkish coffee. If you simply must have alcohol, there's an Irish bar, Sissy McGinty's, on the same block.

For a little souvenir from your hookstravaganza, you can buy a hookah or brass lantern from one of the shops on Steinway. Strategically place the item in your living room to help steer the conversation at your next cocktail party toward "that time you smoked the hookah."

AFTER WRESTLING, THESE PIANOS HIT THE SAUNA
Astoria, Queens

From a classical concert at Carnegie Hall to Billy Joel's world tour, have you ever wondered where those gorgeous grand pianos come from?

You might guess that they are created at a big factory in China where a small, goggle-clad man presides over a massive machine that drops in each key with robotic staccato before it glides down the conveyer belt.

In fact, most concert grands are made by Steinway & Sons at a small factory right here in Queens, land of the Mets and Archie Bunker. There aren't giant robotic machines. Rather, each piano is made (technophiles, cover your eyes for this part) *by hand.*

Hey, buddy, can you throw some water on the coals?

Actually, it's more like 600 hands. It takes about 300 people to assemble the 12,000 parts that comprise a Steinway grand piano. And it takes one year to make.

You can take a tour of the Steinway piano factory, which is like Willy Wonka's Chocolate Factory for the Chopin set. There aren't Oompa Loompas, but there is a full cast of characters and some surreal sets the piano encounters on its journey. There are the burly rim benders, who wrestle eighteen sheets of hard rock maple into that signature piano curve and then clamp it down with a piano-sized vise. There's a "sauna room," where the piano goes for a little R&R after all that wrestling, and a "belly room," where rows of women at long wooden tables toil over small parts with miniature hammers. There are men shaving keys and stringing strings. True to Wonka form, a lacquer waterfall recycles the runoff after each coat of gloss.

And then, the finale, when the piano gets its voice. Voicers poke, prod, soften, harden, and balance each note to perfect pitch. A voicer's office has all the usual cubical fare—staplers, pens, pictures of their kids, and so on—but a few key differences: There's a rolltop door like a garage, and a huge piano parked in the middle!

Upon exiting the factory, you'll notice a pile of wood in the parking lot. But don't even think of snagging some for your winter kindling—what may look like a "scrap" heap to you is actually piano wood left out to dry for a year and could be the Piano Man's next grand!

Steinway & Sons offers factory tours a few days a week, but only seasonally and the tours fill up quickly, so book in advance. For more information go to www.steinway.com or call (718) 721-2600.

WHAT THE JETSONS LEFT BEHIND
Corona Park, Queens

In 1964 space was the great new frontier and *The Jetsons* showed us how to make a sandwich when we got there. The World Trade Center was merely a blueprint, and the Beatles announced to the world that they wanted to hold your hand.

★ ★

The 1964–1965 World's Fair, held in Flushing Meadows Corona Park in Queens, was a portal into the future, as envisioned by the likes of various countries, states, and major U.S. corporations. GM's "Futurama" exhibit showed us we could live anywhere—even on the moon. IBM dazzled visitors with a 500-seat hydraulic stadium and high-tech presentation to explain that computers were our friends and not to be feared. (HAL came along a few years later and nearly ruined it for us all.) Disney brought the diorama screaming—well, more singing and frolicking—into the 20th century with the debut of the animatronic "It's a Small World" ride. Wisconsin offered the world's largest cheese and Belgium introduced the world to its culinary future: the Belgian waffle.

When the fair ended, many of the exhibits were carted off to other cities or countries, but there are a few curious hangers-on that

The Unisphere, the world's largest world.

remain in Flushing Meadows Corona Park. The most famous is the Unisphere, the world's largest globe, which is made of stainless steel and stands twelve stories tall. You might recognize it in the opening credits of *The King of Queens.*

The Unisphere is pretty well preserved, but not so much for the New York Pavilion, a roadside oddity visible from the Grand Central Parkway. Huge columns support a spiky metal circle with wires stretched like bicycle spokes. During the fair, it was covered in a colorful canopy and housed New York's "Tent of Tomorrow." Nearby are the crumbling remains of three giant fair-observation decks, which once featured futuristic pill-shaped elevators. Several movies were filmed here, including *Men in Black.*

The Queens Museum, located inside the park, is home to a 9,335-square-foot panorama of all five boroughs of New York City that was one of the fair's most popular exhibits. You can't take a simulated helicopter ride over the "city" anymore, but it's still pretty cool.

Today, there isn't much evidence of *The Jetsons* in Queens, except for two very tall curiosities outside the Hall of Science, also in the park.

On the number 7 train to Queens, a little boy looks out the window. "Look, Daddy, a rocket!"

That's cute. As for me, I'm still holding out for the jet pack.

DAISY FROM THE BLOCK
Floral Park, Queens

Bing, bong. Stand clear of the closing doors, please. Honk honk! Waieeeeeeeeerrrrrrrrowaieeeerrro! Hey, watch it, buddy! Taxi!

Ah, the sounds of the city.

Er er er er errrrrrrrrrr!

Wait, who was that last guy? He wasn't from New York, right?

Actually, that rooster *is* a New Yorker and he lives on a farm in Floral Park on the far eastern border of Queens. When you get there,

★ ★

Hey, have you guys tried that new restaurant in SoHo? Any good?

you'll find him wandering the roads of the farm, so don't drive like a New Yorker lest you run over him, OK?

The farm has been around since 1697, and holds the distinction of being the last working farm in New York City. It sits on forty-seven acres, which in New York City terms is like an entire neighborhood.

The farm was in private hands for many years, before the state bought it for the Creedmoor Psychiatric Center for produce—and therapy. It was about to be shuttered in 1973, but the local townfolk rallied to save the farm, and it's now a museum.

But don't let the museum part fool you: They've got one hundred hens that produce eggs and a beehive that makes honey, both of which are sold at the farm. Plus, forty sheep and lambs, twenty-five goats, three pot-bellied pigs, a coupla turkey, and a cow named Daisy. They also grow and sell a variety of fruits and vegetables including apples, pears, corn, tomatoes, and pumpkins, and have a vineyard where they make their own wine!

The location is a favorite for television, film, and magazine crews. Both *Sex and the City* and *Law & Order* have filmed there. The next time you see a bridal magazine spread set on a farm, check the credit! That farm may very well be in New York City.

You don't have to be Sarah Jessica Parker to get into New York's farm; anyone can stop by and say: "Well, howdy doo, Ms. Daisy?" There are guided tours on the weekend, and the farm is open for self-guided tours every day of the week.

The best times to go are during the fall, when the crops are in full swing. There are a variety of cool events, including an interactive corn maze—a maze of maize, if you will—plus pumpkin picking, an apple festival, and an American Indian Pow Wow.

For more information go to www.queensfarm.org or call (718) 347-FARM.

THE MYSTERIOUS ROCK MAN
Staten Island

One day about ten years ago, mysterious rock formations began appearing on Staten Island's south shore. The local paper, the *Staten Island Advance,* was on the case immediately. It brought in experts on demonic worship, who concluded that this was clearly the work of a Satanic cult. Textbook evil. They ran the story on the front page.

This outraged Doug Schwartz, keeper of the rain forest at the Staten Island Zoo, for one very good reason: He was the one who built those rock formations. And he's no Satan worshiper.

Schwartz likes to pile the beach rocks, in rich earthy tones of brown and tan, as a way of showcasing nature's beauty. For Schwartz, personally, the rocks provide a spiritual, artistic, and emotional balance to his work at the zoo, which is all about science. And, he believes that art isn't something you keep to yourself, but something you share with the community.

He's out there working on new formations at least once a week, in rain, sleet, or snow. There are now dozens of the shoulder-high rock piles, known as cairns, on the beach. A path marked with— what else—rocks and logs for benches offer beach-goers an opportunity to get up close and enjoy the art.

"I figured, well, if they see these things, they'll think somebody really cares about the beach," Schwartz says.

Some people know who he is—the man behind the rock formations—but others don't. There are still wild theories circulating that the cairns are some sort of vampire graveyard or a message to aliens. Schwartz likes the interactivity of public art, so he'll walk right up to

Staten Island's mysterious rock man, revealed!

Staten Island Chuck

If you think Doug Schwartz, builder of the rock formations on Staten Island's south shore, looks familiar, it's because he's famous for something else.

In addition to maintaining the rain forest at the Staten Island Zoo, Schwartz is also the handler for Charles G. Hogg VII, aka Staten Island Chuck, New York City's very own winter-prognosticating groundhog.

Chuck basks in the limelight in February for Groundhog Day, meeting city dignitaries and making the media rounds. But the rest of the year, Chuck keeps a pretty low profile. During the week, he lives just down the hall from Schwartz's office under the rain forest. "In my day, I'll just do some of my regular work, then go in there and throw him a paper towel. Play with him and go back to work," Schwartz says nonchalantly, as if we all have such exotic office mates.

And, while he's whisked around in limos for Groundhog Day interviews, on normal weekends, Chuck takes the bus like everyone else. He spends weekends at Schwartz's house, where he enjoys running around on the deck, playing tag, and hiding. "He has a whole series of games," Schwartz says. "He hops back and forth from front to back feet. When he gets really excited, he hiccups. If you've got a hiccupping groundhog, you know you're on the right track," Schwartz says.

About a month or so after Groundhog Day, you're likely to find Chuck singing. Is he sad that his fifteen minutes are up? Upset that Regis doesn't return his calls anymore? Nah. He's just letting the ladies know that he's available.

Unfortunately there isn't an exhibit at the zoo where you can visit Chuck, but mark your calendar for February 2, when he takes center stage at the zoo for his shadow-finding mission. The rest of the year, you can stop by the rain forest Sunday through Thursday and talk to Schwartz. Send your regards to Chuck or put in a request for the next winter forecast.

"Slip me a note about an extended ski season and I'll see what I can do with the hog!" Schwartz says.

★ ★

visitors and introduce himself as the creator of the cairns. Often, they don't believe him.

"I get this vague sense that people who meet me are sort of disappointed," Schwartz says. They expect him to be bigger—capable of lifting all those heavy rocks. Either that, or a crazy old man. "Perhaps wearing a loincloth with one eye open, gesturing to the heavens!" he adds.

In fact, Schwartz is very down to earth and has a great sense of humor about it all. "I'd love to call myself a mystic. Act it out with the whole loincloth thing," Schwartz says. "But the wife wouldn't allow it. So, I have to create a more vivid projection of spirituality."

The cairns are located on the beach near Sharrott Avenue, just south of Hylan Boulevard, on Staten Island's southern shore.

THE JEWELED GATES OF STATEN ISLAND
Rosebank, Staten Island

There have been many shrines built in the Virgin Mary's honor, but nothing quite like Our Lady of Mt. Carmel Grotto in Staten Island.

It's been described as "the city's most elaborate yard shrine" and "a fairy tale of a jeweled city." It looks like ruins from an ancient temple, or what the gates of Heaven would look like if they were designed by Antonio Gaudí.

It's a twisting and turning ornamental concrete wall, with one main altar in the middle. Set into the concrete structure, which is about 20 feet tall by 50 feet wide, are hundreds of smooth beach pebbles, as well as bits of blown glass, seashells, and even bicycle reflectors.

It all started with Italian immigrant Vito Russo, who built a small homemade shrine out of cardboard and tinfoil. Russo wanted to go bigger, so, one day in 1935, he convinced his buddies down at the Society of Our Lady of Mount Carmel to help him build a courtyard grotto. The construction workers handled the heavy stone blocks, sanitation workers gathered the pebbles, and a few of the guys

★ ★

worked at the glass factory down the street, which is likely where the blown glass came from. The men came from all over Italy, so the resulting architectural style is a mosaic of Italian styles.

"This was before television," says Mike DeCataldo, treasurer of the society, whose father and grandfather helped build the grotto. "So, the guys would come down to the town hall at night, drink wine, eat, and build things in the basement. That's just what they did back then."

The shrine is open twenty-four hours to offer a place for anyone and everyone—not just Italians or Catholics—to say a prayer or clear their head at their time of need—even if that time is 3:30 a.m.

A peaceful place in Staten Island.

People bring photos of loved ones, rosaries, flowers, or other objects. It's also become a popular place to leave that religious sculpture-turned-albatross you inherited when your grandmother died. You know the one: It doesn't go with your decor, but you feel way too guilty to toss it.

"We don't throw anything away," DeCataldo says, to the collective sigh of relief from guilt-ridden Catholics the world over.

The grotto is located at 36 Amity Place in Rosebank, Staten Island. A good time to go is in July for the big feast, when you can hear these stories firsthand while listening to an Elvis impersonator and eating a piping-hot zeppole.

It doesn't get much better than that.

THE TUGBOAT GRAVEYARD
Rossville, Staten Island

They stand there, tipped to the side or backside drooping, like a couple of drunken sailors.

But these guys aren't going to wake up tomorrow and continue about their business with a slight hangover. This is it for them. A couple of old souls trapped in shallow water, rusting away the time.

This is the Rossville Boatyard, where the pier crumbles off into slippery sand and a handful of old boats of all denominations—cargo vessels, tug ships, dredging barges—have come to their final resting place.

It's located off the southwestern shore of Staten Island, the end of the New York City line, just before the Outerbridge Crossing whisks the living off to New Jersey. It's a discreet enough place to just slump over and hope no one notices, tucked between the now-retired Fresh Kills Landfill and the Arthur Kill Correctional Facility. The woods nearby are loaded with unwanted cars; a seaside cemetery hosts graves more than 200 years old. Here, graffiti artists hone their craft, and paintball players obliviously make their mark. The shops sell topsoil, tile, and concrete.

The water is shallow here, so you can get a really good view of the boats. Some urban adventurers have risked the busted-up pier to get a closer look, but you can see the boats from the shore. As you gaze through the tall marshy grass, Canadian geese gliding in and out of the wreckage, you can't help but wonder what tales they might tell if these old-timers could talk.

"Hey, Jimmy. Did I ever tell you about the time we were bringing in this aircraft carrier? One of these new guys—thinks he's a real hot shot—he falls straight off the edge! Took 'em two hours to get that kid back on the ship! I mean, those things are like 1,000 feet long."

Blink again, and they're asleep. Some appear to be dozing, others down for the count, as the tide washes in and out.

Nah, you go on ahead without me. I'm just taking a little snooze.

★ ★

FROM THE MALL TO THE POORHOUSE

Willow Brook, Staten Island

How many times have you said something like, "Whoa, I'd better stop spending money or I'm going to wind up in the poorhouse!"?

We say such things absentmindedly, but the truth is, if this were 1902, that could actually happen.

One of the charming English holdovers in this country, which lasted well into the 20th century, was the poorhouse, also referred to as the poor farm. Essentially, it was a place to sweep the poor out of site from the rest of society. I have no idea why this was what we chose to keep instead of, say, the English garden or the English accent, which would've been pretty cool.

The New York City Farm Colony opened on Staten Island in the early 1900s. The idea was to have the poor be self-sustaining— growing fruit and vegetables, and tending to pigs and chickens—to ensure that the rest of the community would never see them. Each person was assigned a set of work clothes and a small dorm room, not unlike prison. This particular farm colony did well in that department for a few decades, but there's one teensy-tiny problem with keeping a population isolated like that for an extended period of time: They get old. So, the facility quickly became a geriatric center and the farming part petered out. The facility was eventually shut down in 1975.

Staten Island, which seems to have a problem with throwing things away (not only will you find boats left at sea, but cars and other unwanted items dumped in the woods), still has that poor farm, or what's left of it. Apparently, there were efforts to try to sell the land for residential development, but such plans got buried under a mound of red tape, and at some point, Staten Island just said, "Aw, what the heck. Let's make it a historic district."

And so, there it stands today, a series of decrepit buildings penned up behind a fence, tangled in a jungle of vines, trees, and trash. To look at this monstrosity, you might be inclined to think that the only

The historic district that was once the New York City Farm Colony.

"historic" things it's preserving are the fine art of graffiti and the cultural institution of the late-night teen party.

There are an abundance of photos online from urban thrill seekers who dared trespass on this tetanus-friendly site. They show rusty cots with mattresses askew, toilet bowls lying on the floor, piles of papers, and thirty-year-old laundry waiting to be claimed. It's as if the inhabitants were suddenly called away all at once, and never returned.

The ironic thing is that the Staten Island Mall is just down the street. It makes you wonder if shoppers ever realize that they're *literally* just a hop, skip, and a jump away from the poorhouse.

THE GREAT SPHINX OF FONTANA

Bayport, Long Island

Not that it's terribly easy to steal heavy hunks of concrete, but just in case, a giant sphinx, an Egyptian symbol for guardian, presides over Fontana Concrete Products in Bayport, Long Island.

The 20-foot-tall solid concrete sphinx was built in the early 1900s by Will Graham as a way of attracting politicians and movie stars to his hotel, the Anchorage Inn, in Blue Point, Long Island (which, incidentally, is also home of the tasty Blue Point oyster).

The inn burned down in the late 1920s, but the sphinx squatted the property for a few decades more. (It's probably not that easy to evict a concrete sphinx, whether he's paying his rent or not.) But, in the 1970s, the jig was up for the squatting sphinx and he was bulldozed to make way for a new gas station.

Louis Fontana, co-owner with his brother John of Fontana Concrete Products, was driving by and told the demolition workers to toss the 10,000-pound head on the back of his truck. He drove it back to Bayport, where he let the weary head rest for about seven years, before beginning restoration.

It took two years, but they rebuilt the body of the sphinx and it now keeps a watchful eye over all sorts of Fontana Concrete products, everything from paving stones to birdbaths and planters.

Don't even *think* about stealing that bird feeder.

The inscription on the bottom of the sphinx reads: "She who climbs to the Sphinx's head, a millionaire will surely wed." But please, ladies, don't climb on the sphinx. Put on a pair of pumps and a little makeup instead.

The Great Sphinx of Fontana is significantly easier to get to than its more famous counterpart in Giza. It's located at 890 Montauk Highway in Bayport, just across the street from the 7-Eleven and Starbucks. Visit www.fontanaconcrete.com or call (631) 472-1600.

THE EAST COAST AREA 51
Camp Hero State Park, Long Island

You might want to put on your tinfoil hat for this next story.

Out on Long Island's eastern tip in Montauk, a popular summer spot for New Yorkers, is a former military base called Camp Hero, which is now a state park. Used during World War II, Camp Hero had all the usual fort fare—docks, hangars, bunkers, and barracks. But some say that a huge underground facility, located under the camp's giant radar, was subsequently used for secret government experiments.

The Montauk Project, as it's known, traces back to the 1943 Philadelphia Experiment, also known as the Rainbow Project, when the government was allegedly tinkering with radar invisibility and successfully made a ship invisible, though in the process removed it from the space-time continuum for fifteen minutes. As the story goes, several crew members were killed and others were left with psychological damage.

The conspiracy theorists, several of whom are brilliant scientists and claim to have been involved with the experiments, allege that the government used the massive underground facility in Montauk to rekindle the time-travel experiment—opening a portal between 1983 and 1943—and to conduct other experiments in telepathy, mind control, and other equally bizarre subjects. They allege that homeless people were abducted for some experiments, and that young boys

Site of a conspiracy theory, and a lovely place for a picnic.

with heightened psychic abilities were able to materialize objects from their thoughts! Alien reptoids, a psychically generated Yeti, and a professional wrestler may or may not have been involved, but let's just leave it at that.

Today, there is no shortage of Internet sleuths who note the abundance of "do not enter" signs at the park as well as the generators, cords, and other signs of activity at the allegedly decommissioned site. Some even say that armed soldiers have shooed them away from poking around the site.

The park is open to the public, so check it out at your own risk: Drive past the boarded-up guard checkpoints, get up close to the giant radar installation, or picnic in the abandoned military camp nearby.

To get to Camp Hero State Park, take Route 27/Montauk Highway all the way to the end, just before you hit the ocean. Pack some sandwiches, chips, soda, and maybe some mini-Snickers. But don't forget to wrap it all in tinfoil so you can make a hat.

ALL HAIL THE QUEENS!
Fire Island Pines, Long Island

Guy walks into a bar. (You've heard this one, right?)

He's wearing full drag. (OK, maybe not *this* one.)

The bartender says this isn't appropriate attire and refuses to serve the man/lady.

The guy returns home and tells the newly crowned (homecoming) queen what has happened. A few days later, the queen returns with an entourage. The bartender does the math. Drinks are served.

This is how the Invasion of the Pines, now an annual event, started thirty years ago.

Fire Island, on the southern side of Long Island, is a top summer spot for New York's gay community. Cherry Grove and the Pines are the most popular, but they couldn't be more different. The Pines, which came out of the closet in the 1950s, about twenty years after Cherry Grove, is home to a wealthy, conservative gay population that would never dream of dressing in drag. (Heck, some of its residents may still be rummaging around in the closet.) For its artsier sibling, Cherry Grove, anything goes. Gay, lesbian, straight, drag, leather— you'll see all the colors of the rainbow in Cherry Grove.

So you can imagine that, when the Grove's Teri Warren showed up in all of his glamorous lady glory for dinner at Botel, a Pines hotel, on July 4, 1976, the fireworks were flying. But when Homecoming Queen Panzi led the follow-up invasion, Pines residents were so surprised and entertained that they treated the ladies to a drink at the Botel's Blue Whale restaurant and bar, and a tradition was born.

★ ★

And so, every Fourth of July, hundreds of cross-dressers board a two-deck ferry in Cherry Grove and "invade" the Pines. They come in their best summer dresses, ball gowns, bikinis, big wigs, and of course, perfectly accessorized. Some dress as celebrities—Britney Spears and the Brady Bunch have appeared in past years—or in themed getups, like the Cherry Grove Airline Stewardesses and the beer-stein–toting Heidi Hoes.

Once the boat reaches the Pines, the ladies strut that dock like a catwalk, to the delight of the shorts-and-sandals-clad Pines folk. They drink, they dine, they mingle. And just before Macy's kicks off

Photo by Marco Herrera for fireislandqnews.com

The drag queens are coming! The drag queens are coming!

The Man-Eating Lake

Legend has it that the spirit of an Indian princess lives in Lake Ronkonkoma in central Long Island. She drowned herself in the lake after the man she was to marry was murdered by a white man. It is said that each year she claims the life of one man as revenge.

There are many variations of this story and more than a handful of stories on the Internet from men who claim to have heard the voice of a woman beckoning them to the center of the lake—a very deep lake, once rumored to be bottomless—but managed to escape.

So, are men afraid to swim in the lake?

"Well, there's this one guy who comes into the bar," says Mickey Quinn, a bartender for the last nine years at Parsnips Pub on the north side of the lake. "He says to me, 'Anyone drown yet, Mick?' If I say, 'No,' then he says, 'OK. Then I'm not goin' in.'"

Quinn, an Irishman who fashions himself a bit of a *shanachie* (Gaelic for storyteller), has a million stories about what's in that lake. A lot of cars, from days gone by when people used to try to drive across the ice, and at least one raccoon. (It's a long story, but the short of it is that the fuzzy little bandit was punished for eating kittens.) Few of his stories about the lake involve a lady. Well, except for that one about a date that ended with a moonlight dip and a misplaced car. But that might be getting a little too personal.

After nine years, surely Quinn has heard more than his share of tales from men who come into the bar, claiming to have been summoned by the lady in the lake, no?

"Well, maybe at four in the morning they heard something," he says, chuckling. "The girls get prettier at four in the morning, too!"

"Hey, did you hear about that new designer dog they got there?" Quinn asks with a sly grin. "Yeah, they crossed a bulldog and a Shih Tzu. You know what they call that?"

Hmmm. I guess it's not a dog zu, now is it?

its fireworks in Manhattan, the ladies return home to Cherry Grove, mission accomplished.

For more information check out www.fireislandqnews.com and www.fireislandinvasion.com.

NOW THAT IS FOWL!

Flanders, Long Island

Long Island's eastern end is home to the Hamptons, a summer playground for the rich and famous. But let's face it, Long Island is for the birds.

To be more specific, ducks. Long Island, once home to a lively duck-farming industry, commemorates its fowl past with a building shaped like a big duck. It's located in Flanders, just down the road from the tony Hamptons.

The duck was the brainchild—or brainfowl, as it were—of duck farmer Martin Maurer in 1931. Inspired by a giant coffeepot he saw while on vacation in California, Maurer got the flighty idea that it might help his business if he made a big duck on the side of the road. So, he hired a local carpenter and a couple of theater-set designers to create the 29-foot-tall duck, which is appropriately called "the Big Duck." They used wood, mesh, cement, and Model-T taillights for the eyes.

"The duck is pure fun but nevertheless an important historic icon," says Barbara Bixby, curator of the Big Duck, who also proudly goes by the name of the Duck Lady. "It's a symbol of ingenious advertising, architecture, agriculture, and all-around Americana in the automotive age." (Say that one five times fast!)

Inside the Big Duck, Maurer used to sell his ducks. Today, thanks to the preservation efforts of the state, it's the home of a gift shop for duck-a-bilia—everything from Big Duck T-shirts to wind-up ducks and, of course, rubber duckies.

But make no mistake, the Big D's legacy is much more than bath-time fun. It spawned the architectural term "duck," meaning

Whoa! Now that's a mighty duck.

a building shaped like the products or services sold within, as well as a Duck Design Theory. Part of the DDT, coined by architect James Wines, goes, "Form follows fantasy, not function, for architecture that cannot offer fantasy fails man's need to dream."

Stop by and see the Big D on Route 24 in Flanders, Long Island (631-852-8292).

index

index

317

index

index

★ ★

Cindy Perman is a native New Yorker, a freelance humor writer, and an experienced journalist, who wrote for the *Wall Street Journal* Online for nine years. She knows the state up, down, left, and right, having grown up in Rochester, attended school in Syracuse, and lived in New York City, where she's made her home since 1994.